Idea of a New General History of North America

The deeds of Boturini

Idea of a New General History of North America

An Account of Colonial Native Mexico

By *Lorenzo Boturini Benaduci*

Translated and edited by *Stafford Poole*

Foreword by *Susan Schroeder*

UNIVERSITY OF OKLAHOMA PRESS : NORMAN

Also by Stafford Poole

Pedro Moya de Contreras: Catholic Reform and Royal Power in New Spain, 1571–1591 (Oakland, Calif., 1987)
Our Lady of Guadalupe: The Origins and Sources of a Mexican National Symbol, 1531–1797 (Tucson, Ariz., 1995)
Juan de Ovando: Governing the Spanish Empire in the Reign of Philip II (Norman, Okla., 2004)
The Guadalupan Controversies in Mexico (Redwood City, Calif., 2006)

Library of Congress Cataloging-in-Publication Data

Boturini Benaducci, Lorenzo, 1702–1751, author.
[Idea de una nueva historia general de la América Septentrional. English]
Idea of a new general history of North America : an account of colonial native Mexico / by Lorenzo Boturini Benaducci ; edited and translated by Stafford Poole ; foreword by Susan Schroeder.
pages cm
Includes bibliographical references and index.
ISBN 978-0-8061-4833-5 (hardcover : alk. paper)
1. Indians of Mexico—Antiquities. 2. Indians of Mexico—Early works to 1800. 3. Mexico—History—Early works to 1800. I. Poole, Stafford, editor, translator. II. Title.
F1219.B7513 2015
972'.01—dc23

2015019423

The paper in this book meets the guidelines for permanence and durability of the Committee on Production Guidelines for Book Longevity of the Council on Library Resources, Inc. ∞

1 2 3 4 5 6 7 8 9 10

Contents

List of Illustrations / ix
Foreword, *by Susan Schroeder* / xi
Acknowledgments / xv

Introduction / 3
Some Principles of Translation / 16
Select Glossary of Spanish Terms Translated in This Book / 17

Idea of a New General History of North America Based on Copious Material of Figures, Symbols, Characters, and Hieroglyphics, Songs, and Manuscripts of Indian Authors, Recently Discovered / 21

Dedication to the King / 22
Evaluation of the Most Reverend Father, Master Pedro Fresneda / 24
License of the Ordinary / 26
Declaration of Doctor Don Joseph Borrull / 27
Permission of the Royal Council of the Indies / 33
Approbation of the Most Reverend Father Fray Juan de la Concepción / 34
Permission of the Royal Council of Castile / 38
Official Price / 39
Invocation of the Muses / 40
Sonetto and Epigramma / 50

Index of the Sections / 56
Preliminary Disclaimer / 58
Prologue for the Reader / 60
1. The Excellence of the History of New Spain / 62
2. Procedure in Writing This History / 67
3. First Age / 68
4. Second Age / 91
5. Divine Heroic Symbols of the Planets / 93
6. Divine Heroic Symbols of the Days of the Year / 99
7. The Days Are the Following / 100
8. Divine Heroic Symbols of the Months / 102
9. Symbols of the Indian Months, according to Father Fray Martín de León / 104
10. Symbols of the Indian Months, according to Gemelli Careri / 106
11. Divine Heroic Nocturnal Symbols of the Year / 111
12. Other Examples of Transformations as Means of Reward and Punishment / 113
13. Heroic Military Symbols / 123
14. Heroic Political Symbols / 128
15. Of the Knots and Songs, Both Historical and Poetic / 135
16. Origin of the Indians of New Spain / 146
17. On the Passage and Crossing that the Indians of New Spain Took to Arrive There / 167
18. Giants / 170

Division of the Kingdoms of New Spain / 175

19. The Olmec and Xicalanco Indians / 175
20. The Toltec Indians / 176
21. Third Age / 178
22. The Chichimeca Indians / 180
23. The Tepanec Indians / 182
24. The Mexican Indians / 183
25. The Teochichimeca Indians / 187
26. Conquest by the Spaniards / 188
27. Observations on What Has Been Said / 189
28. The Usefulness That This Work Can Produce / 194

Catalog of the Historic Indian Museum of the Knight Lorenzo Boturini Benaduci, Lord of la Torre and Hono / 201

Preliminary Statement / 203
Index of the Sections / 205
Toltec History / 207
Chichimeca History / 209
Tepanec History / 213
Mexican History / 214
Tlatelolco History / 222
Various Histories / 224
History of Michoacan / 225
Matlaltzinca History / 228
History of Huejotzinco / 229
History of Tlaxcala / 230
Various Other Historical Sources / 234
Pictorial Documents of Tribute / 238
Manuscripts of Tribute / 240
Rare Books / 241
Other Various Learned Manuscripts / 242
Christian Doctrine in Figures and Ciphers / 246
Printed Books in the Nahuatl Language / 247
Indian Calendars / 249
History of the Conquest / 258
Ecclesiastical History / 261
History of Guadalupe / 263
Observations / 273

Bibliography / 275
Index / 281

Illustrations

Figures

The deeds of Boturini / *frontispiece*
Title page of the 1746 edition / 19
Lorenzo Boturini Benaduci / 59

Tables

Symbols of the Four Parts or Corners of the World / 109
Symbols of the Four Seasons of the Year / 109–10
Symbols of the Four Elements / 110
Symbols of the First Days of the Year / 110
Symbols of the First Days of the Year, Corresponding to the Character in Which the Year Begins / 110
Dating the Confusion of Tongues Based on the Year of the Flood / 164

Foreword

Susan Schroeder

Lorenzo Boturini's arrival in New Spain in 1736 was auspicious. The Bourbon king, Philip V, had been on the throne for three decades (r. 1700–46). Major wars had been won, or at least settled, during that time, and the long reach of the Spanish Crown still extended west to the Philippine Islands and east to parts of the Italian peninsula. In the Americas, royal reforms were under way but were less draconian than in later years. Over the course of the previous century, an incipient patriotism had come to full form, and American Spaniards, especially in New Spain, were increasingly optimistic about their situation.

Creole intellectuals, such as Carlos Sigüenza y Góngora (1645–1700), had taken stock of Mexico's past and potential and found that the great indigenous monuments of Mesoamerica were on par with anything known in classical Europe. Sigüenza studied Nahuatl, the language of the Aztecs, and collected and analyzed the natives' manuscripts, determining that their authors had sophisticated sociopolitical systems and profound knowledge of mathematics and calendrical reckoning. Their achievements were illustrious and should be esteemed, he and other creoles believed.

Perhaps as a Christian theological counterpoise to Sigüenza's allusion to Greek and Roman antiquity, an account became known and was soon widespread about the dark-skinned Virgin of Guadalupe. The Catholic Virgin, it would appear, had favored the Indians, a true sign of New Spain's preeminence and American particularism. Guadalupe was thereafter adopted as the patron saint of Mexico City, and all manner of devout peoples across the countryside considered themselves privileged by her blessing. The coincidental popularity of the Virgin of

Guadalupe served to augment and legitimize the creoles' fervor for their American *patria.*

Boturini had been well positioned socially and politically in Milan—where he was educated in civil and canon law—and later in Austria, and he had important connections in Rome. He eventually made his way to Spain, where he was received into the circles of numerous individuals of high rank and influence. He came to know doña Manuela de Oca Silva y Moctezuma, countess of Santibáñez and a distant relative of Moteuczoma Xocoyotl, the infamous last Aztec emperor (r. 1502–20). The countess encouraged Boturini to travel to New Spain to settle some affairs on her behalf and provided him with funds for the endeavor. Soon after his arrival in North America, he became fascinated with the devotion to the already legendary Guadalupe and set out to establish the authenticity of her glorious patronage by bringing together and scrutinizing indigenous records about her apparition. Almost accidentally Boturini became one of the foremost scholars of Aztec antiquity of the time. In the course of doing so, he too subscribed to creole ardor in support of an autochthonous and splendid American Indian civilization.

Because of his activities relating to the Virgin of Guadalupe and because of his exceptional archive of documents in the Museo Indiano, as he called his collection of antiquities, Boturini ran afoul of the authorities. In 1743 he was arrested, and his manuscripts were confiscated. He was also sent back to Spain. To secure his release and to recover his Museo, he wrote the *Idea of a New General History of North America* as a précis of sorts in anticipation of a much-expanded account of the past of New Spain's native peoples. The *Idea* highlighted their history along with their deities, their rulers, their literacy, and their extraordinary culture. He included the *Catalog*, an itemized, annotated list of the precious documents in his Museo that might serve as absolute evidence in support of all that he claimed in the *Idea.* The work was dedicated to the king and published in 1746.

Philip V died in the same year that the *Idea* and the *Catalog* were published. Nevertheless, the Council of the Indies released Boturini and favored him with an honorable title and position but unfortunately never enough money to return to Mexico City to regain his Museo. Moreover, his collection of antiquities had been indiscriminately relegated to the basement of the viceroy's palace, resulting in the scattering or disappearance of many items, a genuine loss.

What the king and his Council of the Indies thought of the *Idea* has not been established, nor is it known if they all read it. One member of the Council did, Doctor don José Burrull, an attorney, judge, and former member of the faculty at the University of Salamanca. Burrull wrote a glowing report in support of Boturini and his project. Indeed, the *Idea* was endorsed by an interesting cohort of esteemed dignitaries: a Jesuit, a bishop, and a Discalced Carmelite, who also served the Holy Tribunal of the Inquisition, as well as a member of the king's Council of Castile. Could one have wished for a more authoritative approbation? Yet the *Idea* is florid, convoluted, obtuse, and long, and it is written in French, Italian, Latin, Nahuatl, and Spanish. We cannot know if all the signatories were equally multilingual, or if they all supported Boturini's claim of American exceptionalism.

The *Idea* is an invaluable exercise in realizing how and what learned men thought and wrote in Bourbon Spain. The approbations alone are telling of what was involved in publishing a book in the eighteenth century—a formal address to the king, the support of any number of intellectuals and politicians who wrote of what they knew of Boturini and his proposal, the role of the Church in the process, the pricing of the book (by the number of sheets of paper, it seems), and the tentativeness of the entire business. Although in many ways important at the time and eventually translated into Italian and reprinted in Spanish, occasionally with minor additions, the *Idea* was dismissed by later scholars, and according to the historian Benjamin Keen, it "fell into the limbo of forgotten things."[1] On the other hand, the *Catalog* became an invaluable tool for collectors and scholars because of the information it contained about heretofore unknown or now-lost indigenous materials and because it was ostensibly the only reference work of its kind available.

In 2011 anthropologist John Glass telephoned me, wondering if Stafford Poole might consider translating Boturini's *Idea* into English. It was a daunting proposition considering especially the various languages in which it is written, the ponderous style, and the content of the work. To describe Glass as a Boturini enthusiast misses the mark. Nearly everything we know of Boturini has been the result of Glass's

1. Benjamin Keen, *The Aztec Image in Western Thought* (New Brunswick, N.J.: Rutgers University Press, 1971), 236.

diligence over the years, particularly when it came to the Museo. He has painstakingly reconstructed and tracked the permutations of the items listed in the various inventories that resulted in the *Catalog*. Not everything in Boturini's possession came to be recorded, but most was. We are all the better for Glass's assiduity.

Always interested in the Virgin of Guadalupe and the history of early Mexico, Stafford Poole immediately set himself to translating Boturini's work. There could not have been anyone better suited to the task. Poole, fluent in the requisite languages and abundantly knowledgeable about the classical and theological substance of the *Idea*, has brought forth an erudite critical translation that is an invaluable contribution to the fields of Latin American colonial indigenous and intellectual history. He expounds the bewildering biblical and literary references from antiquity and elucidates the many classical Latin citations; he sagaciously standardizes and explains the Nahuatl; he untangles the Spanish text; and he exactingly furnishes translations of the poems and sonnet, finding purpose and meaning in Boturini's enterprise.

The *Catalog* continues to serve as master template for researchers interested in the indigenous histories of New Spain. Most items listed in the Museo Indiano of eighteenth-century Mexico City are long dispersed. John Glass, in the *Handbook of Middle American Indians*, contributed significantly to bringing the Museo up to date, and since then those of us working with former Boturini manuscripts have complemented Glass's contributions with detailed information regarding repositories, authorship, and dates.[2] Boturini said that he rescued the early history of Mexico's Indians from "the tomb of oblivion."[3] We are fortunate that Stafford Poole has delivered the *Idea* and the *Catalog* from further neglect and time lost.

---

2. John B. Glass, "The Boturini Collection," in *Handbook of Middle American Indians*, vol. 15, *Guide to Ethnohistorical Sources*, pt. 4, ed. Howard F. Cline (Austin: University of Texas Press, 1975), 473–86. See also, in the same *Handbook*, Charles Gibson, "A Survey of Middle American Prose Manuscripts in the Native Historical Tradition," 311–21; Gibson and Glass, "A Census of Middle American Prose Manuscripts in the Native Historical Tradition," 322–400; and Glass, "A Checklist of Institutional Holdings of Middle American Manuscripts in the Native Historical Tradition," 401–72.

3. Boturini's dedication of the *Idea* to King Philip V.

Acknowledgments

First, credit must be given to the work of John Glass, whose dedication to Boturini has achieved so much. I also wish to thank Professors Susan Schroeder and Louise Burkhart for their invaluable contributions to this work and Reverend John O'Malley, S.J., for his suggestions about the introduction. A special word of thanks is due to Alessandra Jacobi Tamulevich of the University of Oklahoma Press, without whose help and encouragement this work would not have been possible. Without all of these generous colleagues it would never have been completed. My gratitude also extends to the two anonymous reviewers for the University of Oklahoma Press, whose suggestions proved invaluable. I owe special thanks to Katrin Flechsig, whose meticulous and careful copyediting contributed so much to improving the original manuscript, and to Emily J. Schuster, the manuscript editor whose patient answers to my questions were of such great help.

Idea of a New General History of North America

Introduction

Lorenzo Boturini Benaduci was one of the most fascinating and frustrating personalities in the history of colonial Mexico.[1] He was born at Sandrio on April 18, 1698, in the bishopric of Como in the Duchy of Milan, at that time under Spanish rule.[2] Thus he was technically born a Spanish subject. The original spelling of the name was Botturini, but he adopted the Spanish form, Boturini, around the year 1745. He was educated in Milan, where he studied both canon and civil law. It is clear from his writings that he had an extensive classical education: at times he wrote letters in Latin. He was also a person of intense intellectual curiosity, a trait that grew with the years.

Boturini claimed the title of Lord of la Torre and Hono and Knight of the Holy Roman Empire, though the authenticity of these titles and even his place of birth have been questioned today. During his lifetime, though, no one questioned his origins, and if he had falsified them, that fact could easily have been discovered and he discredited.

1. Information on Boturini's life and work is surprisingly sparse. This material relies in great part on Glass, *Boturini in Spain*, 7–9, and Cañizares-Esguerra, *How to Write the History*, 135–40. Other references include Keen, *Aztec Image*, 227–37; García Icazbalceta, "D. Lorenzo Boturini Benaduci"; Poole, *Our Lady of Guadalupe*, 192–93; León-Portilla, Introduction, ix–lx.

2. According to Glass, he was born between August 1702 and November 1703 (*Boturini in Spain*, 14). Milan passed to Austrian rule by the Treaty of Utrecht, 1713. Antei (*El caballero andante*), however, reproduces his baptismal record, which clearly states the date given here.

He was a disciple of the famed Italian historian Giambattista Vico (1668–1744), and so was probably exposed to Enlightenment ideas. It is significant, however, that he never mentions Vico in the *Idea of a New General History of North America.* As a matter of fact, Boturini moved away from Vico by accepting native documents as trustworthy.[3]

"Wanting to learn languages and see courts," as Boturini wrote to the marqués de Ensenada in 1754, he undertook extensive travels.[4] In 1725 he left Italy for Austria, where he held various responsibilities in the court of the Holy Roman Emperor, Charles VI (r. 1711–40). Because of these duties he spent a year in the port of Trieste. Around the year 1726 he accompanied the emperor on various tours of his dominions. Boturini seems to have been a young man ambitious to be associated with royal courts. León-Portilla asserts that he spoke German, French, and Spanish, though in the *Idea* there is evidence only for the last two.[5] He also asserts that Boturini visited Bohemia, Hungary, Croatia, and Slavonia. All of this, of course, is based on Boturini's own testimony.

In 1734 he had to leave Austria because of the War of the Polish Succession (1733–35).[6] After a brief visit to Great Britain he went to Portugal and then in 1735 to the Madrid of Philip V (r. 1700–46). Armed, as he claimed, with a plethora of letters of recommendation and testimonials, he became associated with the royal court. He found a patron in the marqués de Ensenada, to whom he directed several reports. He also made the acquaintance of doña Manuela de Oca Silva y Moctezuma, the countess of Santibáñez. She persuaded him to go to New Spain in the following year and subsidized his journey from a pension that she received from the crown as a descendant of Moteuczoma Xocoyotzin. Part of Boturini's mission was to collect debts owed to her. He arrived in Mexico City in February or March 1736, after enduring

3. Cañizares-Esguerra says that Boturini "stood Vico on his head," *How to Write the History*, 139.

4. Cited in León-Portilla, Introduction, xii. Most of the information in this paragraph is derived from this study.

5. Ibid.

6. Cañizares-Esguerra says that the Spanish Bourbon king, Philip V, threatened "to punish and confiscate the property of any Italian serving under the Habsburgs." See *How to Write the History*, 136. This animosity may have been connected to the war, which pitted the French and Spanish Bourbons against the Austrian Habsburgs.

shipwreck at Veracruz.[7] He quickly developed an interest in the history of New Spain and especially the devotion to Our Lady of Guadalupe. In fact, he became an enthusiast of the Dark Virgin (*Virgen morena*).[8] Aware of the lack of documents supporting the traditional account of her apparitions, he determined to find some. For the next seven years he traveled throughout the colony, enduring hardships and dangers, often without sufficient funds. He gathered documents, pictures, and maps of every description. The result was a collection of some five hundred books and documents, both pre- and post-conquest, that dealt not only with the apparitions but also with different aspects of indigenous history and culture. It was, in John Glass's words, "the most important collection of Indian manuscripts for ancient Mexican history ever gathered by a single individual."[9]

It was against the background of a devastating epidemic (*matlazahuatl*) in 1735–36 and the decision by royal officials to proclaim the Virgin of Guadalupe as patroness (*patrona*) of Mexico City that Boturini conceived the idea of having a coronation or crowning of the image. This was uncommon at that time and required papal approval. He wrote to Rome in 1738 to seek approval.[10] In the summer of 1740 he received a papal bull of approval.[11] This document also described the crown that was to be made and specified the ceremonies and prayers for the occasion. The crown was to be inscribed with the arms of the Vatican and those of an Italian count who had left a legacy for the purpose. Unfortunately for Boturini, the response came to New Spain without the clearance (*pase*) of the Council of the Indies, because communications with Spain were hindered by a war between Spain and England. For that reason the archbishop of Mexico, don Juan Antonio de Vizarrón y Eguiarreta (1730–47 term), refused to accept it. Boturini turned to the royal audiencia, the tribunal ruling New Spain in the absence of a viceroy, and secured its approval (March 1742). Since he lacked money (the coronation was to be at his

7. Cañizares-Esguerra gives the date as 1735, ibid.

8. On Boturini and Guadalupe, see Poole, *Our Lady of Guadalupe*, 192–95.

9. Glass, *Boturini in Spain*, 7.

10. Cañizares-Esguerra says that he wrote to Jesuit friends in Rome, *How to Write the History*, 136.

11. Cañizares-Esguerra, ibid., says that it was a brief, and unexpected.

own expense), he sent appeals throughout New Spain together with copies of the Vatican response, but the returns were disappointing.

On October 5, 1742, a new viceroy arrived at Veracruz. This was don Pedro Cebrián y Agustín, fifth count of Fuenclara (viceroy 1742–46). In Jalapa, en route to the capital, he was given a copy of one of Boturini's circulars. At Guadalupe, the customary stop for important personages on their way to Mexico City, in November, he was greeted in person by Boturini and given a copy of the Vatican document. In that same month, the new viceroy, who was concerned about Boturini's actions, ordered an inquiry by the crown attorney (*fiscal*). The conclusion was that Boturini was a foreigner who had entered New Spain without license, something about which the Spanish crown was very exacting. In pursuing the coronation he was acting beyond his authority. The engraving on the crown with the arms of the Vatican and a foreign nobleman infringed on royal prerogatives (*patronato real*). During the next seven months the government endeavored to retrieve Boturini's circulars. It investigated the finances of his campaign to see if there were any irregularities. On February 2, 1743, Boturini was arrested and his collection of documents confiscated.[12] Some weeks later, on February 28, Fuenclara wrote a complete report on the matter to the king. While under arrest, Boturini composed a catalog of his collection.[13] In September, 1743, after refusing four times, he was compelled to cooperate in an inventory of the collection. On October 7, the viceroy ordered his deportation to Spain for further investigation and judgment.

Boturini left New Spain in December of 1743. On the high seas, his ship, the *Concordia*, was captured by English pirates (March 7, 1744), and more of his papers were lost.[14] In New Spain his collection was neglected by the government. A long series of ever shorter inventories testifies to its gradual diminution and dispersal.[15] Today some of these documents are found in repositories throughout the world.

In Spain Boturini stayed with his friend and fellow historian Mariano Fernández de Echeverría y Veytia (1718–80).[16] A criollo, Veytia was born

12. Glass, *Boturini in Spain*, 17. Cañizares-Esguerra says that he was arrested in December 1742. *How to Write the History*, 137.

13. On this see Glass, *Boturini in Spain*, 253–60.

14. For a detailed description of these events, see Glass, *Boturini in Spain*, 19–24. For the report by the English captain, see ibid., 291–92.

15. Ibid., 8.

16. On Veytia, as he is commonly called, see Poole, *Our Lady of Guadalupe*, 200–201.

at Puebla to a family with a longstanding legal tradition and had come to Spain in 1737. His father, in Puebla, had sent to his son in Madrid a letter of recommendation on Boturini's behalf. The two soon became good friends, and after Boturini's death, Veytia continued the Milanese's studies of Guadalupe.[17]

During this time Boturini sought to justify himself to the Council of the Indies and to seek redress from the king. He was helped by having powerful friends, including José Burrull, formerly *catedrático* of civil jurisprudence at the university of Salamanca,[18] prosecuting attorney and judge of Granada, and a member of the Council of the Indies. On November 2, 1745, Burrull submitted a *dictamen* to the council, recommending approval of Boturini's project. In addition he suggested that Boturini be awarded the title of *escritor general de la* Nueva España (general chronicler of New Spain), be given a salary to return to New Spain, and be allowed to finish with the coronation. This *dictamen* was included in the introduction to Boturini's *Idea* but without the specific recommendations.

Burrull was highly critical of previous historians of the Indies. "This is clearly seen in the most classical of authors, such as the scholarly [José de] Acosta, Inca Garcilaso [de la Vega], [Antonio de Herrera], [Antonio de] Solís, and others, who, even though they touch somewhat on these matters in their histories and accounts, it is so much in passing and with such superficiality, that they arouse the desire of the curious reader more than they satisfy it." The Council of the Indies approved Boturini's project.

Boturini had already composed a catalog of his archive while under arrest in New Spain. What he proposed now was to write a comprehensive history of New Spain. This had to be done almost entirely from memory. Benjamin Keen has commented that it "must rank among the most prodigious *tours de force* of memory in the history of scholarship."[19] It stretches credulity that all the detailed material in the *Idea*

17. He was the author of a study of Mexican devotions to the Virgin, called *Baluartes de México*, published posthumously in 1820.

18. He also may have had enemies. Cañizares-Esguerra asserts that opposition came from a group of Aragonese who thought that he was insulting Spain (*How to Write the History*, 135–36). The Aragonese, however, had little to do with the New World.

19. *Aztec Image*, 228. As will be seen, Boturini's memory may not have been a good as Keen believed.

and the *Catálogo* could have been written from memory, but there is no clear evidence to the contrary.[20] On numerous occasions Boturini admitted that he could not remember the name of an author or the precise content of a work. Men of his day often had prodigious memories, using mnemonic devices such as the memory palace. In 1749 he completed the first volume of his *Historia general de la América Septentrional*, but it was not published until 1948.

It is difficult to trace the history of the composition of the *Idea* and *Catálogo.* By the time that Burrull penned his *dictamen* (November 2, 1745) Boturini's *Historia* may well have been finished. The first evidence of the existence of the *Idea* was a petition, dated April 26, 1745, to the Council of the Indies to permit its printing.[21] The author's dedication to the king in the first printing, however, is dated February 3, 1745. It does not seem that the *Catálogo* was part of the *Idea.*[22] This is supported by the fact that the *Catálogo* was added to the *Historia* with its own pagination.

It is notable that after all of its author's difficulties in New Spain, the *Idea* received royal approval and introductory letters by prestigious persons in Spain.[23] These letters were not just testimonials to the orthodoxy of his book, but also served as advertisements for its quality. The censor was the Jesuit Pedro Fresneda, a tenured professor (*catedrático*) of mathematics at the Imperial College and the director of all scientific pursuits (*cosmógrafo mayor*) in the Indies.[24] Another letter of approbation was written by a Discalced Carmelite, Juan de la Concepción, a former lecturer in Scripture and assessor (*calificador*) of the Inquisition. These are significant because they show that Boturini had influential friends and supporters in high places and that he was highly regarded for his work and scholarship.

In the same year that the work was published, the king declared Boturini's innocence, restored his honor and reputation, and gave him

---

20. In this context, *Idea* has the connotation of proposal.

21. Glass, *Boturini in Spain*, 31–32. As his source he cites the Archivo General de Indias, Seville, 398, folios 340–41.

22. Glass, *Boturini in Spain*, 42.

23. The story of this approval can be found ibid., 67–85.

24. The name is also spelled Fresnada (used by León-Portilla) and Frisnada. See Cañizares-Esguerra, *How to Write the History*, 153.

the title of royal chronicler of the Indies. He also ordered his return to Mexico, but his collection was never returned to him. The salary that he received as chronicler, if he were to return to Mexico, was inadequate for his needs.

In his remaining years he was unable to overcome opposition to his work, by forces at court hostile to his interests, or to obtain payment of his salary, let alone increase its size. Between December 1745 and May 1746, the Council of the Indies changed its mind again and proposed giving the entire project to a Mexican Indian, a Nahuatl interpreter.[25] This raises an interesting question: how far along was the *Idea* when the Council changed its mind? The writing of the book, collecting the introductory letters, the bureaucracy of taxation, obtaining the permission of the Council of Castile (January 21, 1746), and the work of printing would have taken a great deal of time. The reversal of the Council of the Indies apparently had no impact on the publication of the *Idea*.[26]

Boturini died in poverty in Spain in 1755 at the age of fifty-two without returning to Mexico and without regaining possession of his collection.

Boturini's *Idea* is a work rich in information on pre- and post-conquest Mexican history. Since it was written from memory, it inevitably contains errors. It is written in Spanish but also contains numerous citations of classical Latin, Roman law, Nahuatl terms, and in some cases Italian poetry. There is also a lengthy paragraph in French. His citations of Nahuatl present some problems. He often joins words while retaining the absolutive forms rather than using the combining forms. At times the native terms are misspelled, for example, Matlaltzinco for Matlatzinco, but whether that is the result of Boturini's memory or the printers' mistakes is not clear. There is room to wonder about Boturini's mastery of Nahuatl.

Boturini had a penchant for citing classical Latin sources, but whether this was pedantry is difficult to say. Of the classical Latin authors cited

25. This section is heavily dependent on Cañizares-Esguerra, *How to Write the History*, 140.

26. Pp. 135–36. Cañizares-Esguerra (*How to Write the History*, 135–36) believes that the opposition came from a group of Aragonese who thought that he was insulting Spain. This presents a problem. The Spanish rule in the New World belonged to Castile, not Aragon. The Aragonese in New Spain were on the same level as foreigners.

by Boturini, two stand out. Most frequently quoted is Ovid (Publius Ovidius Naso, 43 BC–AD 17/18), author of the *Metamorphoses*, a retelling of mythological narrative as an epic poem. The other is Vergil (Publius Vergilius Maro, 70 BC–19 BC), Roman poet and author of the *Georgics*, a rural poem, and the *Aeneid*, an epic poem about the founding of Rome by exiles from Troy.

In many ways Boturini exemplified the new Catholic historiography, represented by Vico, the Bollandists, and the Maurists, that was moving away from Baroque piety toward a more scientific and rational approach to history. Boturini's work is fundamental for understanding the history of colonial Mexico. He varied in his approach, at times precise and analytical, at others naïve and credulous. Since he was seeking largesse from the king, the tone is that of a conversation with the monarch to persuade him to support Boturini's project.

Boturini's opus was not written in isolation. As a modern historiographer tells us, "From the 1740s on, writing a new history of America became the central preoccupation of one of the new institutions for cultural renewal created by the Spanish Bourbons, the Royal Academy of History."[27] Spain was in the midst of a historiographical revolution, sparked in part by the Enlightenment and the accusations of Spain's enemies, and the argumentation was intense. Boturini's work appeared at the height of the controversy, though in some ways he seems to reflect an earlier school of Renaissance historiography.

Boturini's literary style was typical of his age. It reflects the innovations of the Baroque poet Luis de Góngora y Argote (1561–1627), who devised a style known as *culteranismo* or *gongorismo.* It was characterized by a deliberate obscurity of style that was also flowery and convoluted. It made use of neologisms and employed many words for simple concepts. There were also references to Greek and Roman mythology, often obscure. All of this is reflected in the text of the *Idea* and to a lesser extent of the *Catálogo.* The most egregious examples of gongorismo are to be found not in Boturini but in the introductory letters and poems he includes, the meanings of which at times are obscure—perhaps what their authors intended. Boturini is at his most obscure when he discusses the various ages of humanity and when he deals with the Indian calendars vis-à-vis the European ones.

27. Cañizares-Esguerra, *How to Write the History*, 3.

One thing is clear: Boturini was educated in the classical style typical of that age. He shows an extensive knowledge of Classical Latin literature, Greek and Roman mythology, and elements of medieval canon law. He was also well acquainted with the Bible. He had an intense intellectual curiosity, and was a man of many and varied enthusiasms.

Boturini stands out for his exaltation of the Indians, whom he always referred to as "our Indians" (*nuestros indios*). Whereas Rousseau believed that "savages" were "noble" because they were untouched by modern civilization, Boturini considered the Indians noble precisely because they had always been civilized. He claimed that they were descendants of the Hebrews of the Bible and of the ancient Greeks and Romans. Thus he asserted that the Toltecs were present at the Tower of Babel. Boturini was at pains, however, to deny that native languages or institutions owed anything to foreign influences. It can be argued that he stands in the same tradition as Bartolomé de las Casas, Toribio de Motolinía, and Bernardino de Sahagún, but without the fire. However, times had changed. Boturini was a historian of the Catholic Enlightenment. His view was not apocalyptic.

Boturini's attitude toward the "native races" places him squarely in his age. Whereas earlier defenders of the Indians had approached the question in millennial and charismatic terms, Boturini's approach was more historically oriented and rational. Other Europeans and criollos in New Spain had a more negative view of the Indians. In the Guadalupan dramas, whether in Nahuatl or Spanish, there is usually a comic Indian who is selfish, undisciplined, concerned only about his next meal, and an indifferent Christian. Boturini glorified the natives, at least in their past. Occasionally, he does let slip a pejorative opinion of contemporary Indians.

One of the ideas that permeates the *Idea* is that urban or city life was the civilized way of living, while the nomadic was not (*políticamente* vs. *bárbaramente*). Spaniards of that age could not conceive of life without cities and the institutions that went with them. One of the first things that Fernando Cortés did, in order to legitimize an otherwise rogue expedition, was to found the city of Veracruz. By doing this he theoretically emancipated his expedition from the governor of Cuba.

The reforms of the Bourbon monarchs tended toward greater uniformity and a rejection of Baroque religious practices. In the atmosphere of the Enlightenment everything was subject to the test of "reason."

Native religious practices, including confraternities (*cofradías*), pilgrimages, devotion to local saints, and the power of the mendicants over the natives were in theory severely restricted. There was even an attempt to get the Indians to abandon their native languages in favor of Spanish.

In this regard Boturini was at pains to refute the Black Legend of Spanish cruelty and exploitation in the New World. He criticized Englishmen like Richard Hakluyt and Samuel Purchas for their historical errors. "At this point I would happily undertake the task of rescuing this history from very many errors about it that Samuel Purchas, an Englishman, published in his work on the description of the world." Others, he criticized for simply being incompetent, like Francesco Gemelli Careri. This latter, who lived from 1651 to 1725, was an Italian judge who after an unsuccessful career in law devoted himself to world travel and travel writing. His most famous work was the multivolume *Giro del Mondo*, whose sixth volume was devoted to New Spain.[28]

He also judged the Indians by the degree to which they aided in the conquest and their acceptance of western Christian life. Thus he has lavish praise for the Tlaxcalans. "I have no doubt that this glorious city and nation have an eminent place in the history of New Spain, full of laurels and applause."[29] "The exploits that it carried out in the time of its paganism, and more in the conquest, deserve to be written with letters of gold." He went so far as to say of the Nahuatl language that it "in my opinion, surpasses Latin in beauty," an astounding claim for his time. He deplored the wanton destruction of native documents. "These fires have been frequent and very fatal in New Spain. The Indians and learned Spaniards bemoan them, and I lament them because it is clear to me that in the ancient pictorial documents there are individual accounts not only of great literary treasures but also of some immense riches kept in their paganism and hidden at the time of the conquest."[30]

In general, the *Idea* divides human history into three "ages," that of the gods, that of heroes, and that of men. Boturini does not seem to

28. Boturini often spells the name as Carreri, though Careri is the form commonly used today.

29. P. 105.

30. Pp. 143, 108, 179, 189.

follow the classical models of Hesiod or Ovid, his favored poet. Rather, he seems to depend more on Augustine of Hippo, the great doctor of the Church, and the ideas of Vico, though without acknowledgment. Thus, whereas the classical pattern begins with a golden age, Boturini begins with a first age, which followed on the confusion of tongues in Genesis. Mankind wandered without purpose and deified the forces of nature. The second age seems to be a mythical time, characterized by heroic, warlike symbols that are simultaneously religious and political. The idea of the heroic age is a strong motif in the *Idea.* The final age is rather idyllic, with the spread of the Spanish empire and the flowering of Christianity in the New World. This division of ages appears to be unique to Boturini.

The most valuable part of the work is the *Catálogo.* It is a vast enumeration of the works that Boturini had been able to gather in New Spain. First composed in New Spain in 1743, it was revised in Spain two years later. The *Catálogo* is an entirely distinct work from the *Idea*, even to the point of having its own pagination, and the *Idea* contains no reference to the *Catálogo.* Boturini seems to indicate that the *Catálogo* was not done from memory. On the other hand, when discussing the miracle of Diego Lázaro, he admits, "I do not remember the name of the author." He later repeats the same assertion at least four times. At another point, he says of a work, "Its author, if I am not mistaken, was someone by the name of Avilés, a priest. . . . For the life of me I cannot remember what the said separate papers are like." At another point he asserts, "because of the weakness of memory and the vast amount of papers, I cannot remember them all, because when I wrote this catalog I was separated from my archive."[31]

Many of the entries in the *Catálogo* are familiar to modern-day scholars. He lists these works according to the various nations and city-states of New Spain and their histories. Some of his entries are unfortunately obscure, and in cases in which he names the authors, they cannot be verified from other sources. Thus, for example, Boturini is our principal source for the works of Joseph Pérez de la Fuente or the so-called will of Gregoria María. The lacunae highlight the tragedy of what happened to Boturini's lifetime of work. If his collection had remained

31. Pp. 170, 173, 174, 179.

in one place and not been dispersed, it would be an invaluable source for modern researchers.

How or why Boturini became interested in the history of devotion to Our Lady of Guadalupe is not clear. He claimed that his interest was spurred on his first visit to her shrine at Tepeyac. His sympathy with the indigenous peoples may have played a role. He declares in an opening letter, "I had scarcely arrived there when I felt myself stimulated by a higher, tender impulse to investigate the miracle of the apparitions of our patroness of Guadalupe." He immediately ran into a difficulty cited by many modern historians. "On that occasion I found their history based on tradition alone, without its being known where or in what hands the documents of such a precious wonder had ended up."[32] The fundamental problem was that from 1531, the traditional date for the apparitions of the Virgin, until 1648 and 1649, when the story was first published by Miguel Sánchez and Luis Laso de la Vega, there was not a single clear reference either to Juan Diego or the apparitions. Of Laso de la Vega's account, Boturini says that he did not mention "any authors from whom he took it, and I believe, rather, that by chance he found some ancient manuscript by an Indian author, and he did not more than publish and put his name on it, quite simply taking away, not only from the natives the honor of having written it, but also the antiquity of the history."[33]

Until recently, biographies of Boturini and studies of his works, especially of the *Catálogo*, have been confined to an earlier period, mostly in the nineteenth and early twentieth century. But in 1974 the edition of the *Idea* published by Miguel León-Portilla contained a lengthy "Estudio preliminar" that examined both Boturini and his work. It also included an exhaustive bibliography. Unfortunately, the citations and translations of classical Latin were not always accurate. The facsimile edition published by Porrúa in 1999 is an invaluable aid for anyone interested in the great Milanese. The present translation is from that edition. The truly outstanding work in recent years has been that of the independent scholar John Glass. His meticulous studies of every aspect of Boturini's life and works is invaluable and merits the gratitude of scholars and researchers everywhere.

32. P. 2.
33. P. 172.

In 2007 the Museo de la Basílica de Guadalupe published a biography of Boturini by Giorgio Antei.[34] It is lengthy, lavishly illustrated, and beautifully produced, almost a coffee-table book. It is extremely detailed, and the author has sought to include all data, not all of it relevant. Still, it presents problems for the historian. Not all the illustrations are pertinent to the text. The list of archives and repositories consulted is exhaustive, but the notes are few in number and rarely cite sources. There is no essay on sources, bibliography, or index. The author sometimes resorts to speculation, such as raising doubts about Boturini's noble titles. All of these factors diminish the usefulness of the book.

34. Giorgio Antei, *El caballero andante: Vida, obra y desventuras de Lorenzo Boturini Benaduci, 1698–1755*. Mexico City: Museo de la Basílica de Guadalupe, 2007.

Some Principles of Translation

The original formatting and the general layout of Boturini's work have been retained as much as possible here. Many capitals have been changed to lowercase. But his spelling of Nahuatl place and proper names, which follows the practice of the eighteenth century, has been modernized to that familiar to contemporary readers. Thus, Ixtlilxochitl is used rather than yxtlilxochitl, Olmec rather than Hulmeca, Toltec rather than Tultec. Boturini consistently uses the accent grave (`) to indicate vowel stress. These have been omitted since they are not in accord with modern practice. He also tends to join Nahuatl words without using the combining forms; these have been left as is. Some of Boturini's paragraphs, which can run on for a whole page, have been shortened for the sake of clarity. Some passages in Latin or Italian have been left in the text to give the reader a sense of what reading the book was like; they are translated in footnotes. Biblical citations have been translated to English directly from the Latin Vulgate. Similarly, classical Latin citations have been translated from the original after comparison with the Loeb Classics.

Select Glossary of Spanish Terms Translated in This Book

cacique	Of Arawak origin, it has been left in the original because there is no single good English term to convey its meaning. It is standard in modern English usage.
cifra	Generally does not refer to numbers but has the meaning of "symbol."
fábula	Not exactly "fable," but more like "story, narrative."
gente	This has a twofold meaning. Sometimes it refers simply to "people," sometimes to "pagan."
gentes mayores	Ancestors.
Gentilidad	Refers to pagan times.
hojas útiles	Documents in good, readable condition.
lienzo	Literally, cloth. Here, indigenous paintings on cloth. The Spanish word has been retained because it is now acceptable among scholars.
mapa	Map or chart and by extension, a drawing, painting, or pictorial representation. Used in the eighteenth century as a generalized description of Indian pictorial manuscripts, not necessarily a map in the European sense.

metáfora	Not a metaphor in the strict sense but in the broader sense of "figure of speech."
monumento	Usually, historical sources, here usually translated as "records."
papel de marca, papel de marca mayor	A stamped sheet of paper or official paper for legal documents.
pliego	Full-size sheet of paper. Forms two folio leaves when folded in half. Also, a sealed or folded sheet of paper forming a cover for an enclosed document.
rueda	Literally, "wheel." A native language document in the form of a circle.
símbolo	Symbol; see tabla. The Latin original means a profession of faith, or a creed.
tabla	Table or tablet, but can also refer to a posted notice.

IDEA

DE UNA NUEVA

HISTORIA GENERAL

DE LA

AMERICA SEPTENTRIONAL.

FUNDADA

SOBRE MATERIAL COPIOSO DE FIGURAS, Symbolos, Caractères, y Geroglificos, Cantares, y Manuſcritos de Autores Indios, ultimamente deſcubiertos.

DEDICALA

AL REY N.TRO SEÑOR

EN SU REAL, Y SUPREMO CONSEJO DE LAS INDIAS

EL CAVALLERO LORENZO BOTURINI BENADUCI, Señor de la Torre, y de Hono.

CON LICENCIA

EN MADRID: En la Imprenta de Juan de Zuñiga. Año M. D, CC. XLVI.

Title page of the 1746 edition

IDEA

OF A NEW

GENERAL HISTORY

OF

NORTH AMERICA

BASED

ON COPIOUS MATERIAL OF FIGURES,

Symbols, Characters, and Hieroglyphics, Songs,

and Manuscripts of Indian Authors,

Recently Discovered

THE KNIGHT LORENZO BOTURINI BENADUCI,

Lord of la Torre and Hono,

Dedicates it

TO THE KING, OUR LORD

IN HIS ROYAL AND SUPREME COUNCIL

OF THE INDIES

With Permission

IN MADRID: at the Press of Juan de Zúñiga

1746

SIR:

Divine Providence which guides men per ambages et judicia maxima[1] *has transferred me from other courts of Europe to that of Your Majesty and destined me for the Indies in the year 1735. I had scarcely arrived there when I felt myself stimulated by a higher, tender impulse to investigate the miracle of the apparitions of our patroness of Guadalupe. On that occasion I found their history based on tradition alone, without its being known where or in what hands the documents of such a precious wonder had ended up. The same history of pagan times, which was on the verge of disappearing, cried out for a devotee who would rescue it from the tomb of oblivion. My inclination was not slow in thinking about the one and the other, and although the undertaking seemed impossible to many, confident in the help of the Almighty, who never fails one who has a good intention, I daringly went ahead, and exposed to the inclemency of heaven and an infinite number of other discomforts, I traveled over vast territories, and often without finding lodging, until after eight years of unceasing determination and ever-growing expenses, I had the good fortune, which nobody can recount, of having collected a museum of materials so precious in both ecclesiastical and secular history, that it can well be considered among the richest treasures of the Indies. As a firm testimony of my loyalty and humble submission, I sent its Index to Your Majesty, whom I wished ever to serve, with the intention of my returning to court. I considered it a strict duty to give Your Majesty an account of the historical materials of that New World.*

---

1. "Through winding ways and highest judgments."

I humbly carry this out, placing at Your Majesty's feet the present Idea of the General History of North America, which I wrote in a short time, emptying the small treasury of my memory, and these are the first fruits of the burning zeal that I profess for Your Majesty's service. May God protect Your Majesty's Royal Catholic person, as Christendom has need.

Madrid, February 3, 1745.

SIR:
At Your Majesty's royal feet,

Lorenzo Boturini Benaduci

EVALUATION

of *the Most Reverend Father, Master PEDRO FRESNEDA of the Society of Jesus, Catedrático de prima*[2] *of mathematics in the Imperial College, and Cosmógrafo mayor of His Majesty in matters of the Indies.*

By order of Your Excellency I have seen the book titled *Idea of a New General History of North America* written by the knight don Lorenzo Boturini Benaduci, lord of la Torre and Hono. I have read it with some care because, since the proposal that he presents is the bulk of the work, seeing that it is so expanded in its size, out of curiosity I wanted to see where I could underline the lack of proportion in this mass; I saw the parts, which are presented proportionally, the well-founded means that are proposed; and believing that the construction would correspond to his original design, I reveled in the newness of his method, in the inexhaustibility of his labor, in his revealing of such a diversity of species, in his genius for such small details of information, and, finally, in an extensive, brilliant, well-fitted architecture. The book is only an Idea, but if a lion is known by one claw, *ex ungue leonem*[3] the greatness of the work can be known just by this outline when only one footprint indicates its oversized stature. He proposes clearly what so many published in such an obscure and unlearned way, and while his genius outlines the vastness of the material, he illuminates, like the light, new things, *labore et constantia*,[4] with work and application the most arduous enterprises are achieved, and this is the motto that is inscribed on what is most difficult. And the author, by force of labor,

2. Tenured chair that was taught at the canonical hour of Prime.
3. "The lion from the claw."
4. "By work and application."

at the cost of his means, by nourishing his strength, achieved what others did not find, perhaps because out of weariness their talent grew lazy. The Work teaches what the most inquisitive people did not succeed in discovering, and thus it will resound in the echoes of eternal fame, the name of the author will live in common usefulness, and the presses will declare how genius, work, application and care achieve what is most difficult. And because the Work does not contain anything against our faith and good morals, I judge that it is worthy of the permission that he requests. This is my opinion in this imperial college of Madrid, February 9, 1746.

JHS[5]
Pedro Fresneda

5. First three letters of the Greek name for Jesus.

License of the Ordinary[6]

We, the licentiate don Miguel Gómez de Escobar, inquisitor ordinary and vicar of this town and its district, etc. By the present [letter], and in accord with our office, we grant license so that the book titled *Idea of a New General History of North America*, its author being don Lorenzo Boturini Benaduci, lord of la Torre and Hono, can and may be printed, seeing that by our order and commission it has been seen and examined, and it does not contain anything opposed to our Holy Faith and good morals. Given at Madrid, February 9, 1746.

Lic. Don Miguel Gómez
de Escobar
By his Command
Felipe Ignacio Vázquez de Neira

6. "The ordinary" means the local bishop.

DECLARATION

of Doctor don Joseph Borrull, *formerly catedrático de prima of civil jurisprudence at the University of Salamanca, prosecuting attorney and judge of Granada, and at the present time [member] of the Supreme Council of the Indies.*

By order of the Royal and Supreme Council of the Indies I have seen and perused very slowly and in detail and with the help of a skilled and intelligent interpreter, who was necessary for understanding the various American languages, hieroglyphics, and pictures cited in the *Idea of a New General History of North America, Based on Copious Material of Figures, Symbols, Characters, and Hieroglyphs, Songs, and Manuscripts of Indian Authors, Recently Discovered,* which the knight don Lorenzo Boturini Benaduci, lord of la Torre and Hono, has assembled and dedicates to the King, Our Lord, in the Royal and Supreme Council of the Indies. And on the certain supposition that it may not contain anything contrary to the dogmas of our holy faith, good morals, nor the rights of His Majesty, I proceed without delay, in fulfillment of the command that has been imposed on me, to make known my declaration on the subject of the proposed Idea. It is not new (and if only it were more frequent, and we would not be mocked so often, moved only by the specious titles and inscriptions in the books) that before beginning and undertaking the devised work, the materials should be collected, the outline and design should be formulated and given to the public, in order that, after being seen and examined by many persons, its usefulness and importance should be recognized, and being received, as is appropriate, the author may enter into it with new vigor and with the morally certain hope that it will merit the approval of learned men, who also can contribute to its greater perfection with their observations. Not only is this practice to be seen in material constructions and buildings that serve for the benefit and profit of the body, but also in the intellectual things that have as their purpose to adorn and enlighten the human mind. We have a good example in Cardinal de Aguirre,[7] the immortal splendor and honor of our Spain, who before publishing the four volumes of the Councils of Spain with notes, discussions, and analyses, published at Salamanca in the year 1685, an explanatory notice or brief summary of the councils of this nation, decretals, and other instruments pertaining to it, which he desired to bring to the public, and he dedicates it to His Majesty, the lord don Carlos II, and asks for his royal help and protection. It seems that the knight don Lorenzo Boturini follows in these same footsteps, explaining in this *Idea* or design the matters that he will deal with, the books, papers, parchments, and other documents that his diligence has been able to collect at the cost of extreme work, dedication, and expense, from which he forms an extensive and individual index that he locates at the end of this *Idea*, and they are the materials with which he will construct this great edifice, and he seeks and requests royal protection for such a costly undertaking. The usefulness and importance of this well-planned work are easily recognized by drawing a parallel and connection between the histories that we have of that vast American continent and the one that this author offers. Those that have been published up to the present time, whether general or whether particular to a certain region or province, have been satisfied merely to recount the condition in which the province or kingdom found itself at the time of its conquest, without seriously investigating and inquiring into the origin of the Indians, their coming to those regions, their transmigrations, government, political structure, customs, religion, language, signs, hieroglyphs and pictures, with which would explain their concepts to those who were absent, and left to posterity the memory and notice of their deeds and actions. This is clearly seen in the most classical of authors, such as the scholarly Acosta, Inca Garcilaso, Herrera,

---

7. Joseph Saenz de Aguirre (1630–99) was a cardinal and a learned Spanish Benedictine. His more important works are on philosophical and theological subjects, but he also produced valuable writings on ecclesiastical history, commentaries on the theology of Saint Anselm, two volumes of *Miscellanea*, and a book to prove that the *De Imitatione Christi* was written by the scholar Jean Gerson (1363–1429).

Solís,[8] and others, who, even though they touch on these matters somewhat in their histories and accounts, it is so much in passing and with such superficiality, that they arouse the desire of the curious reader more than they satisfy it. And, without a doubt, either these despaired of obtaining them or did not dare to penetrate these materials, to free themselves from the arduous and costly work of inquiring and collecting the memorials that the ancient Americans left, of seriously applying themselves to the knowledge and understanding of the languages, and principally of the characters, signs, hieroglyphs, and pictures, of dealing with the chiefs and persons of standing among those of that nation, who would have preserved something. However, our author, following the style and historical method used by the sacred authors and the most celebrated secular ones, both Greek and Roman, having as his purpose that commonplace but true pronouncement of the divine Maro:[9]

Book 1 *Georgics*, verse 145.

Labor omnia vincit
Improbus . . . .[10]

With his indefatigable work and application, he has been able to collect so much material (as the index, which has already been mentioned, makes clear) and like another Oedipus,[11] to clarify and decipher the characters, hieroglyphs, and pictures that the Indians used in their histories, of which many others are the most obscure enigmas, and comparing these labors with the works of the fabled and fictitious

8. José de Acosta (1539–1600) was a Jesuit missionary, naturalist, and historian. He was the author of *Historia natural y moral de las Indias* (1590). Garcilaso de la Vega (1539–1616), also known as Garcilaso El Inca, was the son of a Spanish conquistador and an Inca noblewoman. He was the author of a comprehensive history, *Comentarios reales de los Incas* (1619). Antonio de Herrera y Tordesillas (1559–1626) held various important posts in the Spanish government. He wrote numerous histories while serving in government. Antonio de Solís y Ribadeneyra (1610–88) was a dramatist and historian. He was the author of *Historia de la conquista de México* (1684).

9. That is, Vergil (Publius Vergilius Maro).

10. *Sic* for *Labor improbus omnia vincit*, "Unceasing labor conquers all." Vergil, *Georgics*, book 1, vols. 145–46.

11. A reference to the legend that Oedipus solved the riddle of the Sphinx.

Alcides,[12] this latter remains on a much lower level. One of the most celebrated antiquarians of this century, and revered as such in all Europe, attempted several times to form an alphabet or ABC of the ancient Spanish language to understand and read the letters or characters that the Spanish used before the Latin ones were introduced into these provinces. There are many medals or coins from that time, whose fronts and backs are written with them, making them useful for their formation of the Phoenician, Samaritan, Ionic, and other nations that ruled Spain, but after many sleepless nights and application he composed one but with the greatest fear and diffidence that he had not achieved his purpose, as he himself admits. Their alphabet, if it had achieved the appropriate perfection, would deservedly have gained for the said author among the learned men of Europe who eagerly consulted him, such credit and applause as he who as among princes and sovereigns had discovered or would discover, amid the changing waves of the sea and the unstable winds, the sought-after point of geographic longitude. But of what praise, honor, and reward is our author not deserving? With only the light that the renowned don Carlos de Sigüenza was able to provide[14] and the traveler Careri in volume 6 of *Journey to New Spain*,[15] which [light] given to him, has penetrated what is the innermost and unknown, that is, the true origin and progression from those parts to North America, its government, sciences, and principally having deciphered its characters, hieroglyphs, and pictures. . . .[16] This point is not just curious to satisfy scholars and lovers of antiquity but also useful and necessary for enabling those tribunals of justice to administer it to the wretched Indians, who, on the basis of their lawful titles, explained with hieroglyphs and pictures, without an interpreter

The Dean of Alicante[13] Marti, book II, letter 6

12. Another name for Hercules.

13. Manuel Martí, the dean of the Cathedral of Alicante, apparently wrote with some levity in his *Epistolario* about the accomplishments of the American Indians. There is not much information about him.

14. Carlos de Sigüenza y Góngora (1645–1700), Mexican savant, scientist, historian, and polymath.

15. Giovanni Francesco Gemelli Careri (1651–1725), Italian traveler and adventurer. His most important work, *Giro del Mundo* (*sic* for *Mondo*), describes a tour around the world. Volume 6 is devoted to New Spain.

16. Periods in original.

capable of deciphering them, miserably lose their rights and the exercise of them. I admit, with the simplicity that I profess and ought to profess, that when I began to read this *Idea*, I thought that it was the author's dream, or even delirium, and that no person would find himself capable of carrying it out without divine inspiration and help. However, having read the index of the books that he has collected and that are stored in his archive or museum, and having observed what he now makes clear and uncovers in the *Idea*, and most of all having dealt with this person with sufficient frequency, I have changed my assessment entirely, for with my dealings and conversation with him I have reached the point of probing his singular genius, his supreme penetration, indefatigable labor, pointed judgment and well-founded criticisms, a universal ornamentation of all the sciences, not being a foreigner in anything, but a very good native, both in the purely mathematical and in the physical-mathematical, natural and moral: in both jurisprudences, civil and canonical, and in every kind of learning; skill in European languages, and ultimately in his stay of nine years in America, in those [languages] of that country, to which he traveled, not in order to discover material mines and what human greed so esteems, but to unearth those previously buried in oblivion, in order to enrich his understanding and cast light on the nation and even all of Europe. That is not strange but very frequent in many foreigners, who, moved only by curiosity and without any further interest, circulate through various countries, observing in each one what is most singular; of this there are as many witnesses as there are books published by travelers, for which reason I think that only this person is capable of putting into practice the *Idea* proposed and fulfilling the expectation, and that this most opportune occasion should not be wasted; if lost, so much collected material is frustrated, for it is a priceless treasure, which, under the control of someone other than the author, will be useless for lack of use and knowledge, and with him we can promise a complete history, which we do not have, of the most valuable part of America, which is the north,. Because after what the chronicler Antonio de Herrera wrote in his universal history and don Antonio de Solís with what regards New Spain, ending with just the conquest of Mexico, there has been no progress, not even by those to whom its continuation was entrusted, nor is there hope that it will be finished later on. In view of what has been explained up to now, I am of the opinion, not only that the requested permission be given, but many thanks for the work carried out up to now, with the hope of greater ones, as soon as what is proposed in the *Idea* be brought to perfection. This is my feeling, *Salvo*, *&c.*[17] Madrid, November 2, 1745.

Doctor don Joseph Borrull

17. Apparently the beginning of a declaration that his opinion is subject to the teaching authority of the Church.

PERMISSION OF THE ROYAL COUNCIL OF THE INDIES

I, don Pedro de la Vega, of His Majesty's Council, its secretary and major official of the secretariat of the Council and Court of the Indies, of the administration of the provinces of New Spain, certify that the approbation given by the señor doctor don Joseph Borrull of His Majesty's Council and fiscal of the same for the Indies, of the book titled *Idea of a New General History of North America*, written by the knight don Lorenzo Boturini Benaduci, Lord of la Torre and Hono, having been seen by the gentlemen of the aforesaid council, have agreed on the thirteenth of the current month to grant permission to the aforesaid don Lorenzo that he may be able to publish the aforesaid book, as is evident from the agreement cited and from the approval, the original of which remains in this secretariat, to which I refer, and in order that there be evidence of this, I give the present [permission] as directed by the aforesaid gentlemen. Madrid, December 15, 1745.

Don Pedro de la Vega

J[esus] M[ary] J[oseph]

APPROBATION OF THE Most Reverend Father fray JUAN DE LA CONCEPCIÓN, Discalced Carmelite, formerly lector in Sacred Scripture, writer of his religious order, examiner of the Supreme and General Inquisition, theologian to the household of the Most Serene Lord Prince Cardinal, and Academic of the Royal Spanish Academy.[18]

V[ery] [Powerful] [Lord]

In obedience to the order of Your Highness, I have read the book titled *Idea of a New General History of North America*, which its author, the knight *don Lorenzo Boturini Benaduci, lord of la Torre and Hono*, seeks to have published, together with the *Index of the Historic Museum*, which the author himself has collected. And although I have carried it out with almost excessive reflection because he has increased in my natural inclination, which many have judged to be rigorously critical, he has given extra attention to the *new*, the *very ancient*, the *extensive*, and the *arcane* of the matter. I have not known how to avoid changing a censure into praise. I must say with the most sincere candor that the intent of the Knight *Boturini* in writing this history of America is no less worthy of applause nor less an object of admiration than the daring[19] of Columbus and the heroism of the fortunate Cortés in discovering it and conquering it.

---

18. Juan Bautista de la Concepción was a native of Catalunya, provincial of the Barcelona province of the Discalced Carmelites, *visitador* of New Spain, and author of *El silencio panagírico*, 1718, and *La mejor madre: Elogio de Nuestra Señora del Carmen*, 1719 (Beristáin de Souza, *Biblioteca*, 1:326–27).

19. *Arresto*, which may also mean "determination."

Against the discovery of the New World, no arguments were raised except in the negative. (I use this word keeping in mind the opinion of Saint Augustine, Lactantius,[20] Vergil, and others). *No one has had news of it* (they commonly said): *therefore it does not exist.* Those who might oppose our author's intention have a large number of positive arguments; because after two centuries America is now populated with Spaniards, its ancient inhabitants extinguished, its rivers taken over, its mountain ranges trekked, its mines worked, its idols buried, its temples turned into churches. It hardly seems credible that everything that can be investigated about that country has not been investigated. The idea, as erroneous as it is widespread, that the Indians were *barbarians*, gave birth to skepticism about finding records which would recount how they used to be, among some men of whom it has been written more than once that even they themselves doubted that they had once been. So the author has had to fight not only against neglect and forgetfulness, but to show that they were only neglect and forgetfulness, which up to now usurped the names of diligence and care.

The hero *Cortés* had to combat the valor and multitudes of the Americans, but with the advantages of European military arms and strategies, unknown until that time in those regions. Finally, he proceeded like the light in overcoming the darkness, and our author has seen himself compelled to introduce himself and (let us say so) to make friends with the darkness in order to find the light. Familiarizing himself with the Indians, admitting and giving them hospitality in the privacy of his office and to the confidences of his table, has been not the least and almost the most, useful of his laborious sleepless nights. No one can doubt that, despite the advantages I mentioned earlier, the conquest of North America was an achievement greater than what human strength is capable of and pertains to the finger of God, manifested in a thousand repeated wonders: and I will have no doubt that Divine Providence has shown special care to this knight, giving him the means for such a vast, difficult enterprise.

---

20. Saint Augustine of Hippo (Aurelius Augustinus Hipponensis, AD 354–AD 430) was one of the most influential of the early church fathers. He was the author of the *Confessions* and *The City of God.* Lactantius (Lucis Caecilius Firmianus Lactantius, ca. AD 240–ca. AD 320) was an early church theologian and historian.

The great problems of *by whom, when, and where those countries were populated, and if, when our Spaniards entered them, they found the light of the gospel unknown or just forgotten*, for even in hope, they were considered inseparable, will occupy, when the edition of this history is published, the category of truths. The *Idea* alone uncovers so many and such noble species of which not even our imagination has notice, which almost satisfies curiosity although it stimulates it. Early examples are the notices about the primitive, most glorious *Toltec Nation*, whose very name most of our authors did not make known to us. The *theogonia* or descent of the American gods, so closely related with the Greek, Roman, and as a result, the Egyptian. The system of *computation*, so mysterious, so unchangeable, so well ordered. The artful method and division of the *calendars*, and another thousand species, as notable as they are unknown.

Effort is the daughter of the heart, just as writings are born of the understanding, and this is of a quality so rare that in order to undertake it and carry it out, our author has had need of all the highborn efforts which his very noble, even almost royal, lineage affords him, and all the learning that enriches his understanding, even if the very great renown of Encyclopedia does not come to him. In order that the thought of this work be not avoided in terror and be embraced as a pleasure is not the operation of any spirit of mediocrity. Who knows if it might be said that this daring was no less than that of Aeneas when he went to take account of the riches of the dark kingdom, not leaving out the similar act of giving the golden bough at the entrance, in the great quantities that the author has expended in order to acquire the wealth of so many monuments.[21]

From this day forward the Spanish nation should recognize him as earning all its applause and all its gratitude. I will always revere him for this quality, although with some feeling (not base, I think, though it seems so) that the master of such a glorious action should not owe his birth to our Spain. I now know that it can be a satisfaction that the author is a Milanese whose fellow countrymen have continuously proven to be very Spanish in feeling. I do not know what connection

---

21. The reference is to book 6 of the *Aeneid*, in which Aeneas seeks to visit his father in Hades and bring a golden branch to Proserpine.

Providence has placed between America and Italy that one Italian [Columbus] rescued it from the immensities of the Gulf and another Italian vindicates it from the injuries with which slander, forgetfulness, and time want to debase it. The former, even serving the fifth Ferdinand,[22] among whose high virtues liberality was not the greatest, did not fail to win a prize. How can our [Italian] not expect the highest reward when he has the good fortune to serve the fifth Philip, to whom munificence is natural, and to whom the world of letters owes all of its exaltation?

A work in which the triumphs of our religion are described, the errors of paganism are uncovered, the spread of the gospel is facilitated, and the means are given for governing the American dominions in peace and justice, not without usefulness to the monarch, most certainly does not contain any doctrine or proposition that is not in conformity with our holy Catholic faith, good morals, or His Majesty's royal rights. For all of which, not only do I think the author worthy of being authorized with permission for publication, but also that he be awarded it quickly. This is my opinion, *Salvo, etc.* In this convent of the Discalced Carmelites of Saint Hermenegild, Madrid, January 18, 1746.

Fray Juan de la Concepción

22. Another title of Ferdinand II of Aragon.

PERMISSION OF THE ROYAL COUNCIL OF CASTILE

Don Miguel Fernández Munilla, secretary of the king, our lord, his senior notary of the law court and of the administration of the Council. I certify that its gentlemen have granted permission to the knight don Lorenzo Boturini Benaduci, lord of la Torre and Hono, that a book that he has written can be printed once and sold, titled *Idea of a New General History of North America*, with which the printing may be made from the original, which has a rubric and at the end is signed with my signature, and which, before it may be sold, the said printed book be brought to the Council, together with the original and the certification of the corrector that they are in agreement in order that it may be taxed according to its sales price, while observing in the printing that which has been established and foreseen by the laws and pragmatics[23] of these kingdoms. And as evidence I have affixed my signature on January 21, 1746.

Don Miguel Fernández Munilla

23. Royal order with special formalities that added to fundamental law.

OFFICIAL PRICE

I, Don Miguel Fernández Munilla, secretary of the king, our lord, senior notary of his chamber[24] and of the government of the council, certify that the book titled *Idea of a New General History of North America*, having been seen by its members, its author, the knight don Lorenzo Boturini Benaduci, lord of la Torre and Hono, who with the permission of the said gentlemen granted to him, has been printed, they have set its price at eight maravedís[25] per sheet and the book referred to seems to have thirty-three, without the introductory matter or tables, which in this respect involves two hundred and sixty-four maravedís, and they ordered that it be sold at the said price and no more, and that this certification be placed at the beginning of each book so that it may be known to the seller. And in order that it may be evident I signed it in Madrid, May 21, 1746.

Don Miguel Fernández Munilla

24. *Escribano de cámara.*

25. A fictional unit of Spanish currency, used as a standard of value.

THE AMERICAN MUSES

UNKNOWN TO MANY, NOT BELIEVED IN BY MOST, CONSIDERED DEAD BY A FEW, having overcome, with the help of the knight Boturini, the oppressions of forgetfulness and the impediments of time, present themselves to the European [muses], asking to be introduced at the feet of the Great Jupiter of Spain, whom they venerate as the better Apollo, in this

HEROIC ROMANCE

Beautiful throng, sacred honor of Pindo,[26]
To whose sweet, powerful influence
You show your intelligence, you do not have
The indocile stock, the rough crag
Fair daughters of Apollo who hasten
To his luminous rays, in order that being spread about,
You may raise crystal to the melodious fountain;
You may produce fodder for the winged brute:
You [muses], through whom Europe has now
Succeeded in having imposed a noble yoke on the world;
Accomplishing that the invasion, what could be an insult
Is considered a gift,

26. *Sic.* Perhaps another form of Pindar?

Recognize some of your sisters,
 To whose names an unjust fate wanted
 To give, building obelisks from waves,
 The whole ocean as a tomb.
We are sisters, yes; because we were born by an act
 Of the divine knowledge that begot us
 For mankind, and we endure
 narrow veins of the greatest torrents.
We, having moved from Asia
 By hitherto unknown routes,
 Egypt and Boecia,[27] we go forward
 To the world, new today, at that time old.
From Isis there, from Astrea, from Minerva,
 And from Phoebus[28] we formed a thousand students,
 From the first lintel of Puerto Rico,
 To the eastern seaport of Acapulco.
To Ephoros and Quirites[29] the white robed ones
 Could give norms for what is just.
 Being envious beforehand of Pompilius,
 And early imitation of Lycurgus.[30]
They devised symbols and understood
 Them as so proper, so concise, so profound,
 That even having seen its pyramids, the Nile
 Could learn lessons from the Amazon.
It is true that they multiplied the number of deities,
 But the error of belief had a bitter aftertaste;
 Since just accepting the benefits
 Was an indication of consecrating the cults;

---

27. Boeotia, a fertile region of Greece.

28. Isis was an Egyptian goddess who had a following in ancient Rome. She was the spouse of Horus and represented the ideal mother figure. Astraia was a goddess of justice. Phoebus was the Greek god of light; god of prophecy, poetry, music, and healing; son of Zeus and Leto; twin brother of Artemis. Often associated with Apollo.

29. Rather obscure terms. The Ephores were highly regarded ancient Spartans, and the term passed to a class of Romans. The Quirites were originally Romans with the full right of citizenship.

30. Numa Pompilius was the semi-legendary second king of Rome. Lycurgus probably refers to the author of the Spartan constitution.

The ardor of poetic enthusiasm
    Strongly inflamed their discourse
    So that their verses were the annals of the
    Past age and the teaching of the future one.
Music moves the emotions
    With such a smooth, irresistible impulse
    That now to the Epicedio,[31] now to the Epinicio[32]
    The morning blossomed,
    the pleasure was excessive.
The twisted fibers of the magueys offered many volumes
    Of history, in which colors were the pages,
    Forming letters from knots,
Better pens were the brushes
    Which passed over the cotton cloth
    Such a living reflection of the heroes,
    That even the touch judged its subject by its appearance.
Exquisite mechanical agitation softened
    The hardest metal,
    And the polished trunk, sharp flint,
    Substituted for the lack of iron.
The ingenious raced with such speed
    The rational, technical course
    That the rest were unaware of their progress,
    All the extent of their learning.
In other times we were so venerated,
    Until the furious horrors
    Of renewed Mars succeeded in mingling
    Peacefulness with disturbances.
Therefore when your children ask us
    About the frightening kingdom of Neptune,
    They perceived our remnants so badly
    That they believed them to be false because they were confused.
We saw ourselves so close to nothingness
    That on the threshold of its dark breast
    To finish casting us into the center
    Five years would be like a thousand centuries.

31. Poetic composition that mourned and praised a dead person.
32. Song of victory.

Possessed by this unhappy state,
 And misfortune now made eternal,
 The reestablishment even of hope
 Was madness, when a refuge was longed for.
When the benign, provident heaven
 Great genius placed us in Insubria[33]
 That neither the poor man nor greedy man (this is the wonder)
 Would resolve to enter our world.
In accidental tragic remains
 He found traces of our ancient honor;
 Incentives that made them search
 For a treasure lost because it was hidden.
Almost ten times the fleece, the fish scale
 Depicted the four brutes[34] of the sun
 Each spray offering impetus to the Januaries,
 By giving impetus to the burning Julys.
With regard to Lelius,[35] attentive to the uprising
 That his noble spirit proposes
 It penetrated the household gods of royal Troy,
 It registered the smoke of humble Ithaca.
Neither did he find the most flowered valley enchanting,
 Nor did he pardon the wildest forest,
 Which in trees, crags, and even in cliffs,
 He had to restore, which he had to learn.
Not without a shudder did America look
 At the guest counted among their frequent ones,
 What the noble son of Phoebus spent
 To achieve an effect of Mercury.
Of such great expense, of such great effort,
 He achieved the result in a copious museum;
 Where sweet swans are able to preen themselves
 To the confusion of portentous owls.

33. Apparently a reference to the area around Milan and to Lombardy in general.

34. A reference to Apollo's four horses.

35. An obscure reference. It may refer to Caius Laelius, a Roman general and statesman, about whom little is known.

With the examination of so many monuments
He reduced us to the life of the world;
Transforming the sulphurous bitumen of the Muses
Into the currents of Lethe.[36]
As if to hinder our recovery,
What is fragile has immense strength,
For this beginning to achieve progress,
An arm no lesser than that of Augustus is required.
Only that of Philip can achieve
To whose good fortune, to whose judgment, to
Whose valor Neptune yields the wet trident,
And Jupiter the rapid three-pointed spear.
He who scorns, overcomes, weakens, treads on
Now the despicable acts of cunning Simon,
Now the shape changes of deceitful Proteus
Now the daring of the mighty Enceladus.[37]
He who has taken care of your guardianship,
Consecrating a thousand temples to your worship;
For whose protection Spain succeeds in being
The pledge of France, the fright of Britain.
To this greater Jupiter, more famous Apollo,
Faithful tribute binds our yearnings;
Waiting for our Laurel to be reborn,
From a happy contact with their classic theater.[38]
You [European muses] are their most favored [Greek deities]:
Present us, then, before their throne,
Whose place of honor they judge by the words
Of the fierce Chilean and the barbarous Mollucan.

Written by
Fray Juan de la Concepción
Discalced Carmelite

36. In Greek mythology, Lethe was one of the five rivers of Hades and caused complete forgetfulness.

37. "Simon" may refer to Simon the Magician. See *Acts of the Apostles* 8:9–25. Proteus was a sea god, and Enceladus was a giant son of the earth goddess Gaia.

38. Conthurno, originally a buskin or footwear worn by actors in classical Greek and Roman theater, also meaning the theater itself.

THE EUROPEAN MUSES RESPOND

To the American Muses in this

SPANISH HENDECASYLLABLE[39]

Sacred deities, gala of the lyre
    That Apollo plays, where the
    Soul is endowed
    With the advantages of the body
    Which Osiris[40] makes golden
    Which you infused in its strings.
Divine beings of the west, your
    Light rivals in its rays that of Phoebus,
    Surrendering to the triumph you achieve as garlands
    The flowering laurel, which was its eclipse.
O, our sisters, not that short fanfares
Are equal to elevated tones
    Indeed, because your elegance grants us
    The honor that the Graces forbid to us.
That image came to our admiration,
    Which without crossing the plain of Amphitrite[41]
    Writ on the space of the heavens
    Overcame distances that the pilot measures.
An image by that lively and wise pen
    Which when it now flies, now when it writes,

---

39. A varied form of eleven syllables originally borrowed from Italian poetry.

40. Osiris was the Egyptian god of life, vegetation, and the annual flooding of the Nile.

41. Sea goddess, wife of Poseidon.

With your impulse and influence,
They applaud Tully,[42] they celebrate the swan.
Heraldry of apple orchards which in the cloister or gardens
Of sacred poems the letters of their names form portraits:
One is grace, the other is conceived in grace.
This happy student of your lights
Painted the great spirit for us with the finest shades;
Yes, he alone can be its brush
Who paints souls.
The great spirit of that man,
The hero who was able, not in bloody battles,
But in famous reasoned battles,
To find triumphs, like the wise Ulysses.
Boturini: now the Po[43] with such renown,
Full of vanity, is not restrained,
And overflowing with honor, seeks to flood
With his glory the ends of the earth.
Boturini: the Solon,[44] he who in a notable way
Facing Medea and even Circe,[45]
In order to discover hidden treasures,
He enchanted (great accomplishment!)
Your caciques.
He who by enhancing so much the name of the
Great Cortés, and his advances declare,
With deeds and with polite terms
He conquered unconquerable wills.
He who in order to know these histories,
Preserved on pita fiber[46] and images,

---

42. Anglicized version of Marcus Tullius Cicero (106 BC –43 BC) Roman orator and politician.

43. A river in Northern Italy.

44. Synonymous with a lawgiver.

45. Medea in many Greek legends was an enchantress. She was the niece of Circe, who figures prominently in the *Odyssey* and who transformed her enemies into animals.

46. Pita was a New World plant from which was made a delicate thread comparable to linen.

Acquired, by negotiating at great cost
With the language of gold, the language of the pagans.
He who in his breast alone brought us
More riches than the mainland, Peru,
And New Spain, have given to the Spaniards,
Stomachs which are those of pitch black vultures.
We believe that full of honor, the useful vassal,
Rewarded by the Royal Grace which binds
The Crown of two worlds, the undaunted,
Famous, great king, the fifth Philip:
He will again carry out the enterprise
That has been started: sorrow will not pain us,
Because the glory that is lost is not pain,
If the adored idol achieves it.
Boturini will return (O sweet muses!)
To your hemispheres, that he may imitate
The eagle and the phoenix which in tasks
Find the lights that are fond of fame.
The worsening condition of Hesperia[47] prevents it
Repairing the ship, which to Thetis[48] makes
Turbulent the skeins of waves; and its bonds
are to be delights of Turkish leaves.
He will pass the great salon of two thousand leagues,
He will see its curtains to be invisible,
Inflamed by Favonius;[49] and there will be cornucopias
Of wings and the dolphin's scales.
They will show crystaline garzotas[50]
When they populate the wide expanse;
And because they have lights in the night,
The salt residue will produce Saint Elmo's fire.[51]

---

47. The term refers to two peninsulas, Spain and Italy, most often the latter.

48. In Greek mythology, a sea nymph.

49. Favonius, one of the Roman wind gods, who held dominion over plants and flowers and was generally equated with the Greek god Zephyrus.

50. A species of bird whose feathers were used for adornment.

51. Figuratively, a savior, someone who favors a certain cause.

There will be as many mirrors as there are crossings-out,
They are seen in the high spheres,
In order that in their spaces
The copy of man as such may be multiplied
In a living way.
You will have precursors of the two moons in the
Sixty suns, which will inform you there
Of their arrival at these sands; and the
Last will see to it that in the ovens
There will be no danger.
In prison, overcoming the strong north wind,
It will guide the ship until it reaches
[San Juan de] Ulúa to the leeward of Castile.
And tie up the ropes on its rings
Here, sisters, take away from the Nereides[52]
The shores that they occupy and change
The beaches into lush gardens and firmaments
In order that our sailor may set foot on them.
When, covered with the naval carriage
Among the small boats on the pier may he scan the horizon
Bring him to the garden of your arms
From the zephyrs of the longboat.
He wears on his breast finely wrought jewels,
Emeralds, diamonds, and rubies,
Where our hopes are counted
His constancy and his zeal for the good that follows.
Your docile Indians in their dances
Weave together respect and love,
And adorned with such precious cloth,
From their plants they bring forth blouses.[53]
Permit that this time (fair deities)
For so many reasons you may drink a toast without reason;
Because there cannot be vile effects of fiery pulque
With noble causes.

---

52. The Nereides (or Nereids) were fifty Haliad nymphs or goddesses of the sea. They were the patrons of sailors and fishermen, and came to the aid of men in distress.

53. *Huepiles, sic* for *huipiles*, Nahuatl *huipilli.*

Put aside what concerns navigation, and let
The wanderer stop, in which three times
Your sacred favor distinguishes him,
His circumstances and
And the perseverance to travel through so many countries.
May that giant who yawns flames
(when his skirt smells) enlighten him;
And the fortune that the Orizaba[54] bestows,
Mongibelo[55] and Vesuvius may envy.
Of Moteuczoma, Bogota, and the Inca,
Those which were empires, may they dedicate to him,
As much as the influence of Phiton[56] engenders,
As much as the honor of Venus conceives.
You are his tutelary deities; and because he has
Had such happy beginnings in the enterprise
Grant him the means necessary
For him to achieve his heroic purposes.
Let the great work be finished, projected
By his great heart, from which follow
Service to the king, honor to the Indies,
Glory to you, and crests for Spain.
God keep you, divine spirits.
Europe, in the best of Aprils;
Year of our union. Your sisters,
Who will make coats-of-arms from your crests.

Don Joseph de Toca Velasco

54. Volcanic mountain in Mexico.
55. Reference not clear.
56. The earth god of Delphi, usually depicted as a serpent.

AL SIGNOR CAVALIER BOTURINI

in occasione della nuova, bella, ed erudita Storia delle Indie, data in luce con vantaggio, ed applauso della Republic Literaria,

SONETTO[57]

Tempo già fù, che dalla Tosca Arena,
E dall' Onda Ligustica partìo
Colombo, e poi Vespucci, che desìo
Solo di scoprir Mondo invita, e mena.
Quindi con alma intrepida ripiena
D'alti pensieri, e coraggioso brio
Dell' Elemento falso infido, e rio
Mirano entrambi le procelle à pena.
Del gran' disegno al' fin' si scuopre, e trova

---

57. "To the lord knight Boturini, sonnet on the occasion of the new, beautiful, and learned history of the Indies, brought to light with the advantage and applause of the Republic of Letters."

There was a time when from the coarse sand
And from the Ligourian sea Columbus
Departed, and then Vespucci, who desired only
To discover a world, entices and leads.
Therefore with an intrepid soul
Filled with lofty thoughts and courageous spirit,
Not trusting any false element and channel,
Both scarcely look at the tempests.

Oltre i termini già di Battro, e Tile[58]
Nuovo ciel', nuovo Mondo, e Terra nuova.
Ma perde il pregio l'opra, e sembra vile,
Se con lei pongo, ò Boturini à pruova
L'erudita tua Storia, e 'iculto stile.

In segno d' ossequio
un' Amico dell' Autore

---

58. Apparently Italian proper names to indicate boundaries.

At the end of the grand design, there is discovered and found
Beyond the limits of Battro and Tile,
A new heaven, a new world, and a new land.
But the work loses its value, and seems worthless,
If with you, O Boturini, I put to the test
Your learned history and cultivated style.

In sign of homage,
A friend of the author

AL' MEDESIMO

SONETTO[59]

Se 'l Ligustico Eroe, l'Eroe toscano,
    Stupefatto Lettor, solcando miri
    Dell' onde false i tortuosi giri
    Oprar molto co'l senno, e colla mano.
Per brieve spazio à volger l'occhio umano
In queste dotte Carte ardor t'inspiri,
Forse sia, che di lor' più non ti ammiti

---

59. A sonnet to the same person

Astonished reader, if you see as you sail along
The Ligurian hero, the Tuscan hero
Producing with his good sense and his hands
The tortuous twists of false waves,
To achieve much with heart and hand.
For a brief period ardor inspires you
To turn the human eye to these learned letters;
Perhaps it may be that you no longer admire them
Up to now all wonder is cast aside.
Because if to them a shapeless material
To make known to us was only granted
In conformity with the pure natural state.
This the great Boturini, always undaunted,
Clothed with a soul, while it has various forms,
The glories of the Indies are expressed in a clean style.

The same

Fin' qui gettato ogni stupore in vano.
Poiche se à quegli una Materia informe
Manifestare a noi su sol' concesso
Al' puro stato natural' conforme.
Questa il Gran' Boturin' sempre indefesso
D'almo vestio, mentre hà la varie forme
Dell' Indie glorie in stil' purgato espresso.

Idem

PRÆCLARISSIMUS, AC GENEROSUS Eques Laurentius Boturini Benaduci, Dominus de Turre, & Hono, dum novam septentrionalis Americæ scribi Ideam Historicam æquiparatur Biantis

Omnia namque sua secum portat[60]

EPIGRAMMA[61]

Hostis cum properat celebrem superare Priennem
En Populus secum fert fugitivus opes;
Ast nihil ex illis sapiens mens illa Biantis
Appetit, & secum grandia ferre putat.
Hesperiam, Boturine, redis quoque captus ab anglo;
Atamen Historiæ culmina mente tenes.

---

60. *Sic* for "sapiens omnia sua secum portat." Latin proverb: [The wise man] takes everything he owns with himself.

61. The most distinguished and high-born knight Lorenzo Boturini Benaduci, lord of Torre and Hono, on writing a new historic Idea of North America, is compared to Bias.

Epigram.

When the enemy makes haste to overcome the famous Priene,
Behold, the fugitive people take their possessions with them;
However, that famous wise mind of Bias seeks
Nothing and thinks to take great things with himself.
Captured by the English, Boturini, you turn westward;
But you have in your mind the summit of history.
Why do you hesitate to write? Everything you have you carry with you
And alone surpass yourself with the library.

Doctor don Manuel Barrientos
Lomelín y Cervantes,
professor of the Clementines
in the University of Mexico.

Scribere cur dubitas? Tua tecum cuncta reportas
Et solus superes Bibliotheca tibi.

Doct. D. Emmanuel Barrientos,
Lomelin, & Cervantes, in Universitate Mexica
Clementinarum Cathedrae Moderator[62]

IDEM EQUES BOTURINI nova prætiosa Historia universam Americam locupletiorem facit[63]

EPIGRAMMA

Auri sacra fames binis licet invida sæclis
Sole sub occiduo condita regna petat;
Urgeat illa licet, pressis ibicumque metallis
Indefinitas promere divitias:
Nil nocet: eximio quoniam, Boturine, libello,
Quas alij tollunt, tu modo reddis opes.

D. Antonius Emmanuel Campoy
Morata, in Supremis Concilijs
causarum Patronus.

---

62. Manuel Barrientos was a canon lawyer and *provisor de indios* of the archdiocese of Mexico. There seems to be a confusion of names with Pedro Barrientos Lomelín, also a legist (Beristáin de Souza, *Biblioteca*, 1:137).

63. "The same knight Boturini with a new precious history enriches all of America."

Epigram

The cursed hunger for gold, although malignant, over two centuries
Seeks kingdoms founded under the western sun;
Although it impels, under pressure everywhere for metals,
To produce limitless wealth;
It causes no harm; because, Boturini, in this excellent little book
Which others have seized, you now return the riches.

D. Antonio Manuel
Campoy Morata, defender of causes
in the supreme councils

INDEX
OF THE SECTIONS CONTAINED
in this *IDEA*

§. I. The excellence of the history of New Spain
§. II. Procedure in writing this history
§. III. First Age
§. IV. Second age
§. V. Divine heroic symbols of the planets
§. VI. Divine heroic symbols of the days of the year
§. VII. The days are the following
§. VIII. Divine heroic symbols of the months.
§. IX. Symbols of the Indian months, according to Father fray Martín de León
§. X. Symbols of the Indian months, according to Gemelli Careri
§. XI. Divine heroic nocturnal symbols of the year
§. XII. Other examples of transformations as means of reward and punishment
§. XIII. Heroic military symbols
§. XIV. Heroic political symbols
§. XV. Of the knots and songs, both historical and poetic
§. XVI. Origin of the Indians of New Spain
§. XVII. On the passage and crossing that the Indians of New Spain took to arrive there
§. XVIII. Giants

Division of the Kingdoms of New Spain

§. XIX. The Olmec and Xicalanco Indians
§. XX. The Toltec Indians
§. XXI Third age
§. XXII. The Chichimeca Indians
§. XXIII. The Tepanec Indians
§. XXIV. The Mexican Indians
§. XXV. The Teochichimeca Indians
§. XXVI. Conquest of the Spaniards
§. XXVII. Observations on what has been said
§. XXVIII. The usefulness that this work can produce

There Follows the Catalog of My Historic Indian Museum

PRELIMINARY DISCLAIMER

Although on the occasion of writing this *Idea of a History*, I have had to meditate on the secret and scientific plans of the Indians and to use, especially in the first and second ages, their own concepts in order to explain it, nevertheless, I am so far from separating myself in the least way from the purity of the Catholic religion, in which I was born, that rather I am prepared to die for it, and everything that I say here I submit with the most humble obedience to the censure and correction of our Holy Mother the Catholic Apostolic Roman Church.

Lorenzo Boturini Benaduci

Prologue for the Reader

Two words of warning occur to me at the threshold of my undertaking. The first, that in order to formulate this *Idea of a History*, I found myself not only separated from those materials that I had gathered over many years and that could have provided me with more than enough beautiful items to illustrate it, but also robbed of all the notes that I brought with me from the Indies, and so this work becomes a reconstruction that memory makes of what is deposited in it, but so faithful that I have no scruple about giving any notice that is not true. The second, that because I was born outside the kingdoms of Spain, and since I came to it, busy in the Indies with studying the pictures and languages of that hemisphere, I did not set aside any time to perfect myself in the Castilian language and style. The lofty[64] erudition of the matter will supply for this lack, *Ornari res ipsa negat contenta doceri*,[65] and the desire I have that I will be given the opportunity of explaining myself in Latin. VALE [farewell].

Navigant quidam & labores peregrinationis longissimæ una mercede perpetiuntur, cognoscendi aliquid abditum remotumque. Hæc res ad spectacula populos contrahit, hæc cogit præclusa rimari, secretiora exquirere, antiquitates evolvere, mores barbararum audire gentium. Curiosum nobis natura

64. *Peregrina*, see Glass's note, *Boturini in Spain*, 35n1.
65. "The thing itself refuses to be adorned, content with being taught."

ingenium dedit, at artis sibi ac pulcritudinis suæ conscia spectatores nos tantis rerum spectaculis genuit, perditura fructum sui, si tam magna, tam clara, tam subtiliter ducta, tam nitida, & non uno genere formosa solitudini ostenderet. Seneca, De otio et secessione sapientis, chapter 32.[66]

66. "Certain men set sail and endure the labors of a very long journey for one reward: knowing something hidden and remote. This thing draws crowds to spectacles, it brings together hidden things to be examined closely, to seek out more secret things, to unfold ancient histories, to hear of the customs of barbarian peoples. Nature has given us a temperament for curiosity and conscious in itself of its art and beauty, it has given birth to us as spectators of so many spectacles of things. It will lose its benefit, if it does not show to solitude things so great, so famous, so subtly described, and beautiful in more than one way. Seneca, *De otio et secessione sapientis*, chapter 32."

The Excellence of the History of New Spain

§. I

Many are the writers who have kept their learned pens busy in giving to posterity the history of New Spain. Their diligent efforts traverse the literary world [and] deserve the highest praise. Since they have not therefore closed the door on those who come later to dedicate themselves to the pursuit of the same material, and even to attempt to advance it, searching out the truth that is always clear to everyone (according to Seneca, *Letter 33 to Lucilius, Patet omnibus veritas, nondum est occupata: multum ex illa etiam futuris relictum est*),[67] my hope was centered on finding it, and it favored the sacrifice of my efforts, it was made known to me, exemplified in so great an abundance of materials that other historians did not find, and with so much excellence of sublime things, that I dare to say that not only can this history compete with the most celebrated in the world but also excel them.

1 First, because it is the most abundant of all [the histories]that have been discovered up to the present, because it has four ways of entrusting its notable matters to the public memory. The first, in figures, symbols, characters, and hieroglyphics, which encompass in themselves a vast amount of learning, as will be seen later. Second, in knots of various colors, which in the language of the Peruvians are called *quipu*, and in that of our Indians *nepohualtzitzin*. The third, in songs with exquisite figures of speech and lofty concepts. The fourth and last, after

67. "The truth lies open to everyone, it is not yet restricted: much of it has also been left to future generations."

the Spanish conquest, in manuscripts in both languages, Indian and Castilian, some on native paper, others on European paper, by means of which one comes to know the specifics of civil life.

2 Second, because they are embellished with a chronology so precise that in its skill it surpasses that of the Egyptians and Chaldeans, since it explains its years with four characters, *Tecpatl, Calli, Tochtli, Acatl*, which mean *Flint, House, Rabbit,* and *Reed*, mysteries of the four elements and of much astronomic learning, weaving them into *triadecatrridas*[68] and with four of them forming fifty-two years, which is the *Indian solar cycle*, in which is shown a perpetual and unfailing system, which is the most genuine property of true science. Their year is *lunisolar*, and in former times did not differ from that of the Egyptians, until the mathematicians, noting that about six hours were left over each year, met together in the city of Huehuetlapullan[69] and aligned the year with the vernal equinox, some years before the Incarnation of Christ, Our Lord. On the basis of the said four characters and the triadecateridas, the Indians of New Spain divided the world into four periods. The first was from the creation until the universal flood, and they called it Atonatiuh,[70] which means *Sun from the water*, that is, *the first course of the sun that destroyed the waters.* The second, from the flood to the destruction of the giants,[71] former inhabitants of the interior[72] of New Spain, they called Tlachitonatiuh,[73] *the sun extinguished by the earth*; as they say, *the second course of the sun, ending with earthquakes.* The third, from the destruction of the giants until the great hurricane that in America leveled all the trees, homes, and strongest buildings,

68. A period of thirteen days, four of which constituted the Indian century of fifty-two years.

69. The place of departure of the Toltecs (Siméon, *Dictionnaire*); Gerhard, *Historical Geography*, mentions a Tlapala in Chalco but no Huehuetlapullan; see Davies, *Toltec Heritage*, 272, 274; Codex Chimalpahin, 181. I have been unable to find any reference to Huehuetlapullan in Bernal Díaz del Castillo.

70. First age of the world, sun of water, marked by a general flood.

71. This may refer to the legendary giants mentioned in Genesis 6:4.

72. *Riñón*, interior or center of a terrain.

73. Uncertain meaning. *Tonatiuh* is sun, but what is *tlachi*-? *Tlachia* means to see or observe. It does not fit the meanings that Boturini gives. Perhaps it derives from *chittiloa*, to twist or fold.

they called *Ecatonatiuh*,[74] *the sun, the third course of the sun, destroyed by the air.* The fourth, from the hurricane to the end of the world, they gave the name of *Tletonatiuh*,[75] that is, *the final course of the sun that will end with fire.* For this reason the Indians, who now found themselves at the end of this fourth period, believing that at the end of each cycle of fifty-two years the destruction of the world by fire was near, made great sacrifices to their gods, asking that they not put an end to the world and grant them another, longer-lasting cycle. The months of the year were eighteen, from twenty days each month, based on a lofty system of *neomenias lunares*,[76] and thus their years were like ours, three hundred and sixty-five days, of which three hundred and sixty covered the months and five remained separate, as if useless, unlucky, and unfortunate, regarding the astronomical observations, not the chronological calculation, and for this reason they called them *nenontemi.*[77] The days of the year were also shown with twenty symbols in the form of a wheel and tables. The first thirteen represent a triadecaterida, and another seven follow in order, with a perpetual plan of most exquisite design, having seen and considered that most of the Indian systems are based on the numbers 4, 18, and 20 of a quantity *alicuota*[78] and 7, 9, and 13 of *alicuanta.*[79] The astronomers had their signs and planets, very different from ours, and they predicted which would be auspicious and inauspicious; those that ruled by day, and the nine that accompanied them, or as they would say, *lords of the night.* They would use four calendars which our European historians did not distinguish. The first was *Natural*, by which agriculture was regulated. The second, *Chronological*, and it served history. The third, *Ritual*, and the priests studied it for the order of the movable and fixed feasts of their gods. The fourth, *Astronomical*, whose calculations the mathematicians studied in order to act in accord with the course of the sun and the situation of the planets. The first two I have explained, and the rest will be explained in due course, which there is much to discuss.

---

74. *Ecatl*, wind, + *tonatiuh*, sun.
75. Fourth age of the world, or sun of fire; *tletl*, fire, + *tonatiuh*, sun.
76. New moons.
77. *Sic* for *nemontemi*, the five days left over at the end of the year.
78. Exactly divisible.
79. Not exactly divisible.

3 To such a well-ordered chronology corresponds their geography, and it is a wonderful thing to see the kingdoms, provinces, cities, and lands of each people, with mountains, water, and everything necessary for sustenance drawn on the pictorial documents of the Indians. It is known that *Teuhtili*, governor of the North Coast,[80] ordered the unforeseen arrival of the Spaniards painted on a lienzo, their ships, arms, peoples and dress, the way in which they formed squadrons, bringing it all to his monarch *Moteuczoma Xocoyotl*,[81] as if he were seeing it personally. No less outstanding was that map of the roads that the Indian kings gave to the victorious don Fernando Cortés for the very arduous expedition that he carried out in penetrating the various provinces of *Guatemala.*

4 Even more outstanding is the truth and simplicity with which the ancient historians, both in pictures and in songs, mentioned things worth remembering. Whether they won or lost battles, they depicted the event with the greatest precision, and the experts in language composed some songs of rejoicing or lamentation, celebrating or weeping, to the sound of their musical instruments, *teponaztli*[82] or *tlapahuehuetl*,[83] the most detailed circumstances of their good or bad fortune. The love of truth had such power over them that the lower lip of a liar was cut off in order that he might be known in the republic, and the cheat paid for his crime with his life. And for this reason the aforementioned songs do not fail to bring with them such sublime figures of speech and ongoing allegories, which present much to understand to be able to arrive at their true meaning.

5 There is no pagan nation that relates primitive matters as precisely as the Indian one. It gives us an account of the creation of the world, the flood, the confusion of tongues at the Tower of Babel, the other periods and ages of the world, the long wanderings of their peoples in Asia, with specific years in their characters; and in that of *Seven Rabbits* it calls to mind the great eclipse that occurred at the death

---

80. *Sic* for Teuhtile, governor of Cuetlachtlan, one of the first areas captured by Cortés.

81. Moteuczoma the Younger.

82. A log drum.

83. Tlapanhuehuetl or tlalpanhuehuetl drums are well known. Tlalpan seems to mean something like flattened to the earth.

of Christ, Our Lord,[84] and the first Christian Indians who at that time understood perfectly their chronology and studied ours with total curiosity, left us notice of how, from the creation of the world until the blessed birth of Christ, 5,199 years had passed, which is the same opinion or computation of the LXX.[85]

6 Of this precious history I have an extraordinary amount of material in my archive of Mexico, where a great accumulation of ancient pictorial documents on paper made of *metl*,[86] palm, worm,[87] and European paper; on cotton cloth, and on cured animal skins; a large number of manuscripts of Indian and European papers in two languages, Toltec and Castilian, is contained, totaling twenty volumes between large and medium, with an equal number of fragments. One of these skins I brought with me to present to Your Majesty, and the English took it from me, with other papers of great importance, clothing, and valuables, on the ship named *La Concordia*, on which I was made prisoner. Nor can sufficient consideration be given to the immense work and expense that the said archive cost me, after the heavy task of eight continuous years that the discovery of so many different documents kept me occupied, through widespread journeys, and at a cost of endless inconveniences.

84. See Matthew 27:45; Mark 15:33; Luke 24:44.

85. This is the standard symbol for the Septuagint, the translation of the Hebrew Bible into Greek by seventy Jewish scholars of Alexandria.

86. Native paper, made from tree bark.

87. *Gusano*, "worm." Does this perhaps mean silk?

Procedure in Writing

This History

§. II

1 In accordance with the idea of the famous division of time that the Egyptians taught, I have divided the History of the Indies into three ages. The first, that of the gods; the second, that of the heroes; the third, that of men, to come down through successive stages until the time when our Indians were established in their human governments and spread their empires, kingdoms, and rule in America, and finally, conquered by Spanish arms, abandoned their former idolatry, embraced the Catholic faith, in which they live with constancy under Your Majesty's just and temperate rule. As a result I determined to deal with the matters of the said three times, Divine, Heroic, and Human, which is the same as the very learned Varro[88] explains as a different three ages: Dark, Mythical, and Historic.

88. Marcus Terentius Varro (116 BC–27 BC), historian of the late republican period in Rome.

First Age

§. III

1 Divine Providence, architect of the world and author of nations, seeing that multitudes of Noah's descendants, having forgotten the true religion of their ancestors, wandered after the confusion of tongues, spread out, lost, and scattered through the wilderness of the earth; and wishing to take them from that brutal wandering and restore them to the delights of civil life, determined at different times that some of them, frightened and trembling because of thunder and lightning from heaven, others, admiring its greatness and its most beautiful body, observing in it so many varied but regular movements which (as the Royal Prophet[89] said, make known the glory of their creator), they mistook the first causes for the second ones, to which they mistakenly attributed divinity and worship, not daring in the presence of such a luminous portent to worship[90] the shameless Venus and they settled down, seeking out caves as their first dwelling, in which by reason of the innate and superior force of the male sex, they seized certain women as their own, raising up certain famous sons who would then be the seed of other families, peoples, and nations.

2 And even with the passage of time, our Indians who were descended from them, invented different kinds of gods composed of beings superior to human powers. As a result, at the same time there

89. David in the psalms. The reference is apparently to Psalm 18 in the Vulgate enumeration.

90. *Ejercitar.* This may be stretching the meaning a bit.

arose among them idolatry and divination. With the same idea the Latins derived the word *divinitas a divinando*,[91] which is to ascertain, through some external signs, the future, known only to the gods, and they thought that it would be a silent speech of the same divinity.

3 But they believed in this first age that all things necessary and useful for the support of human life were truly deities, and for this reason they depicted them with divine mental hieroglyphics, which are imaginary divine genera, which human understanding taught them, through that natural propensity to take delight in what is uniform. And what they could not do with the abstraction of forms by means of universals,[92] they did with portraits and likenesses, which I will be explaining with a natural, clear, and evident interpretation, unknown until the present day, and even closed off to the Indians' understanding, avoiding nonetheless the error of those who exalt the meaning of the hieroglyphs to the highest peak of the sciences, as did the Greeks who celebrated Orpheus as their founder, rich in wisdom acquired by having been, as they say, a disciple of Atlante, and the latter [a disciple] of Trimegistus and Zoroaster,[93] to whom are attributed works based on metaphysics. None of them would have flourished except in popular wisdom, in the same way as our Indians flourished in matters pertaining to religion, marriage, and the education of children, the woman entering into the religion of her husband and the children keeping that of their parents, and finally, burying their corpses, considering it true wisdom of humankind. For this reason it was nicely said, *Humanitas ab humando*,[94] and from this pious act and from the site where the graves were located arose the origin of property rights and of the division of the fields, as well as the validity of noble lineages, drawing up genealogies by means of the graves.

4 And in order that the first events should not be forgotten through carelessness, the Indians composed and recounted to the

---

91. "Divinity is from divination."

92. This probably refers to the scholastic idea of reasoning through universal concepts.

93. Atlante may refer to Atlas, the titan of mythology, who supported the world on his shoulders. Trimegistus was Hermes Trimegistus, a Greek god associated with esoteric ("hermetic") philosophy. Zoroaster was a Persian religious founder.

94. "Humanity comes from burying" (Latin *humare*).

people the ancient history with some divine legends, which I will separate from the rest of other times, calling them up at their appropriate place and explaining them in their authors' own sense. They were theologian poets, and under the guise of various deities they sought to write the history of religious matters and the customs of their times.

5 The aforesaid legends were based on the same congruence of common needs; through which understanding these first pagans invented, with images of frightening religious figures, first some gods and then others, almost like a natural generation of them. Nonetheless, the similar *Theogonia*[95] has served from the beginning and brief epochs to be able with clarity to coordinate the interpretation of the events of this obscure time.

6 We see in Greek history that it preserved for us what there is of value in antiquity, that their ancestors counted twelve principal deities; but, as I understand it, confused and interspersed between the two times: the dark and the mythical. The Indians, on the other hand, distinguish their own and special [deities] in this first age numbering thirteen, corresponding to the *triadecatéridas*, with which they tied together both the characters of the years and the symbols of the days, and *neomenias lunares*, and they are as follows.

7 *TEZCATLIPOCA*,[96] hieroglyph for Divine Providence, the primary Indian deity, meaning that, as our pagans acknowledged, the world was governed by a divine wisdom that had its seat in heaven and all human things in its care. *Vis illum providentiam dicere? Recte dices.*[97] Seneca agrees, *Naturales Quaestiones*, book 2, chapter 45, *Est etenim cujus concilio huic mundo providetur ut inconcussus eat, & actus suos explicet.*[98] Grateful for this, they combined him with *teotlamacazqui*,[99] hieroglyph for the priests and wise men dedicated to the service of the divine, so that they would know what they were to achieve, not only through the art of divination to explore his wishes, but also to

95. Greek for "begetting of the god," translation conjectured.

96. Nahuatl: Smoking Mirror.

97. "Do you want to call it Providence? You will speak correctly."

98. "For it is by his plan that provision is made to this world that it go forward unshaken and unfold its activities."

99. León-Portilla has *teotlamacuzqui* (Boturini, *Idea*, 1974:36). Boturini (1999) has *Teotlamacazqui*, a minister charged with carrying a god on his shoulders.

propitiate him with unceasing offerings and sacrifices. Likewise they called him *ti itlacahuan*, which means *we are your slaves*,[100] as if we live through your providence. A true feeling for these divine and harsh times, although later the mythmakers corrupted it by applying to him the character *of the god Cupid.* For that reason, lovers in the third immoral age, with this invocation of *Ti itlacahuan*, carried out their unruly feasts and sacrifices to *Tezcatlipoca* in order that he might favor their disorderly love affairs, in the same way that the corrupt European poets considered the *Cíngulo*[101] which covers what is most indecent about *Venus prónuba* as a base incentive for disordered appetites.[102] Corresponding to this first Indian deity is that of the Greeks, who was *Heaven*, of whom their legendary history tells us that he was the father of the other gods, and that he reigned on earth, having left on it great and very outstanding benefits.

8 *TLALOC*, whose image I have in my archive and of whom there is a copy in the history of the *Giro del mundo*[103] by the doctor Francisco Gemelli Careri,[104] volume 6, page 83; it is a hieroglyph of the second deity and, as it were, minister of Divine Providence, because by carrying out the orders of *Tezcatlipoca* he dried out the earth after the universal flood, spewing out his natural exhalations, which are the material for lightning flashes, illuminations, and lightning bolts, Heaven began to make known his anger. And forewarned by his thunder, as if by a divine tongue, the most docile men took refuge by living in caves, not daring to make use of the immoral Venus[105] in the presence of Heaven, whether serene or angry, and they went forth to look for some women; they brought them to their refuges, in which were established the beginnings of human society. For that reason, in the aforementioned image, *Tlaloc* is seen crowned with a diadem of feathers, which

---

100. More correctly, "we are his slaves."

101. Belt or cincture.

102. Pronuba was a Roman matron who arranged and directed marriage ceremonies.

103. *Sic* for *mondo.* It is strange that Boturini, an Italian by birth, would make this mistake.

104. *Sic* for Giovanni Francesco Gemelli Careri.

105. This may be an indirect reference to sexual intercourse.

should be white and green, holding a thunderbolt in his right hand and a shield in the left, made beautiful by many other feathers of a sky-blue color. With these three colors, they symbolized, with white, those first children who were to be born pure-white in the beauty of marriage; with green, the propagation of their lineages; and with blue, the care imposed on them to keep their religion pure and the sacrifices to the gods constant. And in this they reflected the legend of Daphne, because Apollo, on seeing that this lost[106] girl was going about a fugitive from social life, refusing to subject herself to the domination of a chaste marriage, followed her, seized her, and changed her into an ancestral[107] laurel tree, forever green in its true and well-known growth. Also that of Cyparissus, who, while enjoying the different kinds of hunting, inadvertently killed the deer that he loved so much, was transformed by that same Apollo into a cypress tree, the symbol that accompanies the permanent vigor of illustrious houses. And although the Indians of the second and third age considered this idol to be the god of rain, nevertheless those of the first age revered him as the herald of Providence, thinking that he wrote laws with lightning and published them with thunder, which is the same as what an Italian poet said of Jupiter, with an elegant figure of speech:

Ne la primera[108] *etade*
Gli Eroi leggevan le leggi in petto a Giove[109]

9 *MACUILXOCHIQUETZALLI*, the third deity, who sounds so much like the goddess Venus, and in the Indian language *she of the fan of five flowers and feathers*,[110] is a hieroglyph that means that she is noble and chaste. For this reason she is depicted as accompanied by the god *Tlaloc*, who with thunder and lightning subjected her to married life and was the reason why the first pagans, repudiating the brutal wandering, made use of a beautiful Venus with more humane and modest activity; and finally, united with that thundering deity, they

106. *Descarriada*, someone separated from the group, perhaps exiled or gone astray.

107. *Genealogico.* This translation is a surmise.

108. *Sic* for *prima?*

109. "In the first age heroes read laws in Jupiter's bosom."

110. Literally this means five quetzal flowers.

would have, within the decent bonds of an inseparable union, certain children who (according to the Indian phrasing) were the scented flowers and rich feathers of their lineage. In aspiring to that, Peleus entered into lawful marriage with Thetis, who had previously wandered a fugitive and hidden in various forms of beasts, and by her had the great Achilles. Ovid, *Metamorphoses*, book 11, legend 7.

Vix bene virgineos Peleus invaserat artus
Illa novat formas; donec sua membra teneri
Sentit & in partes diversas brachia tendi.
Tum demum ingemuit: Neque, ait, sine numine vincis
Exhibita estque Thetis, confessam amplectitur heros,
Et potitur votis; ingentique implet Achille.[111]

And this is the *Venus Pronuba* of the Greeks, the goddess of solemn nuptials, which our Indians likewise contracted in all the ages with specified ceremonies. Its purpose is hinted at in the legend of Deuca lion and Pyrrha[112] who, situated on top of a mountain in front of the temple of Temis, with their heads covered, transform the rocks at their feet into men by throwing them over their shoulders. This signifies that the first men, lacking understanding because of their solitary and wandering life, had neither wives nor legitimate children, until because of fear of thunder and lightning they awoke to contemplate divine justice, which commands what is upright and decent, and, clothed with the modesty of chaste marriages, they gave birth to legitimate children and accustomed them to civilized life. And those who were once all of stone leave behind them, that is, to their posterity, as a lasting seedbed for the rest of the nations, in which afterward the careful discipline of the natural law of peoples was to shine.

10 *TLAZOLTEOTL*[113] the fourth deity, an immoral, common, and abominable Venus, a hieroglyph of those men and women who were

111. "Scarcely had Peleus skillfully invaded the virginal confines, she changed shapes; until she felt her members to be held and her arms stretched in different directions. Then, finally, she moaned, she says, 'you do not conquer without divine help"'and she has appeared as Thetis, the hero, embraces the one who has admitted him. And he fulfills his desires, and impregnates her with the mighty Achilles." [Lines 260–65.]

112. A couple in Greek mythology who survive a major deluge.

113. Literally, the "garbage goddess."

still nomadic, and when the former encountered the latter, they satisfied their animal appetites and then parted company, not recognizing each other again, in the same way as the rest of the animals. Perhaps the poets placed Tantalus, a commoner, exiled to the lower regions to suffer always from hunger and thirst, with apples being placed over his head without his being able to reach them, because, separated from the splendor of marriage, he was in the low and vile places of base pleasure, far from the fertile fields occupied by married people, longing for the sweetness of the apples that he could not grasp because they were in the high and noble place of the happily married.

11 *PILTZINTEUCTLI*, the fifth deity, means *god of the children*,[114] but the hieroglyph is of those who were born of solemn marriage ceremonies, were raised in the religion of their parents, and learned from them the rites of sacrifices and how to seek the good will of the gods with auguries. This custodian or child-guardian is pictured with a beautiful face, of a tender age, in a house which serves her as an altar hanging and signifies the government that awaits them in their families after the deaths of their parents because they will be adorned with civil beauty which is the same with which in Greek histories, Theseus, Bacchus, Bellerophon, and Ganymede, who was carried off by the eagle and mastered the wisdom of auguries and ministered to Jupiter at his table with sacrifices, were resplendent.

12 *TEOTLACANEXQUIMILLI*, the sixth deity, which means *ash-colored bundle, bundle of darkness and low-lying clouds*,[115] or a god without feet or head, is the opposite, the hieroglyph not only of those who have remained in the nomadic life, like vague, dark shapes of humanity who the Indians' legends say were transformed into stones and monkeys, but also of the children born outside of the marriage chamber, lost children, so to speak, who were not pleasing to the gods, who had neither feet nor head in civil life. Our Indians look on this race of peoples with the same disdain as the other nations, just as one reads about the Roman plebeians who, deprived of auguries and solemn

---

114. More correctly, "ruler of children."

115. *Bulto ceniciento, bulto de obscuridad y neblina. Bulto* has several meanings, including "vague shape," "shape in the distance," "volume or size of something," "statue," "box," or suitcase"; Covarrubias gives pretty much the same meanings. In this context "bundle" seems to be the best translation.

weddings, *agitabat connubia more ferarum*,[116] and of Pan, who, born of the hero Ulysses and the plebeian Penelope, with the contradiction of discordant natures, could not be anything other than a monster, a mingling of man and goat, obliged to live in the woods, playing his reed pipes among the satyrs. Similar monsters are those that the Spartans ordered thrown from the mountain *Traigeta*, and the Roman Decemviri by the law of the Twelve Tables threw into the River Tiber.[117] And Minos, in order to remove from the sight of the people of Crete the infamous fruit of his wife's adultery, ordered the Minotaur buried in Daedelus's labyrinth. He had been born part man, part bull, that is, of an illustrious matron and a lower-class man. Ovid, *Metamorphoses*, book 8, legend 2.

Creverat opprobrium generis: fœdumque patebat
Matris adulterium monstri novitate biformis.
Destinat hunc Minos thalamis[118] *removere pudorem,*
Multiplicique domo, cæcisque includere tectis.
Dedalus ingenio fabrae celeberrimus artis
Ponit opus.[119]

A companion to this image of darkness was the goddess Venus, whom we have called crude and immoral, because both were lacking the beauty, the fair light of auspicious and chaste marriages, and in latter times *Tlalteuctli*,[120] the god who punished adulteries with rigorous penalties. A person who died because of this crime was called generically *Tlazolteominqui*,[121] and if he was a man, *tlazolteotlahpaliuhqui*,[122] which means

---

116. "They entered into marriages after the manner of wild beasts."

117. I have not been able to locate Traigeta. *Decemviri* (literally ten men) is a Latin term that designated legal experts in the Roman republic, whose duties included judgments and writing of laws.

118. *Sic* for *thalamo.*

119. "The disgrace of his line had grown; the shameful adultery of the mother was made clear by the biformed monster. Minos decides to distance this shame from his marriage bed, and to keep it in a maze-like dwelling and blind passages. Daedalus, most famous for his genius in the art of construction, takes on the work."

120. "Ruler of the land."

121. *Sic* for *Tlazoteomiqui*, "Tlazolteotl's divine dead."

122. "*Tlazolteotl's* groom or nubile young man." Boturini's translation is erroneous.

he whose head is flattened with a flagstone, and if a woman, *tlazolteocihuatl*,[123] which in Latin means *sacred to Venus*, and in Castilian, offered to the goddess *Tlazolteotl*.

13 *XIUHTEUCTLI*, the seventh deity, and one of the most principal ones that the Indian nations had, because it meant *fire*,[124] which they said was the first element, and I think that they discovered it when they rubbed sticks together or by piling and splitting rock with rock. So it is that Festus *in the Calepino*[125] *under the word ignis* [fire], Pliny, book 16, chapter 40. *Calidæ morus, laurus, hedera, & omnes ex quibus igniaria fiunt. Exploratorum hoc usus in castris, pastorumque reperit; quoniam ad excudendum ignem non semper lapidis est occasio. Teritur ergo lignum ligno, ignemque concipit attritu excipiente materia aridi fomitis fungi, vel foliorum.* Seneca, *Naturales. Quaestione*, book. 2, chapter 2. *Videamus quomodo apud nos fieri soleat ignis —— Duobis modis: uno, si excitatur sicut ex lapide percusso; altero si attritu invenitur, sicut cum duo ligna inter se diutius trita sunt. Non omnis hoc tibi materia praestabit, sed idonea eliciendis ignibus: sicut laurus hederae, & alia in hunc usum nota pastoribus.*[126] Because both methods for producing [fire] are celebrated in Indian history, not only with the flint that they used in order to symbolize this element, but also with the two sticks rubbed one on the other, which was later on an oft-repeated ceremony in the *New Fire*.

---

123. "Tlazolteotl's woman."

124. *Xihuitl* + *tecutli*, "ruler of the year or of grass or of fire." *Xihuitl* has all three meanings.

125. The Lexicon of Festus (*De uerborum significatu*) is a Latin dictionary compiled in the Roman imperial period. It preserves information about the history, society, religion, and topography of Rome and Italy in earlier centuries. The *Calepino* was a work by the Italian Renaissance lexicographer Ambrogio Calepino (c. 1440–1510) whose name later became synonymous with dictionary or lexicon.

126. "Hot are the mulberry, laurel, ivy, and all from which combustible materials are made. The experience of explorers in camps and of shepherds makes this clear, because a stone is not always available for producing fire by striking. Therefore wood is rubbed against wood, and it produces fire by rubbing, drawing it from the material of very dry tinder of fungus or leaves." Seneca, *Natural Questions*, book 2, chapter 2. "Let us see how fire is usually lighted among us. . . . In two ways: One, if it is started from a stone being struck. Second, if it is brought about by rubbing, as when two pieces of wood are rubbed together for a long time. Not everything will do this for you, but things suitable for making fire, such as the laurel, ivy, and others known to shepherds for this purpose."

Under the cloak of this deity and in his presence women gave birth from the first pastoral age on, and it was observed as something sacred in homes and temples. In the second [age], the cult grew and on the fourth day after childbirth, they passed the newborn four times through fire after the manner of purification and baptism, calling the ceremony *tlequiquiztililiztli.*[127] It was an ancient custom of their ancestors, the descendants of Ham, according to Philo the Jew.[128] *Tunc coeperunt hi qui habitabant in terra inspicere in astra & incohaverunt ex his imaginari & divinationes facere, & filios & filias traijcere per ignem.*[129] But fire must have been the most respected and sublime of their gods, because Thare,[130] who was an idolater of fire and father of Abraham, having accused his son before Nimrod of not wanting to adore it [fire] and follow the religion of his family, ordered him to be thrown into it, and he emerged untouched by the work of God. Aram[131] was struck with wonder by this miracle and admitted that the law that his brother Abraham professed was true, as Lyra writes in chapter 11 of Genesis & chapter 12, on the authority of Saint Jerome. *Vera est igitur Hebraeorum traditio, quod egressus sit Thare cum filiis suis de igne Chaldeorum, et quod Abram vallatus babilonico incendio, quia illud adorare nolebat, liberatus sit auxilio dei, & ex illo tempore reputetur ei tempus aetatis, ex quo confessus est Deum spernens idola Chaldeorum.*[132] And for this reason I

127. Etymology uncertain. *Tletl* means fire or flame, *quiztililiztli* may be a substantive derived from the passive of *quiza*, to emerge or come out.

128. Philo (20 BC–AD 50) was a Hellenistic Jewish Bible philosopher born in Alexandria. This quotation is from his book *On the Antiquities of the Bible.* This book, dating from the late first century AD, is attributed to Philo. However, most scholars agree that it was not written by Philo, and it is hence sometimes called "Pseudophilo." Consisting of a retelling of the Hebrew Bible from Genesis to the end of 1 Samuel, it embellishes and often departs from the narrative, as we know it today, in small and large details.

129. "Then these who dwelt in the land began to look to the stars and from these they began to invent and make divinations, and to pass their sons and daughters through fire."

130. Boturini uses the Vulgate form of the name Terah, the father of Abraham. See Genesis 11:26–28. This story is not found in the Bible.

131. Boturini uses the Vulgate form of the name Haran.

132. "Therefore the tradition of the Hebrews is true, that Thare emerged with his sons and daughters from the fire of the Chaldeans and that Abram, immersed

(*continued*)

am not surprised that the Indians, as descendants of those who were involved in building the Tower of Babel, as will be said later, would celebrate fire so much, to the point of characterizing it by a hieroglyph, and at the beginning of the chronology, and by its divine characters in the Toltec calendar, which was much more ancient than the Mexican one, and that they should call him in the calendar of the natural year *Lord of the Grass*, which sounds so much like *Xiuhtecutli*, and finally, that in the waning of the Indian cycle they would dedicate so many sacrifices to him and bring out with great ceremonies the *New Fire*; likewise, that in the astronomic calendar it would be the first of the nine accompanying signs, or *Lord of the Night*. The sacrifices and rites, which I will refer to in their entirety in the History, rise even more to the point in the third age. I note only that in the ritual calendar the thirteenth moveable feast was dedicated to him; the day on which after great offerings and dances the judges were named and those who were to be chosen or appointed tribute payers of the empire, because the returns from the obligations did not go beyond this term.[133] They had another and very horrible feast in the month *xocothuétzi*,[134] because at the beginning of one of the days they went to a mountain for a large tree which they brought with much reverence and a great accompaniment of music to the patio of this idol's temple, whom they also called

---

in the Babylonian fire because he refused to worship it, was freed by God's help, and the time of his age was reckoned from that time when he professed God, spurning the idols of the Chaldeans." This story is not found in the Bible and reflects a legend. Saint Jerome (c. 347–420) was a theologian, biblical scholar, and apologist. He is best known for his translation of the Bible into Latin (the Vulgate). Nicholas of Lyra (c. 1270–1349), a Franciscan teacher, was among the most influential practitioners of Biblical exegesis in the Middle Ages. His major work, *Postillae perpetuae in universam S[acram] Scripturam* (Perpetual Postillae on all of Holy Scripture), was the first printed commentary on the Bible (Rome, 1471). *Postillae* is a contraction of *post illa verba*, "after these words." Nicholas of Lyra was later considered a precursor of Martin Luther. Hence the saying, *si Lyra non lyrasset, Lutherus non saltasset*, "if Lyra had not played the lyre, Luther would not have danced."

133. *Señalados feudatarios del imperio, porque la devolucion de los Feudos no passaba de este termino.* The translation given here is conjectural. *Feudatario* literally meant those who had feudal obligations. Here it may have the meaning of vassal.

134. The tenth month of the year, corresponding roughly to August; on its first day was celebrated the feast of the god of fire, called *Xiuhtecutli.* It was also written separately as *Xocotl Huetzi.*

by another name, *Izcocauhqui*,[135] and there they removed its bark and lifted it high so that the people would see that it was of the legal size. Then, with much good order they lowered it finally to adorn it, on which occasion each one pressed it with some pieces of paper stained with their own blood, and they again raised it on high with great touching and devotion. Next to this tree they had deliberately lighted a large fire, and the lords who had come to the ceremony with their slaves, not caring what should happen to them, ordered their hands and feet tied, back to back, and their masters who carried them on their shoulders danced with them around the fire, and finally they finished the feast by throwing them into the flames. Also, at various times of the year another very famous feast was celebrated in honor of *Xiuhteuctli*, which they called *the flying pole*, dedicated to the course of the years, which in the Indian language is called *xiuhmolpia*,[136] that is, *one who binds the years*, which up to the present time our Indians use for entertainment, and I will explain in the History because no writer has penetrated its true meaning.

14 *TLATOCAOCELOTL*,[137] the eighth deity, is a hieroglyph that teaches us that, on finding the land totally filled with woods and wild beasts, the founders of pagan humanity had to clear the forests with fire. In that arduous enterprise they pitted their forces against ferocious animals, from which is derived the beginning of wars and of the first triumphs, and for this reason this deity is called *Man Jaguar* because they dressed in the skins of the same jaguars that they had overcome. In the same way the beginnings of agriculture were discovered in this epoch of *Tlatocaocelotl*, because in the act of setting fire to the forests, these pious arsonists discovered some cooked grains of maize and of other seeds, which they found very tasty to the palate; for that reason they kept others that were not damaged by the fire in order to plant them in that same earth, which they recognized had been their mother, and they had harvests corresponding to her wishes. I found in New Spain a wild maize that grows in the woods, especially in the hot lands, with small ears, whose few kernels are of a more delicate flavor

135. This seems to be a combination of *izcoa*, "to burn oneself with fire," and *cahua*, "to stop, permit, suspend."

136. A fifty-two-year cycle.

137. "Jaguar ruler."

than the cultivated [maize], as if nature places in summary all the substance in them. This authentic interpretation is bolstered by the legendary history of the Greeks in the renowned legend of Cadmus,[138] who, obliged by his father Agenor to go in search of his sister Europa, whom Jupiter had taken to the island of Crete *in another land*, circulated through different countries in order to find her, *in order to seek out the most suitable of the so-called people*, and he consulted the oracle of Apollo as to which road he should take, *because without religion no civil body can be established*, who told him that he would find on a desert plain a still undomesticated cow, *not subject to the yoke or labor*, that he should follow, and wherever it might throw itself on grass, there he should build a city, *since all things arise from agriculture* and he should call it *Thebes, which in the Syriac language means the cow which was to be his guide.*[139] And having fulfilled the prophecies of the oracle, at the time when Cadmus ordered a search in the neighboring forests for some permanent source of water, since this element is so necessary for human needs, he found the great *serpent of Mars*, which is the land of heroes. He fought it, dressed in the skin of the Nemeian lion, which vomited flames; because it was necessary to counteract its fire; he wounded it, overcame it, and killed it with a spear, with an iron point, with a plough, and then he sowed its teeth, the grains and seeds from which were born armed men. Outstanding heroes were propagated who in the beginning killed each other, with heroic struggles, and finally, with the five who survived, he founded Thebes.[140] Ovid, *Metamorphoses*, book 3, legend 1.

Pallas adest: motæque jubet supponere terræ
Vipereos dentes populi incrementa futuri.
Paret: & ut presso sulcum patefecit aratro,
Spargit humi jussos mortalia semina dentes.
Inde (fide majus) glebæ cœpere moveri,
Primaque de sulcis acies apparuit hastæ.[141]

---

138. This story is told in many versions.

139. This does not appear to be accurate.

140. In general Boturini's description of Cadmus and the founding of Thebes follows the ancient Greek tales closely.

141. "Pallas comes and orders that on the overturned earth he sow the viper's teeth, the seed of a future people. He obeys. And in the same way that he opens

Once the woods, which were impenetrable, were leveled in this way, the ancestral Indian peoples built their houses right next to their sowed fields, in order to defend them from the ravages of wild beasts, and from these homes our Indians took the second element of their chronology and the meaning of the element of the earth because they [the houses] had been built with crude mud and brick. This was a prosperous age with the horn of plenty of Archeloos, whom the Nyades made divine and filled with sweet-smelling flowers and most delicate fruit.[142] The same, in the aforesaid passage, book 9, legend 1.

Naides hoc, pomis & odoro flore repletum
Sacrarunt; divesque meo bona copia cornu est.[143]

That which the poets perhaps seek to call golden, and perhaps silver, because seeds were the most precious silver of primitive times. The same, book 1, legend 4.

Et densi frutices: & victæ cortice virgæ.
Semina tum primum longis cerealia sulcis
Obruta sunt, pressique jugo gemuere juvenci.[144]

And if Jupiter descends on Danae with a shower of gold, so it is on the earth with a shower of seeds, because Perseus, who was born from her, uses as his crest the head of Medusa, painted with serpents. The same, in the aforesaid place, book 4, legend 16.[145]

---

the furrow with the force of the plough, he sows on the ground the teeth as commanded, mortal seeds, thence (beyond belief) the lumps of earth began to move, and the first sharp point of a spear appeared out of the furrows." [Lines 102–7.]

142. Nyades were water nymphs. Archeloos was a water god whose horn was torn from his brow by Hercules.

143. "The Nyades made this sacred, filled with fruit trees and sweet-smelling flowers, and riches and good abundance are in my horn." [Lines 88–89.] León-Portilla translates *pomis* as "poems." However, the form in the original is "pomis" (fruit or fruit tree), not "poemis."

144. Ovid, *Metamorphoses*, book 9 [Lines 122–24.] "And the tree trunks are dense; and the branches bound to the bark. Then the seeds of Ceres for the first time were buried in the deep furrows, and weighed down by the yoke, the young bullocks groaned."

145. In Greek mythology Danae was a daughter of King Acrisius of Argos. When her father imprisoned her, Zeus came in the form of a shower of gold and impregnated her. She became the mother of Perseus, who slew the Gorgon Medusa, whose shield contains snakes that killed with a glance.

Perseus, quem pluvio Danæ conceperat auro.

. . . .

Gorgonei capitis guttæ cecidere cruentæ:
Quas humus exceptas varios animavit in angues.[146]

In this are signified those [women] of the land, who fled from agriculture, through which others changed them into ears of wheat, which were once the fertile hair of Medusa, and I would name with an elegant figure of speech the hairs on the tight ears of maize, *golden hairs*, since it was always agriculture that was the wizard of my delights. The history of so many Hercules, which the famous Varro numbered up to forty-three, is confused with regard to this deity, of which the most famous are the Scythian, the Egyptian, the Celtic, Gaulic, Libyan, Ethiopian, and Theban, and the god Phydias of the Romans, all of whom were symbols of different persons but of the same office, that is, of great enterprises and exertions, such as clearing the land and cultivating it. And as the Greeks placed the lion which, spewing flames, burned the forest of Nemea and was overcome by their Theban Hercules, among the signs of the Zodiac, so our Indians raised the eighth deity, the jaguar, whom their ancestors killed in the act of burning the woods and cultivating the ancient lands, from which proceed the rights of occupation, acquisition, and alienation[147] of the ancestral peoples, which are the three principles that I will show to be lawful in the General History of the sovereign dominions of the Indian nations.

15 *QUETZALCOHUATL*,[148] the ninth deity, and the hieroglyph of the wind, which is the third character in the Indian chronology, and its corresponding element, depicted as a rabbit, perhaps because the Indians derived *tochtli* from the verb *toca*, which means for the wind to blow or travel, or because, like rabbits, the first men emerged from their ancient caves to search the open fields to have at the ready the

146. "Perseus, whom Danae had conceived in a shower of gold. . . . bloody drops fell from the Gorgon's head, which the earth having received gave them life as various serpents." [Lines 612, 618–19.]

147. These are all terms from Roman law.

148. Often translated as "plumed serpent," it is a combination of *quetzal*, a tropical bird noted for its brilliant plumage, and *cohuatl*, "serpent." By extension *quetzal* can also mean "brightly colored" or "blue."

necessities of life and more purified air, as Ovid sang, *On the art of loving*, book 2.

Aere non certo corpora languor habet.[149]

In this first age they celebrated many feasts to him so that the rains would not come to an end and that he would let them fall on their seeded fields, and they could support themselves like the rabbit which, once the land had been dampened with rain, comes out of its hiding places to graze on the tender grasses of the field. In the second age they dedicated to him the symbol *Ce Ehecatl*, One Wind, which was counted among the divine heroic symbols of the days of the year, and they considered it to be one of bad fortune, believing that those who were born on these days would be witches, enchanters, and necromancers, and among those men whom they called *momacpalitohticque*, and if they were women, *mometzcopinqui.*[150] In the third [age] the sacrifices came to be bloody, and they offered him a certain number of children whom they bought from their parents for this purpose.

16 *CHALCHIUHCUEITL*, the tenth deity, the fourth sign of the Indian chronology, and hieroglyph for water; likewise it is the figure of its corresponding element, which our Indians in a figure of speech call *she of the skirt of precious stones.*[151] As I understand it, they first found her on the plains among the canebrakes, because to depict her, they symbolized her with some of the reeds that grow in humid places, taking, as a rhetorical figure, the effect for the cause, and in this way, on the pictorial document of the ritual calendar, I saw her effigy painted with large puddles at her feet and accompanied by many triumphs, of which

149. "When the air is uncertain, languor takes hold of bodies." Ovid, *Ars amatoria*, book 2, line 310.

150. Siméon has *macpalitotia*, "to enchant someone." Molina (Spanish/Nahuatl) glosses it as "encantar para hurtar." He has the same in Nahuatl/Spanish. The noun form he gives is *macpolitoti. Macpalitohticque* is a plural noun form. It is possible that the *c* is intrusive. *Mometzcopinqui* appears to be a combination of *metzli*, "month" or "limb," and *copina*, "for something to pull loose" or *copini*, "for something to pull loose" (Karttunen, *Analytical Dictionary*). In all probability the correct form is *momacpalitohticque*, "they who dance with an arm, the term for feared ritual specialists who charmed or put to sleep their victims by dancing near them while holding a severed forearm, See López Austin, "Los temacpalitotique," 97–117.

151. Perhaps more accurately, "emerald skirt."

I will give a full interpretation in the General History. Fishermen especially celebrated her feast, and others who conducted their business by water, raising statues to her which they carried in public with great dances and joy; and the lords, on the occasion of being married, dedicated their marriages to her with great ceremonies; and she was a deity very respected by the Indians because of the connection that she had with divine rites and human needs, for even the gods paid her reverence by swearing by the Infernal Lake and other Stygian sources, according to Vergil, 6, *Aeneid*, v. 324.

Di, cujus jurare timent, & fallere numen.[152]

And Ovid, *Metamorphoses*, book 2, legend 1.

Promissis testis adesto
Dis juranda palus oculis incognita nostris.[153]

17 *TEOYAOTLATOHUAHUITZILOPOCHTLI*, the hieroglyph of that god *who sends and disseminates wars.*[154] There follows by epoch and natural order the eleventh deity, because, the cultivation of fields having grown in the first age, many men, who still out of fear of thunder and lightning had not been reduced to social life, were observing that pious people had the benefits of many planted fields, and not wishing to imitate them in work (as do many lazy persons of our times), hurled themselves upon them in the fields to steal the harvests, but as they approached with their arms, they [the pious people] defended them with force. That is how it came about that the fields that had been planted were called *fields of arms and of battles* because in that very place the owners of the planted fields killed the thieving vagabonds; those who remained were by some superstitious displays declared accursed and dedicated to *Huitzilopochtli*, just as one reads about the Romans in the Laws of the Twelve Tables, book 19, table 7, *Ne frugem aratro quaesitam nocte furtim despascunto. Puberes si secanto, Cereri eos*

152. "[River Styx] by whose name the gods fear to swear falsely." León-Portilla's translation is not accurate. He omits *jurare.*

153. "Let the River Styx, which is unseen by our eyes, which is to be sworn to the gods, be witness to my promises." Ovid, *Metamorphoses*, book 2. [Lines 45–46].

154. This seems to be a combination of *teo*[*tl*] + *yao*[*tl*] + *tlahtoa* + *Huitzilopochtli*, that is, "divine-warrior-ruler-Huitzilopochtli."

suspendunto.[155] And even in the Indians' human age, the person who entered another's planted field and stole five ears of maize was an accused subject to death, since they retained some shadow of their ancient customs with doors open in their homes and towns, defended only with the majesty of the law. From these specific wars for the defense of the fruits of the field, there later originated the public and offensive ones, and the captives taken in them were in the same way dedicated to *Huitzilopochtli*, a god who was always thirsty for human blood and who was accompanied by the goddess *Teoyaominqui*,[156] who, as they believed, took care of recovering the souls both of those who died in war and of those whom they sacrificed after being captured. For this same reason the Latins derived the words *hostia* [victim] from *hostis* [enemy], *victima* [victim] from *victus* [defeated], as Ovid teaches, *Fastor.* book 1.[157]

> *Victima, quae cecidit dextra victrice, vocatur*
> *Hostibus a domitis hostia nomen habet*[158]

The most famous of the symbols with which this bloody idol was adorned was the *teotecpatl*, which means *Divine Flint*, because the Indians armed the points of their arrows with some thin flints which wounded in the same way as steel. They were also placed on either side of a stick split down the middle and stuck together with a strong and glutinous material, which served them as a two-sided sword and caused much damage in battles; and I heard from an Indian that with one single blow of the said sword, which they called *macana*,[159] he cut off the head of a horse during the conquest by the Spaniards.[160] In the second age, when the

155. "In the night by thievery they are not to feed on the fruits gained by the plough. If adults do the cutting, they will hang them in honor of Ceres." This Latin is archaic.

156. This appears to be a combination of *teo*[*tl*] + *yao*[*tl*] + *minqui*, "goddess-warrior who pierces." Molina (Nahuatl/Spanish) defines it as "one possessing arms for war."

157. *Sic* for *Fasti.*

158. "He is called a victim who has fallen by the victor's right hand, the sacrificial victim takes his name from the vanquished enemy" [Book 1, lines 335–36.]

159. Actually a Taino word that the Spaniards used for the Nahuatl *macuahuitl.* See Hassig, *Aztec Warfare*, 83.

160. On this see Hassig, *Aztec Warfare*, 83, 289n66.

heroes showed a total warlike anger and superiority in virtue and force, this deity was much feared, and his symbol was placed among the heavenly signs. In the third [age] of the human governors the sacrifices were excessively bloody because, in addition to the very solemn feasts that the Mexicans celebrated in the month *Panquetzaliztli*,[161] with the participation of the emperor, the principal lords, and the people, there was an occasion on which in his honor fifty-thousand persons, taken prisoners in war, were killed.

18 *HAHUIATLTEOTL*,[162] hieroglyph of the twelfth god, in which are expressed the idle, vagabonds, gamblers, and street entertainers, who lived on the bare ground, without esteem, in continual poverty and contempt. This wretched race of men was the one that in the second age found itself obliged by hunger to submit to the heroes, and these took them in the capacity of *Dediticia*,[163] and in the third [age] to sell itself into slavery in order to gain the sustenance for living. Ovid depicted it with lively allegoric colors, *Metamorphoses*, book 8, legends 11 and 12, in the person of the unfortunate Erisichthon, a vagabond without any religion, who having violated the forests dedicated to the goddess Ceres and cut down an oak tree, which was a nymph very beloved by the goddess, that is, *having entered the wood which was used by the neighboring farmers and cut down the oak tree destined for making the ploughs for the field*, he was condemned to a perpetual raging hunger and was compelled to sell his daughter Metra[164] to different buyers, under the various guises of beasts of burden, birds, mares, and stags, *in which are signified all the household things, with which he could have supported himself and his daughter*, and even this short recourse was insufficient for such a great hunger; he was eating himself, that is, *little by little he ate the intestines of his freedom.*[165]

---

161. The fifth month of the year, during the first days of which the feasts of Huitzilopochtli were celebrated.

162. This is a confused form. *Hahuiatl* is not a combining form. Perhaps it is derived from the verb *ahahuiy*[*a*], "to take pleasure" [Karttunen, *Analytical Dictionary*]. Or it may be related to *auyani*, a prostitute.

163. *Dedititius*, Latin for "one who has surrendered." The form is feminine to agree with *raza*.

164. *Sic* for Mestra. Poseidon had given her the gift of changing her shape.

165. This story is found in Greek mythology. King Erysichthon of Thessaly cut down trees in a grove sacred to Demeter [Roman Ceres] and killed a nymph.

Pater hujus erat, qui numina Divum
Sperneret, & nullos aris adoleret honores.
Ille etiam Cereale nemus violasse securi
Dicitur; & lucos ferro temerasse vestustos
Stabat in his ingens annoso robore quercus;
Una nemus: vittae mediam, memoresque tabellae.

. . . .

Saepe pater dominis Triopeida vendit; At illa
Nunc equa, nunc ales, modo bos, modo cervus abibat.
Praebebatque avido non justa alimenta parenti.
Vis tamen illa mali postquam consumpserat omnem
Materiam, dederatque grave nova pabula morbo,
Ipse suos artus lacero divellere morsu
Cœpit; & infelix minuendo corpus alebat.[166]

19 *MICTLANTEUCTLI.* Thus under the representations of imaginary deities who signify the principal pressures of the first parents of our Americans; it remains for me to deal only with the thirteenth and final deity, that is, of the *god of the underworld*,[167] a hieroglyph that explains the pious act of burying the dead and the great respect that these ancient Indians had for graves, believing, in imitation of other nations, not only that there the souls of the dead would assist them, as Vergil sang in book 3 of the *Aeneid*, verses 303 and 304.

Demeter punished him by placing an unrelenting and insatiable hunger in his stomach. He sold all his possessions, including his daughter, Mestra, to buy food, but was still hungry. Erysichthon sold her numerous times to make money to feed himself, but she changed her shape. Eventually, Erysichthon ate himself in hunger.

166. "Her father, who would spurn the will of the gods and would not do sacrificial honors to the altars, is also said to have violated Ceres's forest with an ax and to have defiled the ancient sacred groves with iron. The mighty oak was standing among them with aged strength; one forest: in the middle ribbons and memory writing tablets. . . . Often the father sells to buyers the granddaughter of Triopas, but she escaped, now as a mare, now a fowl, now a cow, now a stag, and she offered an immoderate nourishment to her avid parent. However, that force of evil after it had consumed everything material and given new food to a serious disease, itself began to tear to pieces his joints, and the unhappy person nourished his body by diminishing it." Ovid, *Metamorphoses*, book 8. [Lines 729–44, 872–78.]

167. Perhaps a more accurate translation would be "ruler of the abode of the dead."

Manesque vocabat
Hectoreum ad tumulum[168]

Ibid., 4, verse 35.

Id cinerem, aut manes credis curare sepultos[169]

Except the said relatives were also their gods, *Indigetes, ita dicti, quasi inde geniti.* Their bones and ashes gave that place undoubted and clear signs of the possession that they had of that same land, where they were buried, which they had conquered with the sweat of agriculture and even defended with the respect and mute eloquence of their corpses, which is what the same poet [Vergil] makes clear in book 1, *Georgics*, verses 98 and 99.

Dii patrii Indigetes & Romule, Vestaque mater
Quæ Tuscum Tiberim, & Romana palatia servas[170]

This is how it came about that *humanity* was derived from *bury*,[171] because humanity was founded with the tombs, and even the first poets imagined that the underworld was to be found in them. And thus Ulysses, when the earth opened before his feet, saw the past heroes in the underworld, and Theseus together with Orpheus went to the tombs to found first, the Athenian people, and second, the Greek race; from them is derived the beginning of the humanity of the nations. In the second age our Indians dedicated two months of the year, called *Micaylhuitl* and *Hueymicaylhuitl*[172] to the commemoration of the dead, and

---

168. "And he called the shades of the dead to Hector's tomb."

169. "Do you believe that the ashes or spirits of the dead care for this?"

170. "Ancestral gods were heroes, Romulus, Mother Vesta, who guards the Tuscan Tiber, and Rome's Palatine." The point is that *indigena* is derived from *inde geniti.* This seems to be an inaccurate etymology. In classical Latin *indigetes* meant heroes who after their deaths were elevated to the status of gods and became patron deities of their cities.

171. *Humanitas*, from *humando.* See note 94.

172. *Micaylhuitl.* Siméon gives this in a reverential form with a slightly different spelling, *Miccaylhuitltzintli*, and glosses it as "little feast of the dead." He does not have *Hueymicayilhuitl*, which would mean "the great feast of the dead." Boturini translates *ilhuitl* as "month," when it actually means "feast" or "day." [Siméon, s.v., *Miccaylhuitltzintli*].

in the third [age] they performed various acts of piety in their memory, constant proof that they acknowledged the immortality of the soul.

20 In addition to the thirteen major deities mentioned, the Indians had many other, lesser, ones because in this age, so lacking in testimonies and equal to the others in the needs of life, they had to invent more gods in order to explain them [the needs of life]; nor can I decipher the history of that obscure time with that erudition that the refined scholars of our century claim, unless I form (in imitation of the learned Varro, who in the same topic gathered together, among the antiquities of Latium, three thousand gods, which he explained in his book *Rerum divinarum ac humanarum*,[173] which has been lost) a divine dictionary, placing in it the names and explanation of the lesser gods, whom I will attempt, although with great labor, to gather from the numerous pictorial documents and manuscripts of my archive, in order to fill the empty spaces which intervene from the confusion of tongues to mythical times.

21 In the meantime I point out that while, in this age, the mute language of the gods was current, this must by necessity have begun with the images of some divinity, because without religion there can be no society whatsoever. And, as it was necessary that in coordinating the languages (except Hebrew, which began and remained always as the language of the one and only God), men agreed on one common belief, in this way it was easier for them that it be explained in the beginning with divine hieroglyphics than as mental categories; they brought along with them a compendium of differing concepts, which these first founders could not make understood with an articulate language, which was very rare in this age and usually monosyllabic and imperative, which I infer they were, and they are the roots of this Indian mother tongue, *Nahuatl*,[174] and in which the first parents commanded their children and grandchildren the things that they should carry out, since I imagine that the subjects showed their obedience with silence rather than words. And it is proven by the etymology of the word *Tlatohuani*, which signifies a lord, that is, *he who speaks*,[175] since everyone

173. *Of Human and Divine Things*.

174. The name of the language in the central plateau of New Spain. It is derived from the verb *nahuatia*, meaning "to speak correctly."

175. Singular agentive of the verb *tlahtoa* (*tla* + *ihtoa*), to speak.

else had to remain silent, because; up to the present day the Indians had the custom of being silent in the presence of their pastors, governors, and other superiors.

22 Previously I said that *Tecpatl*, *Calli*, *Tochtli*, *Acatl*, which signify *Flint*, *House*, *Rabbit*, and *Reed*, were divine names, figures of the four elements and almost outlines of the Indian chronology, by which the years were distinguished by adding to each of their characters the word *xihuitl*, which means *grass*; for example, *tecpatlxihuitl*, *callixihuitl*, *tochtlixihuitl*, *acatlxihuitl*,[176] which sound so much like *grass of flint*, *grass of house*, *grass of rabbit*, *grass of reed*, or, more precisely, *year of flint*, *year of house*, *year of rabbit*, *year of reed.*[177] And it is well known that from this first age the years were reckoned by the natural characteristic of the appearance of the first grass in the fields; and the Indians enumerated as many years as new grass, as the Latins, ears, according to Vergil I, *Bucolic Eclogues* 1, verse 70, but with some confusion.

Post aliquot mea regna videns mirabor aristas.[178]

And more clearly, the harvests, according to Ovid, *Letters*, Heroid[es], Letter 6, verses 5 & 6.[179]

Tertia messis erat: cum tu dare vela coactus
Implesti lacrymis talia verba tuis[180]

23 Finally, the government of those times was not just *cyclopic*, because a single eye saw and directed everything or because the first caves had only one entrance, a custom that has endured up to the present day among the Indian commoners; but also *theocratic*, because it was properly the age of oracles, in which the founders of these relationships

176. Footnote in the text: "And in combinations, tecpaxihuitl, calxihuitl, tochxihuitl, acaxihuitl."

177. According to Molina, *xihuitl* can mean year, comet, turquoise, and grass. The difference in meaning may depend on whether the first *i* is long or short.

178. "After several of my reigns, seeing the ears I will be in wonder." Boturini is correct, this does not make much sense.

179. The *Heroides* (Heroines), was a series of letter supposedly written by famous mythological characters to their partners.

180. "It was the third harvest; when you were compelled to set sail, you filled such words with your tears."

mandated only that which they thought was acceptable to the gods,
having beforehand sought it out with the common wisdom
of auguries, and they obeyed without response,
as they were learned men,
priests, and monarchs.

Second Age

§. IV

1 Having seen, then, in the previous age that the state of the first Indian peoples had always grown and increased by means of the observance of religion and solemn marriages, now follows that of the families, which with all appropriateness they are thus called, since the time that those same vagabonds of the first age were joined to the first parents as servants, who, moved both by the hunger that tormented them and by the fame of other pious and strong men, resolved to give them their obedience in order to attain a less painful life. And they, like religious and powerful Orpheuses, took them under their protection and help, but with the natural condition that because the said servants, on account of their inborn backwardness, were not able to contribute anything else but personal work toward the well-being of the families, cultivated the lands and were subordinated to the authority of the parents, who with the noblest part of their understanding governed their domestic affairs, exalted with the lofty titles of *priests*, *kings*, and *fathers*, and because of the new virtue of giving asylum to the weak and unfortunate, they were in this age publicly acclaimed as *heroes.*

2 The greater part of the history of this time is spent in celebrating the heroes' origin, which our Indians believed to have been divine; that is, because the said heroes were born under the sacrament of marriage or because they were deeply involved with sacrifices, and they even believed that because of the right that they had to procure auguries, they were continually conversing with the gods and from them were receiving advice and strength to carry out their great enterprises.

3 The entire method of these nations for writing the history of their heroism consists of two ways: the first, by totally elevating the human nature of their heroes to the divine, but because their poets could not abstract the forms of the subjects, it was necessary, in their minds, to destroy the first forms and the subjects, in order to introduce other new ones and new forms, by making use of some metamorphoses and transformations that were no less lively and acute than those of Ovid. The other, by distinguishing the quality of the said heroes from the rest of men, endowing them with superior virtue that made them renowned to posterity. And I observe that in this time intermediate between the first and last ages, the primitive heroes united with and accompanied their gods, and the latter gave themselves after the manner of human governors.

4 One and the other matter is explained with legends and symbols, partly divine and partly human, and I will give a brief account of both for the better understanding of the history of the Indies.

Divine Heroic Symbols

of the Planets

§. V

1 The propensity that the Orientals had for diligently observing the stars, and even more so the Assyrians and after them the Greeks, is well known. To make the prerogatives of their divine origin understood, they placed their gods among the *wandering* [stars] and the heroes among the *fixed* ones. But the Indians took the opposite view in this, exalting their gods as *fixed* and their heroes as *wandering*, perhaps because the former were situated on a higher altitude and shone by themselves alone, while the latter were closer to common view and were recognized by the light that the sun communicated to them; and because it seemed to them that the heroes, who previously had been of a nature inferior to the gods, and even with the great benefit they received in their union, should be accorded a lower place than the primitive deities.

2 The first and most celebrated symbol of the planets is that of the sun, which the Indians called *Tonatiuh*, and in legend the *Venereal One*, in their language *Nanahuatzin.*[181] The Indian legend of his transformation is that once the gods were satisfied with regard to the heroic virtues that some particular individuals had displayed in this mortal life and were resolved to reward them, they called together on a great plain all the peoples of the second age and commanded that on a

181. According to Siméon and Clavigero, *Nanahuatzin* was a mysterious personage linked to Mexican mythology. The name appears to be related to *Nanahuatl*, "venereal disease."

great bonfire that was there and at the time was spewing forth flames, the courageous ones should hurl themselves in order to be transformed and enter into divine honors. While gathered, then, around the bonfire, the principal lords began to dispute among themselves who had the right to be the first to throw himself in, at which time a sick person, with venereal disease and corrupted, appeared to one of them, the god *Centeotl inopitlzin*,[182] that is, *the orphan god*, alone and without parents, saying to him, *What are you doing here? Do you not see that your companions waste time in useless arguments? Go up to the bonfire. Throw yourself into the flames to put an end to all your ills, which with heroic resolve you have learned to tolerate quietly for so many years, and you will find the beginnings of immortal greatness.* The *Venereal One* did so, and dragging himself unnoticed nobly threw himself into the fire, much to the wonder of the others who saw closely as he was slowly being consumed and transformed into the very flames, and no longer looking like any vestiges of a human body. Under the sky a very beautiful eagle which, entering into the bonfire, carried him to the heavenly dwellings, and it is almost the same as what Jupiter did with Ganymede, young noble of Troy, having sent an eagle to take him to heaven in order that there he would serve as a cupbearer,[183] which gave rise in part to the anger of Juno and the misfortunes that she brought on the Trojans, according to Vergil, book 1 of the *Aeneid*, verse 30 & following.

Manet alta mente repostum
Judicium Paridis, spretæque injuria formæ,
Et genus invisum, & rapti Ganymedis honores[184]

And Ovid, *Metamorphoses*, book 10, legend 4.

Nec mora: percusso mendacibus aere pennis
Abripit Iliadem qui nunc quoque pocula miscet,
Invitaque Jovi nectar Junone manifestat.[185]

182. *Centeotl* was the god of the land and maize. *Inopitlzin* should be *inopiltzin.*

183. In some versions it was Jupiter in the guise of an eagle.

184. "The judgment of Paris remained kept on high in her mind, and the injury to [her] spurned beauty and the hated race and the honors to the seized Ganymede.

185. "There is no delay. In the air struck by deceitful wings he seizes the Trojan boy who now also mixes the potions and, while Juno declines, serves nectar to Jupiter." [Lines 159–61.]

And although some authors, with inept and twisted interpretations, dressed up the true meaning of this unruly legend, what is certain is that the Indians did not want to give it any other meaning except that the sun was a real fire, for which reason some modern philosophers locate this element in the sun and prove that its spots are the smoke that it exhales, without needing anything to support itself or nourish it, because its innate material is very abundant and it cannot squeeze anything from the neighboring bodies and even in case it might have need of it for what it wastes in the ecliptic[186] another bit of delicate matter is added to it on both poles. And Ovid tells us, *Metamorphoses*, book 2, legend 1, that when Phaëthon had obtained from his father, the sun, the gift of being able to drive, though only for a day, the shining chariot, he put the heavens and earth in extreme confusion with his wayward course and going too close to its flames, and to remedy such a great and hitherto unseen disorder, Jupiter was obliged to hit him with the force of thunderbolts, hurling him, dead, over the lands of Italy.[187]

Utque ferant æquos & cœlum & terra calores,
Nec preme, nec summum molire per æthere carrum,
Altius egressus cœlestia tecta cremabis;
Inferius terras . . . . ambustaque nubila fumant.
Corripitur flammis, ut quæque altissima tellus;
Fissaque agit rimas, & succis aret ademptis. . . .
Cumque suis totas populis incendia gentes
In cinerem vertunt. Silvæ cum montibus ardent.[188]

---

186. This is an astronomical term. It can refer to the apparent path of the sun throughout a year.

187. In Greek mythology, Phaëton or Phaethon was the son of Helios (Apollo) and Clymene. According to Ovid Phaëthon sought assurance that his mother, Clymene, is telling the truth that his father is the sun god Helios. When Phaëthon obtains his father's promise to drive the sun chariot as proof, he fails to control it and the earth is in danger of burning up, when Phaëthon is killed by a thunderbolt from Zeus to prevent further disaster.

188. "And in order that heaven and earth may bear equal heat, do not press nor pressure the very great chariot through the air, by going higher you will burn the roofs of heaven, and lower, the lands . . . and the burned clouds pour forth smoke. It is racked by flames like any very high globe, and split, it opens fissures and, with all moisture taken away, it is dry. . . . and they turn all nations together with their peoples to ashes. Forests burn together with their mountains."

What has been said is confirmed by another legend of the same Indians but rooted in historical truth, when by command of Joshua the sun stopped in favor of the Israelites.[189] They say, then, that in the year *Seven Rabbits*, the sun having stopped moving, the heat that originated on the earth was excessive, and the mosquito presented itself before him [the sun], telling him: *Lord of the Earth, do you perhaps wish to burn up the entire earth and reduce the world to ashes, for weary, you cease your regular course, and you remain unmoved by the pleas of mortals?* But seeing that he did not answer and that he was making no movement, it approached him and bit him on a leg, which when it recoiled set [the sun] again on his course. Ovid also recounts the same fact, with other poetic amusements, the aforesaid place, legend 4, when he describes the loss of strength and the stopping of the sun because of the death of his son Phaëthon, and he tells us that at the urging of the gods he again took the reins of his horses and pursued his regular course.

Squallidus interea genitor Phaethontis, & expers
Ipse sui decoris, qualis, cum deficit orbem,
Esse solet: lucemque odit, seque ipse, diemque;
Datque animum in luctus; & luctibus adjicit iram:
Officiumque negat muno. . . .
Talia dicentem circumstant omnia solem
Numina: neve velit tenebras inducere rebus,
Suplice voce rogant missos quoque Jupiter ignes
Excusat, precibusque minas regaliter addit.
Coligit amentes, & adhuc terrore paventes,
Phœbus equos[190]

3 The second divine heroic symbol is the moon, which the Indians call *Meztli*, and the story of its transformation is that after

189. The reference is to Joshua 10:12–13.

190. "In the meantime Phaëthon's father, in disarray and unconcerned about his splendor, such as he is wont to be, when he is absent from earth; and he himself hates the light and himself and the day; he puts his mind to grief and to grief he adds anger; and he refuses his office to the world. . . . All the divinities surround the sun as he says such things; they ask him in a pleading voice not to want to bring darkness on things, Jupiter also excuses the fires that have been sent and like kings adds threats to pleas. Phoebus gathers the horses which are confused and still shaking in fear."

the metamorphosis of the *Venereal One*, one of the sages who was present and who wished to achieve perpetual lodging in heaven, also threw himself onto the bonfire but because it was now diminished from the first volume of flames and had even died down in its activity, was able only to change him into ashes that remained visible on the ground of the same fire, and the sage was transformed into the second planet. That is how it happened that the Indians appropriated the color of ashes for the moon, and by the levels of fire which went up and then down, they symbolized its waxing and waning, always retaining the property of being cold.

4 Both deities were among those of great renown in this age, and even in the third, the Indians worshiped them with many sacrifices of quail which, after their throats had been cut, they offered especially to the sun, to whom they dedicated the fresh blood that they scattered on the ground.

5 There still remain in the city of San Juan *Teotihuacan*, seven leagues distant from *Mexico*, two indisputable testimonies to his notable cult. In the adjoining level fields are seen two high hills made by hand. The one is called *Tonatiuh Itzaqual*,[191] which means *House dedicated to the Sun*, and it is of larger size in comparison with the other one dedicated to the moon. Its building is of four levels which grow narrow toward the top and are symbols of the four seasons of the year and of thc four aspects of the Indian calendars. On the top level, which functioned as a pedestal, was located that great statue of the sun which had in its breast a square sheet of precious metals that reflected the rays of this luminous planet when it rose. The image was called *Tonacateuctli*, *God of sustenance* or *God of our meat*, and it was served by priests called *Papahua Tlemacazque*[192] who, differing from the rest, wore

---

191. *Tonatiuh* + *i* + *tzaqual*[*li*]. Siméon, s.v., *tzaqualli*, defines it as "tower in the form of a small hill, located near the village of Teotihuacan. It is there that the sun and moon gods, *Tecuciztecatl* and *Nanahuatzin*, retired for four days."

192. "He who has a tuft of hair . . . *Papahuaque*, Indian ministers who came together when there was need to choose a chief or king" (Siméon). "Guedejudos" (Molina, Nahuatl/Spanish). *Tlemacazque* may be a misprint for *tlamacazque*, which can mean "mature men" or "priests in the temple" (Durán, *History*, 156n7). Siméon glosses *tlamacazque* as "ministers usually living in the temples and having diverse functions" (s.v. *tlamacazqui*).

their hair long and loose, and at the end of the Indian cycle, they took and sold the *New Fire* to the neighboring towns. In ancient times this hill was perfectly square, whitewashed and beautiful, and the summit was reached by some levels which are not visible today because they have been filled in by their own ruins and the earth that the winds have hurled at it, over which trees and prickly plants have grown. Nevertheless, I was on it and had it measured out of curiosity, and if I am not mistaken, it is two hundred *varas* in height.[193] In the same way, I had it drawn on a pictorial document, which I have in my archive, and surrounding it I saw that the famous don Carlos de Sigüenza y Góngora had intended to drill it but had encountered resistance. It is well known that its center is empty, which the word *Itzaqual*[194] resembles so much.

6 On the left side of the aforesaid house of the sun there is that of the moon, although of smaller size, and it is called *Meztli Itzaqual*, that is, *House of the Moon*, and around it are found the remains of various small hills, all made by hand and dedicated to the rest of the *wandering* stars, which I will explain in the history, being careful to ascertain their number, although the Indians of Chiapas count seven of them, corresponding to the days of their week; and in the wheels and tables of the Toltec symbols of the days of the year, I find after the triadecaterida the number *Septenario*, so notable in sacred scripture,[195]

because it was on the seventh day of the
creation of the world that the most
beneficent creator rested.

193. A *vara* was approximately one yard long.

194. *I + tzqualli.* As noted previously, Siméon glosses it as "towers in the form of a small hill near Teotihuacan" (s.v. *tzaqualli*).

195. In the original this is in a footnote.

Divine Heroic Symbols

of the Days of the Year

§. VI

1 After the Indian nations had observed with great care the *wandering* stars, since they were closer to common view, they went on to contemplate the *fixed* ones, and they calculated the number of the most principal of these as twenty, representing them with the likeness of certain deities, some from the first age, and other semi-deities, which they invented in those times, and the said calculation was of equal service to the astronomers to demonstrate the situation of the signs and to the chronologists to arrange the symbols of the days of the year in order on wheels or tables of the most exquisite kind, in which the entire year revolved, the only difference being that they were distinguished in the numbers.

2 It is proved by the evidence that our Indians took the knowledge of the *wandering* stars before that of the *fixed* ones by the symbol *Ollin Tonatiuh*, that is, *Movement of the Sun*, which in the wheels or tables of the symbols of the days of the year is placed at number four after the triadecaterida, and for greater clarity at number seventeen of the tables, something that proves that the *fixed* stars were found after the *wandering* ones, because with regard to these latter, the existence of the sun came first before its movement being symbolized.

The Days Are the Following

§. VII

Triadecaterida[196]

1. *Cipactli.* Serpent armed with harpoons.[197]
2. *Ehecatl.* Wind.[198]
3. *Calli.* House.
4. *Cueztpallin.*[199] Lizard.
5. *Cohuatl.* Snake.
6. *Miquiztli.* Death.
7. *Mazatl.* Deer.
8. *Tochtli.* Rabbit.
9. *Atl.* Water.
10. *Izcuintli.* Dog.
11. *Ozomatli.* Monkey.[200]
12. *Malinalli.* Twisted cords, from the verb *malina*, to twist.[201]
13. *Acatl.* Reed.

---

196. In the original, this word is perpendicular in the left margin.

197. Simeón glosses this as "shark." Durán says that it was represented "by a kind of serpent's head" (*History*, 307).

198. Also, wind.

199. *Sic* for *cuetzpalin.*

200. Vaillant glosses this as "howling monkey" (*Aztecs*, table 9), while Siméon translates it "a kind of monkey with a long tail" (s.v. *ozomatli*)

201. Siméon glosses it as plait or braid. Vaillant translates it as "grass" (*Aztecs*, table 8).

Septenario[202]

1. *Ocelotl.* Jaguar.[203]
2. *Quauhtli.* Eagle.
3. *Temetlatl.* Stone used in the Indies for grinding.
4. *Ollin Tonatiuh.* Movement of the sun, from the verb *ollini*, to move.
5. *Tecpatl.* Flint, worked into a point for arrows and swords.
6. *Quiahuit.*[204] Rainwater.
7. *Xochitl.* Flower.

1 The first symbol of the days of the year is *Cipactli*, which in most of the pictorial documents, I found painted with the figure of a fish like a serpent armed with daggers like arrowheads. I struggled a great deal over its interpretation but it suited me better to take it from the etymology of its selfsame Indian word, and since *Cipactli* is a combination of the words *ce icpac thatli*,[205] for example, *Cicpactonal*, from *ce icpac tonalli*, it becomes evident that *Cipactli* means the *Father superior to all*, and *Cicpactonal the Father superior to the sun.* And so it is that Cipactli is first father of all human generation, who the Indians say took as his wife *Oxomozco*, and it is as if we would say *Adam* and *Eve*, whom they raised to the honors of divinity.[206]

2 In the history I will continue the interpretation of the rest to the full satisfaction of learned men who, on considering my literary labors, will clearly know, that although some attempted to write about this material, it was little, and they did not have the good luck to succeed due to the lack of the materials that my incessant endeavor has subsequently found.

202. In the original, this word is perpendicular in the left margin.

203. That is, jaguar.

204. *Sic* for *quiahuitl.*

205. This is a confusing etymology. *Thatli* appears to be an error for *tatli*, "father."

206. Siméon gives the form as *Oxomoco*, and says, "wife of Cipactonal, perhaps the same divinity as the Mexican Venus *Tlaçoteotl. Oxomoco* and *Cipactonal* are considered the inventors of necromancy."

Divine Heroic

Symbols of the Months

§. VIII

1 Although the symbols of the Indian months are taken either from the actions which were carried out in them or from the effects of the time in which they fell, nevertheless some of them were divine in themselves, and the rest were sacralized by the great feasts dedicated to particular gods that were celebrated in them with a diversity of rites and ceremonies.

2 In the Indian language the word for month is *Meztli*, which is the same as if we were to say *moon*, and it was by this that they regulated its course, which was twenty days. The year was composed of eighteen months which, at twenty days each, formed 360 days, and at the end of them the Indians added another five, which because they were not included in the reckoning of the months, were considered unfortunate and ill-fated, which in their language is expressed as *Nenontemi.*[207]

3 Whether Indian or Spanish, authors differ in discussing the symbolic pictures of the said months, but this does not take away the certainty of their number nor does it confuse the system of the Indian calendars, it only changes the time of the sacrifices and ceremonies, whose difficulties I will leave to be treated in the history. And continuing for now with the symbols found in the pictorial document and Mexican cycle of Gemelli Careri in volume 6, chapter 5 of his *Giro del Mundo* that he got from don Carlos de Sigüenza y Góngora, I will give an account of some of them, first recounting those of Father

207. *Sic* for *nemontemi.*

fray Martín de León of the Order of Preachers,[208] mentioned in his learned book *Camino del cielo*, and explaining the etymology of the Indian names in Castilian, in order that any difference from one to the others may be seen.

208. The Dominicans.

Symbols of the Indian Months

According to Father fray Martín de León

§. IX

1. *Atlcahualo.* The stopping of the waters.
2. *Tlaxipehualiztli.* The flaying of people.[209]
3. *Totzotzontli.*[210] The small fast.
4. *Hueytotzotzontli.* The great fast.
5. *Toxcatl.* Effort.[211]
6. *Etzalcualiztli.* The eating of *tecojotes.*[212]

---

209. Uncertain translation. *Tlaxipehualiztli* appears to be composed of *tla* + *xipehual*[*o*] + *iztli*, and means to remove the bark or leaves from a tree. This seems to be connected with Xipe Totec, the flayed god.

210. *Sic* for *Tozoztontli.* Vaillant translates it as "small fast" (table 14). Siméon simply says that it was the third month of the year, corresponding to March, the first day of which was dedicated to Tlaloc, the god of rain. Molina (Spanish/Nahuatl), under *Ayuno* and its variants, has nothing resembling this word, nor does he have it in the Nahuatl/Spanish section.

211. León-Portilla translates *Toxcatl* as *esfuerzo*, but Molina (Spanish/Nahuatl) has nothing resembling *toxcatl* nor does he have it in the Nahuatl/Spanish section. Vaillant translates it as "dry, slippery" (table 14). Siméon glosses it as the fifth month of the year.

212. This appears to be composed of *e*[*tl*] + *tzal* + *cual*[*o*] + *iztli.* What is eaten is *etzalli*, which Siméon glosses as a form of gruel or mush. Vaillant glosses *etzalcualiztli* as "bean porridge" (table 14). It actual means a soup of maize and beans. *Tecojotes* is a misspelling of *tejocotes*, Nahuatl *texocotl*, a small acidic fruit from a plant in the hawthorn family. The term *etzalcualiztli* also refers to the sixth month of the Mexica calendar, when the soup was eaten in honor of the rain god Tlaloc.

7. *Tecuilhuiltzintli.*[213] The brief feast of the lord.
8. *Hueytecuylhuitl.* The feast of the great lord.
9. *Tlaxochimalco.* The mat of flowers.[214]
10. *Xocotlhuitzi.* The ripening of fruit.[215]
11. *Ochpaniztli.* The time for sweeping.
12. *Teotleco.* The arrival of the gods.[216]
13. *Tepilhuitl.* The feast of the mountains.
14. *Quecholli.* Turkey.[217]
15. *Panquetzaliztli.* Gold banner or plumage.
16. *Atemoztli.* The altar of the gods.[218]
17. *Tititl.* Stomach, or our stomach.[219]
18. *Itzcalli.* When it sprouts.[220]

---

213. Vaillant gives the form as *tecuhilhuitontli* and glosses it as "little feast of princes" (table 14).

214. *Tlaxochimalco, sic* for *tlaxochimaco.* That is the form given by Vaillant, who glosses it as "birth of flowers" (table 14). Siméon says that *–maco* comes from *maca*, "to give." The form cited by Boturini seems to be incorrect.

215. Again, it appears that words that should be separated are combined, *xocotl huitzi.* Vaillant gives the form *–huetzi*, "to fall," which appears to be more correct (table 14).

216. This is the translation of León-Portilla (54). Vaillant glosses it as "the return of the gods" (table 14). The word is composed of *teotl* "god[s]" and *tleco*, which is glossed by Molina and Karttunen as "to ascend," and Siméon as "to mount" as on a horse.

217. This presents a problem. León-Portilla translates it as *pavón* (54), the same as Boturini, which can mean a turkey or similar bird. Molina and Karttunen give the meaning of a bird with red plumage.

218. A mistranslation. It is actually composed of *atl*, "water," and *temo*, "to fall."

219. Again, confusion. León-Portilla has "vientre o nuestro vientre." "Vientre" is glossed by Molina as *ititl.* Would not "nuestro vientre" be *toti* or *totitzin?* Simeón says that the word *tititl* means "contraction." Vaillant (table 14) translates the word as "severe weather," which seems wide of the mark.

220. Siméon glosses this as "side, right or left flank" (*côté, flanc droit ou gauche*). Vaillant translates it as "resuscitation" (table 14), but Molina (Spanish/Nahuatl) has nothing resembling it under "resuscitar." Neither Molina (Nahuatl/Spanish) nor Karttunen has the word. Molina (Spanish/Nahuatl) has "retoño de arbol," but the Nahuatl is entirely different from *itzcalli.*

Symbols of the Indian Months

According to Gemelli Careri

§. X

1. *Tlaxipehualiztli.* The flaying of people.
2. *Tezoztli.* The letting of blood, or lesser penance.[221]
3. *Hueytozoztli.* Great letting of blood, or greater penance.
4. *Toxcatl.* Effort.
5. *Etzalcualiztli.* Bean stew, called *exotl.*[222]
6. *Tecuilhuitl.* Lesser feast of the lord.
7. *Hueytecuilhuitl.* Feast of the great lord.
8. *Micailhuitl.* Lesser commemoration of the dead.
9. *Hueimicailhuitl.* Greater commemoration of the dead.
10. *Ochpaniztli.* Decoration or sweeping of the streets.
11. *Pachtli.* Moss that hangs from trees.[223]
12. *Hueipachtli.* More fully grown moss that hangs from trees.
13. *Quecholli.* The bird by this name, which has bright-colored feathers.
14. *Panquentzaliztli.*[224] Something that is held aloft, like a banner.
15. *Atemoztli.* Altar of the gods, a combining form of *Ateomomoztli.*

---

221. This word has nothing in common with blood, *etztli*, nor does Molina have any similar words for bloodletting or *penitencia* (Spanish/Nahuatl).

222. Siméon, following Sahagún and Clavigero, gives no meaning other than the sixth month of the year.

223. *Heno* in modern Spanish means "hay." Siméon describes *pachtli* as a parasite that hangs from trees and was used in the decoration of temples during feasts (s.v. *Pachtli*). In Mexico it popularly refers to Spanish moss (*Tillandsia*), used to decorate the streets.

224. *Sic* for *Panquetzaliztli.*

16. *Titit.* Our womb or mother of the gods.
17. *Itzcalli.* New generation or rebirth.
18. *Atlacoalo.* The buying of the waters or *Quiahuitlehua*, a tree that is raised up.

1 *Tlaxipehualiztli.* The symbol of the first month means the *flaying of people*, because on their first day they flayed some men alive dedicated to the god *Toteuc*, that is, *God our lord*, or to *Oxipe*, *God of flaying*, combining form of *Tloxipeuca*, to whom silversmiths dedicated those who had been flayed for having stolen gold and silver jewels or precious stones from them. They carried them beforehand to his temple, dragging them by the hair. This symbol is painted on some pictorial documents with a flayed man stretched out on the ground, and in Gemelli's wheel of the Mexican cycle, the skin of a flayed man is depicted with something like a cap above, in which the priest of the idol was dressed, and he was dancing with it in the partying in the feast.

2 *Tozoztli.* The symbol of the second month means *bloodletting* or *pricking* of the veins because in this way on the first day of this month the Indians, with either *maguey* thorns or with flint knives, as a sign of penance, would draw blood from their thighs, shins, ears, and arms, and they fasted at the same time, and from this the Indians claim that this month took its name, and that in *Tozoztli tozahualo* the *a* changed to *o*, and that it was the combining form of *Tozahual iztli.*[225] This was the feast of penitents, dedicated to the god *Tlaloc, the rain god* in this second age, who is said to have lived in the earthly paradise, called by his name *Tlalocan.* During that opportune time, they used to offer him the first fruits of flowers and roses of that month and year in a high, cube-shaped hill, in the form of a narrow pyramid, and nobody could smell the flowers until they offered the said first fruits. However, those who had the duty of making *xuchiles*[226] or wreaths called *xochimanque*, during the year, celebrated in the third age the feast of the goddess *Cihuatlicue*, which is the same as saying *woman's*

225. *Tozoztli* seems to be derived from *tla* + *çoa* [*zohua*], to skin. It is defined by Siméon as the fourth month of the year (from Sahagún); *tozahualo* is the passive of *toçoa* (*tozohua*), to keep vigil.

226. *Sic* for *xochiles.*

petticoats,[227] or by another name *Coatlatona, goddess of twins.*[228] This symbol is painted in some pictorial documents with a leg, from which ordinarily they drew blood, and with the small head of a bird over it, because it was from the name of the said bird that that of the month is derived, but in Gemelli's pictorial document the whole body of the bird is painted resting on a flint knife that was used for the same purpose of drawing blood.

3 *Hueitozoztli*, superlative of *Tozoztli*, symbol of the third month, means *puncturing* or *great bloodletting*, because with the stopping of the rains, which did not begin until this time, corresponding to our April, penances were increased, the drawing of blood grew, and the fasts were greater, and even the sacrifices. The feast was celebrated to the god *Cinteotl*,[229] god of maize, by placing branches of reeds on the exterior of the temples, houses, and doorways. However, those on the doorways had to be stained with that blood that they drew from their ears and shins, and the interior of the houses with some branches that they called *Acxoyatl*, that is, *small water-palms*,[230] and they would go to the maize fields and bring back some maize stalks that were still small and they crowned the gods with them, and in this way the Indians meant that the water was crowned, they explained it in an elegant way with this word *Acoxochioti in atl.*[231] This symbol is painted in some pictorial documents with the entire bird placed on a pedestal and in Gemelli's with something like a maize granary which has a skylight for ventilation and some tender branches of the same maize, which bloom on top.

4 The other seventeen symbols of the months that remain, I will explain in the history, in which will be seen the difference with which they are painted in one and the other pictorial documents.

5 Here I note that just because the months have twenty days each, the moon is not measured by calculating them alone, but only

227. More correctly, "skirts." *Cihualticue* seems to be an error for *cihuaticue.*

228. The first meaning of *coatl* is snake or serpent, but by extension it can mean twins. *Tona* or *atona* is unattested.

229. More commonly spelled *Centeotl.*

230. Siméon describes this as a plant whose leaves the priests used to draw blood as a penance.

231. Literally, "to place flowers on top of the water."

as thirteen by thirteen, and it is the reason why the Indians divided the movements of the moon into two separate time periods. They called the first figuratively *Sleeplessness*, which was reckoned from the waning of the sun until its waxing, which was thirteen days. The second they called *Sleep*, which concluded with an equal number of days until, according to their understanding, the moon waned in the morning. Gemelli thought that this reckoning of the *neomenias* was impossible to penetrate, and wishing to decipher it, he had recourse to the Indians of his time, who filled him with a thousand follies with their famous legend of the movements of the sun, which they related to him in a very deteriorated and corrupt form, nor can I be anything but astonished that the said author, having a close friendship with don Carlos de Sigüenza y Góngora, chair of mathematics at the University of Mexico, and who perhaps having seen his *Ciclografía indiana*, which I looked for unsuccessfully with such zeal, should write so many absurdities, which I cannot overlook; they are the following, which I correct.

Table 1. Symbols of the Four Parts or Corners of the World

GEMELLI	BOTURINI
1. *Tochtli.* Midday.	*Tecpatl.* Midday.
2. *Acatl.* East.	*Calli.* East.
3. *Tecpatl.* North.	*Tochtli.* North.
4. *Calli.* West.	*Acatl.* West.

Table 2. Symbols of the Four Seasons of the Year

GEMELLI	BOTURINI
1. *Tochtli.* Spring. 2. *Acatl.* Summer 3. *Tecpatl.* Autumn 4. *Calli.* Winter.	This is true and occurs only in the year that begins in *Tochtli*, but in the rest, the symbols are counted as follows. Year of *Acatl.* *Acatl.* Spring. *Tecpatl.* Summer. *Calli.* Autumn. *Tochtli.* Winter. Year of *Tecpatl* *Tecpatl.* Spring. *Calli.* Summer. *Tochtli.* Autumn.

Table 2. Symbols of the Four Seasons of the Year (*continued*)

GEMELLI	BOTURINI
	Acatl. Winter.
	Year of *Calli.*
	Calli. Spring.
	Tochtli. Summer.
	Acatl. Autumn.
	Tecpatl. Winter.

Table 3. Symbols of the Four Elements

GEMELLI	BOTURINI
1. *Tochtli.* Earth.	*Tecpatl.* Fire.
2. *Acatl.* Water.	*Calli.* Earth.
3. *Tecpatl.* Air.	*Tochtli.* Air.
4. *Calli.* Fire.	*Acatl.* Water.

Table 4. Symbols of the First Days of the Year

1. Cipactli.	It is denied that any day of the year begins with these four symbols.
2. Miquiztli.	
3. Ozomatli.	
4. Cozcaquauhtli.	

Table 5. Symbols of the First Days of the Year, Corresponding to the Character in Which the Year Begins

GEMELLI	BOTURINI
1. *Cipactli* corresponds to *Tochtli.* 2. *Miquiztli* to *Acatl.* 3. *Ozomatli* to *Tecpatl* 4. *Cozcaquauhtli* to *Calli.*	Nor does any of these correspond to the character of the year, and it is beyond a doubt that if the character of the year is *Tochtli*, then *Tochtli* should also be the symbol of its first day, and the rest should be interpreted in the same way.

Gemelli's accumulation of errors was thus capable of confusing those who seek to decipher the Indian calendars, because they would never find the thread for getting out of the labyrinth.[232]

232. A reference to the legend of Theseus and the Minotaur.

Divine Heroic Nocturnal

Symbols of the Year

§. XI

1 Our Indians not only had twenty symbols for distinguishing the days of the year, but also another nine that preceded and governed the nights, beginning with the setting of the sun until it rose again, with the one difference that they were not included in the five intercalary days of the year; in other words, because each one in turn had accompanied the symbols of the days forty times and reached the sum of 360, and they paid no attention when they were associated with the said intercalary days because in that regard they considered in their false imagination that these were fateful days and unfortunate. For that reason the priests were vigilant to learn which children were born during the fateful days in order to buy them from their parents and have them ready when the feasts and bloody sacrifices were offered. In other words, because the first nocturnal symbol was *Xiuhteucyohua*, which means *lord of the grass*, and consequently of the start of the year, it was necessary that he should come to accompany the first night of the year, something that could not happen if the reckoning of the passage of time incorporated the intercalary days. These nine were called accompanying *lords and masters of the night*, and they are the following.

1. *Xiuhteucyohua.* Lord of the year.
2. *Itzteucyohua.* Lord of the fire.[233]
3. *Piltzinteucyohua.* Lord of the children.

233. This seems to mean "obsidian lord." The ordinary word for "fire" is *tletl.*

4. *Cinteucyohua.* Lord of the maize.
5. *Mictlanteucyohua.* Lord of the underworld.
6. *Chalchihuitlicueyohua.* Lord of the water.[234]
7. *Tlazolyohua.* Lord of unlawful love.
8. *Tepeyoloyohua.* Lord of the innermost mountains.
9. *Quiauhteucyohua.* Lord of the rain.

2 *Xiuhteucyohua*, first nocturnal symbol, is composed of *Xiuhteuctli* and the word *yohua*, which means night, derived from *tlayohua*, *nightfall*, and it means *night, in which the lord of the year is dominant.* The Indians considered this to be accompanied by evil. In the history, an accounting will be given of the rest.

3 Proof of what has been said is that the first Indian calendar was that of the natural year, because the four divine characters, *tecpatl*, *calli*, *tochtli*, *acatl*, which the years were called, were found in the first age, in which they were explained as the four elements, and the years were numbered by the appearance of the new grass in the fields. Although it was perfected in this second age, the learned men availed themselves of the same characters to divide the year into an equal number of seasons and to foretell in each one of them the times that their respective characters indicated. The other two calendars, the astronomic and chronological, belong to this second age because, as was said previously, the *wandering* stars were deciphered and then the *fixed* ones, whose symbols equally served the astronomers to indicate their properties and better direct agriculture, as well as the chronologists to regulate the days of the year. As for everything else, in regards to the ritual calendar, although it cannot be denied that it had its beginnings in this second age, nevertheless it was brought to completion in the third, and many moveable feasts, which were instituted by the emperors and kings in historical times, show this.

234. An apparent mistranslation. *Chalchiuitlicue* is a variation of *Chalchiuhcueye*, literally "possessor of the emerald skirt," the goddess of water.

Other Examples

of Transformations as Means of Reward and Punishment

§. XII

1 The warlike Mexican nation, which in this second age found itself on the way to seeking new lands in the direction of America, and which greatly prided itself on its bravery in war, wanted to transfer all the fame of the eleventh deity of the ancestral peoples to a famous captain of theirs, by name *Huitziton.*[235] It was he who in the long and dangerous journeys on unknown paths led the Mexicans in particular, and without succumbing to fatigue, looked out for the good of the people. His legendary history recounts that, burdened with years and wisdom, he was taken one night from the sight of the army and all his people, and presented to the god *Tetzauhteotl*, which means, the *frightful god,*[236] who under the guise of a horrible dragon, ordered him to sit at his left hand, saying to him, *You are very welcome, fearless captain. I am very grateful for the good with which you have served me and governed my people. It is now time for you to rest, for you are now old, and your deeds elevate you to the company of the immortal gods. Return to your children and tell them not to be afflicted if from now on they do not have you present as a mortal man, because from the nine places*, which sounds so much like *Chicnautopan*, that is, *from the nine heavens, not only will you view them favorably but in time I will strip*

235. A combination of *Huitzilin*, hummingbird, and the diminutive suffix -*ton*. This is apparently the same deity as Huitzilopochtli. However, I have been unable to find any reference to this name other than in Boturini.

236. A synonym for Huitzilopochtli (Siméon).

from you the remains of humanity, I will leave your bones and skull to your afflicted orphaned peoples so that they may appease their sorrow; they will consult you about the roads to take, and in time you will show them the land which I have destined for them and in which they will have a widespread empire, respected by the other nations. Huitziton did this, and after the sorrowful conversation, he disappeared, taken by the gods, and the Mexicans, who shed copious tears because of their intense sorrow, found themselves with the skull and bones of their beloved captain, which they carried with them until their arrival in New Spain and the place where they later built the great city of *Tenochtitlan Mexico.*[237] The devil always spoke to them through *Huitziton*'s skull and frequently asked them to sacrifice men and women, the source of those bloody sacrifices that this nation later practiced with increased barbarity with prisoners of war. This deity was called *Huitzilopochtli* both in the first and second age, because the ancestral peoples must have believed that he was seated at the left hand of *Tezcatlipoca*, in the same way that they invented that he was at [the left hand] of *Tetzauhteotl* in the second age, in which from his proper name *Huitziton* and from *mapoche*, which is left hand, they composed the name *Huitzilopchtli.*[238] This legend reflects that of the transformation of Aeneas, who, because of his heroic deeds, at the request of his mother Venus, after she had purified him and washed him in the river Numitius and also anointed him with balsam and divine unguents, was received by Jupiter in the assembly of the other gods, according to Ovid, *Metamorphoses*, book 14, legend 15.

Litus adit laurens; ubi tectus arundine serpit
In freta fluminis vicina Numicius undis.
Hunc jubet Æneæ, quæcumque obnoxia mori,[239]
Abluere, & tacito deferre sub æquora cursu.
Corniger exsequitur Veneris mandata: suisque,
Quidquid in Ænea fuerat mortale, repurgat,

---

237. More commonly, Mexico-Tenochtitlan.

238. It is generally agreed that the name is a combination of *Huitzilin*, "hummingbird" and *opochtli*, "on the left" or "on the south." Boturini is a bit confused here. Left hand in Nahuatl is *maopochtli.*

239. *Sic* for *morti.*

Et respergit[240] *aquis, pars optima resistit illi.*
Lustratum genitrix divino corpus odore
Unxit, & ambrosia cum dulci nectare mista
Contigit os; fecitque Deum: quem turba Quirini
Nuncupat Indigetem; temploque arisque recepit.[241]

And [it reflects] even more vividly the metamorphosis of Romulus, who, because of the intense love with which he governed his people, was seized in the shadow of dense clouds and the din of thunder and lightning, to the same Mount Palatine where he gave laws to the people, and in Mars's bloody chariot was transported with a now divine aspect to heaven and given a place among the gods, ibid., legend 19.

Annuit[242] *omnipotens: & nubibus aera cæcis*
Occuluit, tonitruque & fulgure terruit urbem.
Quæ sibi promissæ sensit data[243] *signa rapinæ,*
Innixusque hastæ, pressos temone cruento
Impavidus conscendit equos Gradivus, & ictu
Verberis increpuit: pronumque[244] *per aera lapsus*
Constitit in summo nemorosi colle Palati:
Reddentemque suo jam regia jura Quiriti
Abstulit Iliaden corpus mortale per auras
Dilapsum tenues: ceu lata plumbea funda
Missa solet medio glans intabesceræ cœlo,

240. *Sic* for *respersit.*

241. "She arrived at the shore of Laurentum, where concealed by the reeds, the [river] Numitius creeps into the neighboring channel with a river's waves. She ordered it to cleanse Aeneas of whatever is subject to death and to carry it away under its surface in its quiet course. The horned one carries out Venus's orders and with his own [powers] purged whatever in Aeneas was mortal and spread it on the waters, the best part stays with him. The mother anointed the purified body with a divine scent and touched his mouth with ambrosia mixed with sweet nectar, and made him a god, whom the crowd of Romans called a native and received into their temple and altars." [Lines 598–608.]

242. *Sic* for *adnuit*, another form of *annuit.*

243. *Sic* for *rata.*

244. *Sic* for *pronusque.*

Pulcra subit facies, & pulvinaribus altis
Dignior, & qualis trabeati forma Quirini.[245]

2 However, because there was no lack in the heroes' lineages, and even more so in those of the servants, of those who would besmirch their lives with filthy vices, thus the gods, in the same way as the heroes had degenerated from the noble sphere of humanity, transformed such as these (according to the Indians' belief) into lifeless stones, rugged trees, and noisy birds, and other unclean animals of lesser note, as will be seen below.

3 I mention as the most famous the legend of the penitent *Yappan.*[246] The Indians say of him that when the time for the transformations approached, he moved away in order to win for himself the good will of the gods, his wife, and relatives, and retiring to lead a chaste and solitary life in a desert place, where the stone dedicated to penitential acts was found, which they called *Tehuehuetl*,[247] he climbed up to it and began his penance. The gods watched him attentively, and doubtful of his firmness of purpose, they put another man as guard, an enemy of his called *Yaotl*, which is the same as *enemy*,[248] so that from afar he could continue to spy on him and give an account of his actions. For a long time *Yappan* remained constant and bravely rejected many women whom the same gods sent in order to tempt him. And while the chaste victories of the penitent were being celebrated in the heavens,

245. "The almighty agreed and concealed the atmosphere with gloomy clouds and terrorized the world with thunder and lightning. He [Mars] perceived these things as signs given of plunder that had been promised to him and supporting himself on his spear, fearless Gradivus [another name for Mars] mounted the horses bound to the pole of the bloody chariot, and made a loud noise with a stroke of the whip and falling forward through the air, he set down on the summit of the tree-filled Palatine Hill and took away the Trojan [Romulus] at the time he was delivering royal laws to the Quirites; the mortal body fell through the thin air, just as a lead ball thrown from a sling ordinarily melts in the middle of the air. A beautiful face emerges both more worthy of the high thrones of the gods and as if in the form of the state robes of a Roman citizen."

246. A legendary person who was changed into a scorpion (Siméon; see also Clavigero, *Historia*, 159).

247. Unattested form. Probably a combination of *te*[*tl*], "stone," and *huehue*, "old person."

248. More commonly it means "warrior."

Tlazolteotl, the goddess of illicit love, seemingly unsuccessful and reputed to have little power, began to speak, saying, *Do not believe, O high and immortal gods, that Yappan has heroic resources to complete his penance and merit any of the sublime transformations from your good will. I will go down and you will see how weak his resolve is and how feigned his chastity.* She did so and greeting him pleasantly, she said: *Brother Yappan, I, the goddess Tlazolteotl, amazed by your constancy and taking pity on your labors, come to comfort you*, and seeing him very high up, she repeated to him, *What road shall I take? Or by what path shall I go up to speak with you?* The naïve person did not see the trick and answered her, *You are very welcome; wait, I will come down for you*, and then he was taking her up to the penitential rock, where, fired by an immoral love and covered with the clothing of the goddess, he committed a vile sacrilege with her, thinking that he would not be as guilty because his error had been with a goddess, or because she would keep it secret from the other deities. The gods were angry over the false penitent's having profaned such a divine place, and *Yaotl*, who had seen the abominable happening from afar, having forgotten to forewarn them and blinded by his inner hostility, went straight to *Yappan*, telling him, *Are you not ashamed, hypocritical penitent, because you have failed in your purpose and deceived the supreme gods?* and with a stroke of the *macana* he immediately cut off his head, at which moment the gods changed him [Yappan] into a scorpion, staying in the same shape in which he was found, when with his arms he tried to resist his enemy, who, adding to his greater crimes, went immediately to demand the penitent's wife, whom he abhorred with the same hostility that he had toward her husband. Her name was *Tlahiitzin*, which means, *the burning one.*[249] He took her to the site of the penitential stone and said to her, *You should know, Tlahuitzin, that the gods ordered me to be in this area to spy on the penance that your husband sought to carry out here. He profaned such a revered place; he fell into a vile sin, because of which I cut off his head, which I carry with me. And if by chance you gave him reason to leave you and meanwhile make his feigned and failed retreat, I will do to you what I did to your husband*, and then he cut off her head also, and it was the same fate because of the repugnance he felt for her husband,

249. Or: "the bright red one." *Tlahuitzin* is the reverential form of *tlahuitl*, "red ochre" (Karttunen).

to be transformed into a fiery scorpion, and rushing to the bottom of the penitential stone, she found *Yappan* in the same form. For this reason the Indians say that the bright red scorpions were born from *Tlahuitzin*, and the gray and dark ones from *Yappan*, and that both hid themselves under the rocks out of shame that they felt because of their sin, not daring to appear in public and always fleeing from the light. That is the same thing that happened to Nyctimene, changed into a barn owl because by fraud he soiled the bed of his father the king with nefarious incest.[250] Idem, book 2, legend 9.

An quæ per totam res est notissima Lesbon
Non audita tibi est? patrium temerasse cubile
Nyctimenen? Avis illa quidem: sed conscia culpæ
Conspectum, lucemque fugit, tenebrisque pudorem
Celat.[251]

And in book 4, legend 19, the same poet gives us another metamorphosis of the most beautiful locks of Medusa into frightful snakes because she had consented to the vile advances of Neptune in the very temple of Pallas.

Hanc pelagi rector templo vitiasse Minervæ
Dicitur, aversa est, & castos ægide vultus
Nata Jovis texit. Neve hoc impune fuisset;
Gorgoneum turpes crinem mutavit in hydros.[252]

4 However, the gods were no less angry over *Yappan*'s sin than they were over the disobedience and daring of *Yaotl*; they changed him into a locust, which the Indians called *Ahuacachapulin*, ordering

250. Nyctimene was a character in Ovid's *Metamorphoses.* The daughter of Epopeus, a king of Lesbos, she had sexual intercourse with her father and was transformed by Minerva into an owl.

251. "Or have you not heard what is well known throughout all Lesbos? Nyctimene polluted her father's bed? Indeed she is now a bird, but aware of her guilt, she flees sight and light and hides her shame in the darkness." [Lines 591–94.]

252. "The ruler of the sea [Neptune] is said to have violated her in the temple of Minerva. She was taken by force and Jupiter's daughter covered her chaste features with her shield. Nor would this go unpunished: she changed the Gorgon's hair into foul serpents." [Lines 797–800.]

it henceforth to be called *Tzontecomama*, which means *head carrier*,[253] and in fact this animal seems to carry a load with it, property of telltales[254] who always bear the honors that they have taken from their neighbors, and it is well that they be punished appropriately for their crime, as happened to Phineus, king of Phoenicia, who, because he had ordered his two sons to be blinded, was punished by spending a poor and blind old age; for that reason the harpies not only continuously dirtied his table but always took the food out of his mouth. Ibid., book 7, at the beginning.

Perpetuaque trahens inopem sub nocte senectam
Phineus visus erat; juvenesque Aquilone creati.
Virgineas volucres miseri senis ore fugarant.[255]

5 Likewise there are many legends of the transformation of men and women into trees, like Daphne into a laurel, Phætusa and her sisters into poplars, Leucothoe into the tree that produces incense, and Baucis and Philemon into plants whose branches were covered with floral arrangements and crowns; of Driope into the lotus tree; of Cypressus into the Cyprus; of Myrrha into the tree of this name; of the Bacchantes into oak trees; and of Apulus into the wild olive tree. For this reason when the Indians would go into the forest to gather wood and had occasion to cut some plant, they first asked its pardon and respectful permission to do so, as if, in doing the opposite, it would have become angry and some sorrow and pain would be caused to the one transformed, as Dryope observes, ibid., book 9, legend 8.[256]

Latet sub hoc[257] *stipite mater.*
Stagna tamen timeat; nec carpat ab arbores[258] *flores;*

---

253. Siméon glosses it as an insect that resembles a cicada. It is more likely an error for *tzontematl*, which both Molina (Nahuatl/Spanish) and Siméon gloss as a head separated from its body. The verb *ana* means "to seize."

254. *Malsines*, plural of *malsín*, defined by Covarrubias as "el que de secreto avisa a la justicia de algunos delitos con mala intención y por su propio interés."

255. "Phineus had been seen, dragging out a needy old age under cover of night, and the young men begotten in the north wind. They drove the harpies from the mouth of the wretched old man." [Lines 2–4.]

256. This citation, apparently from memory, contains a number of errors.

257. *Sic* for *latet hoc in*.

258. *Sic* for *arbore*.

Et frutices omnes corpus putet esse Dearum.
Care, vale, conjux, & tu germana, paterque,
Quis siquæ[259] *est pietas, ab acutæ vulnere falcis,*
A pecoris morsu frondes defendite nostras.[260]

At other times, when they would hear the trees creak, they said that they were groaning, in the same way as Myrrha groans in Ovid, ibid., book 10, legend 9.

Quæ, quanquam amisit veteres cum corpore sensus,
Flet tamen: & tepidæ manant ex arbore guttæ.
Est honor & lacrymis: stillataque cortice Myrrha
Nomen herile tenet, nullique[261] *tacebitur ævo.*[262]

6 Nor is there any lack of metamorphoses among birds, in imitation of which the same poet makes up, for example, of Cycno, king of Liguria, changed into a swan; of Semiramis changed into a dove; of the muses into different birds; of Pigas into a crane; of Antigone into a stork; of Philomena into a nightingale; of Periclimene into an eagle; and the Indians thought that the said birds spoke to them with their screeching and would foretell future events, as when the bird *Huatzin*,[263] which was called this because of its screech *huac, huac*, chirped in the valleys and roads, they said that it was warning them that there they were going to fall into the hands of thieves; and when the barn owl would come to screech in their homes, it was foretelling death, especially of the sick who were there, because they considered it a messenger of the god of the underworld, which very much explains its name,

259. *Sic* for *Qui siqua.*

260. "The mother lies hidden in this tree trunk. Let him still fear stagnant waters; neither let him pluck flowers from the tree, and let him think that all shrubs are the body of goddesses. Farewell, dear husband, and you sister and father, who, if it is your duty, defend our leaves from the wound of the sharp pruning knife, from the bite of the herd." [Lines 379–84.]

261. *Sic* for *nulloque.*

262. "Although she has lost her ancient senses together with her body, she still weeps, and the warm drops flow from the tree. There is honor even in tears, and the myrrh that flowed from the bark retains the name of its mistress, and it will not be silent in any age." [Lines 499–502.]

263. Siméon glosses this as a type of bird with a beak.

Yautequihua.[264] For this reason they would insult her, saying, *Stay, remain, O villainess, go away now. Neither I nor the sick can go to the underworld until you have the skulls riddled there with holes from which we are to drink.*[265] Also, when the Mexicans found themselves and the other accompanying nations wandering in the lands of New Spain before arriving at the site of the city of *Tenochtitlan Mexico*, their captains heard a bird singing and then they went to listen to it, and since its chirping was *Tihuique*, which in the Mexican language means *Let's go now*; at that moment they broke camp, thinking that it was warning them that they should go without delay. The same thing is seen clearly in Gemelli Careri's map of the said wandering inserted into volume 6, chapter 4 of his *Giro del Mundo*, in which is depicted the arrival of the said Mexicans at the lake and hill of the stone, which at that time was situated in the middle of the waters and had on its summit a tree of wild prickly pears, which the Indians call *tenochtli*, and perched on top of it an eagle, surrounded by tongues, symbols of what he said to the nobles and leaders of the said nation, persuading them to build their city on that very place, which was called *Tenochtitlan* after the said tree *tenochtli*. In this same way the above-mentioned poet makes up, ibid., book 2, legend 9, that the crow informed Apollo of the love affair of Coronis with the young Hemonius.

Talia dicenti, tibi, ait, revocamina corvus,
Sint precor ista malo, nos vanum spernimus omen.
Ne cœptum dimittit iter: dominoque jacentem
Cum juvene Hæmonio vidisse Coronida narrat.[266]

And in book 5, legend 5, he writes that the nine Pierides,[267] daughters of the king of Macedonia, for the presumption they had in defying the

264. Siméon glosses *yaotequihua* as "captain," "military commandant."

265. This passage is obscure.

266. "To the person saying such things, the crow said, I pray that these things be called back on you as evil. We spurn the vain omen. Nor does he give up the journey he had undertaken, and he recounted to his master how he had seen Coronis lying with the youth Haemonius." [Lines 596–99.] The story of Coronis ("crow") and Haemonius (also called Ichthis) is a mythological explanation of why crows are black.

267. The Pierides, nine sisters who lived in Macedonia, north of Greece, challenged the Muses to a contest. The Muses won and then turned their challengers into chattering birds.

muses, were changed into birds which, placed on their feet in the trees, lamented their unfortunate fate, as the muses and goddess Pallas heard.

Musa loquebatur: pennæ sonuere per auras:
Voxque salutantum ramis veniebat ab altis.
Suspicit; & linguæ quærit tam certa loquentes
Unde sonent: hominemque putat Jove nata locutum.
Ales erat: numeroque novem sua fata querentes
Institerant ramis imitantes omnia picæ.[268]

7 Other transformations abound, which the Indians say happened on hills, waters, fish, grass, and seeds, and to all these natural bodies, with the ideas about the said transformations, they would attribute a certain divinity, calling them lesser gods, whose tales I will be collecting in order to discover in them what there is of history and of moral philosophy, and someday the same ones will be able to invite those noble geniuses, with which both Spains abound, in order that in the two languages, Latin or Castilian, they may make the Indian metamorphoses shine in the world in glorious competition with Ovid.

268. "The muse was speaking. Wings sounded through the air, and the voice of those who were greeting came from the high branches. She looked up, and sought those speaking such certain things from where the tongues were sounding; and the daughter born of Jupiter thinks that it is a man who has spoken. It was a bird, and nine in number, bewailing their fate, the magpies perched on the branches, imitating everything." [Lines 295–300.]

Heroic Military Symbols

§. XIII

1 The same method of explaining things corresponded to this age as was practiced in the first, likewise there were two languages, with which things worthy of lasting memory were celebrated. The first [language] was symbolic, which, with various depictions of animals, birds, and other similar symbols (called heroic even by some philologists who have not delved deeply into the present material); not carved, such as those of the Scythians, Ethiopians, Greeks, and Latins, but painted on the light and portable war shields of rough leather; displayed the accomplishments of the heroes with natural signs. The other [language] was articulate, which I will deal with in section 15, at number 4, in its entirety.

2 With the symbolic language, which was specifically the language of arms, the heroes of the Indian nations spoke in the harsh time of heroism, on the occasion of finding themselves on their long wanderings and one nation encountering another, some seeking to prevent the others from passing through their lands, and the latter, on the contrary, seeking to keep the roads open for themselves, from which there arose public insults and reprisals, and they availed themselves of frequent disputes to explain their feelings and the public law of arms, and on the said shields were painted the symbols of the demands and responses. I have observed of the Toltecs and Chichimecas that their principal heroic endeavors were the *arrows and the bow*; and even in the historic maps, never was a monarch or lord of these nations depicted

without being accompanied with *bow and arrow*; thus when *Xolotl*,[269] prince and leader of his Chichimeca nation, wanted to take possession of the lands of New Spain, he sent his son *Nopaltzin*,[270] who finding them almost entirely empty of their first settlers, went to the summit of a high hill and there shot four *arrows* to the four winds, proclaiming that he was taking it for his father in the manner of a lawful and natural occupation, who would defend them with arms against anyone who would try to invade them in a hostile way. A lighthearted way of explaining sovereign rights, similar to the deed of that Spartan soldier, when asked by a foreigner how far the borders of his republic extended, he answered with this symbolic language, throwing an *asta*[271] as if saying that the borders of Sparta reached as far as that *asta* was able to go; and in the same case that there should be a Chichimeca who shot an *arrow* and would have it understood as

Dove giogne la Freccia è nostro Impero.[272]

3 With this same language Idantura, king of the Scythians, answered Darius the Great who, through his ambassadors, had threatened him with war.[273] In answer he sent him *a frog*, *a mole*, *a bird*, *a plough*, and a *bow*, signifying with these mute symbols that, in addition to the war's being unjust, the defense would be most just, first, because it had originated in the land of Scythia, like the *frogs*, which are born in the same lakes where they live, perhaps showing that [the Sythians] derived their origin from those first men of Lycia, whom the poets imagined to have been transformed into *frogs* for the crime of having, with unjust insults, denied the thirsty Latona the power to quench her thirst in the waters of their lakes, as Ovid sang in the *Metamorphoses*, book 6, legend 5, toward the end.

Distulit ira sitim, neque enim jam filia Cœi
Suplicat indignis; ne dicere sustinet ultra

---

269. A Chichimeca chief who established himself at Tezcoco and is considered the founder of its empire. See Davies, *Toltec Heritage*, especially 47–71.

270. *Sic* for *Nopiltzin*? Heir to Xolotl and king of Culhacan. See Davies, *Toltec Heritage*, especially 43–70.

271. *Hasta*, Latin for spear.

272. Italian, "As far as the arrow may reach is our empire."

273. Darius the Great (550 BC–486 BC) did go to war with the Scythians. Idantura is apparently Boturini's version of the Scythian king Idanthyrsus.

Verba minora Dea: tollensque ad sidera palmas,
Æternum stagno, dixit, vivatis in isto.[274]

Second, because he had built his houses in the same lands, in the manner that the *moles* make theirs in those where they are born; third, and moreover, by means of the *bird* he wanted to announce to him the sovereignty he held over them by right from the auguries; fourth, by means of the *plough*, that he had cultivated them and watered them with the sweat of his vassals; fifth, and by means of the *bow*, that he would defend them with the valor of arms.

4 I still possess an endless number of military symbols to interpret for this purpose, which the heroes of each nation painted on their shields, especially the nine captains of the nations that ultimately came to New Spain with the Mexican nation, which I cannot explain here because I do not remember all the circumstances of their pictures, and this will be a garden of the most refined erudition, because we know that in legendary times the poets summarized on shields the most outstanding accomplishments of the heroes, as they said of Perseus, who with his crystalline shield, that is, *with the mirror of wisdom*, was able, without being frozen into stone, to see the Medusa and cut off her head, so that she would not in the future wreak such havoc on those men and women who gave themselves over in the depths of the forests to foul delights, changing them into frozen stone, as the same poet points out, ibid., book 4, near the end.

Gorgoneas tetigisse domos: passimque per agros,
Perque vias vidisse hominum simulacra ferarumque,
In silicem ex ipsis visa conversa Medusa:
Se tamen horrendæ clypei, quod læva gerebat,
Ære repercusso formam aspexisse Medusæ:
Dumque gravis somnus colubrasque ipsamque tenebat,
Eripuisse caput collo.[275]

274. "Anger prolongs thirst. For neither does the daughter of Coeius now beg for unworthy things nor does she further take it upon herself to say lesser words than the goddess, and raising her palms to the stars she said, you will live forever in this pool." [366–69.] Coeius was one of the Titans.

275. "He arrived at the home of the Gorgons. Here and there among the fields and the roads he saw the shapes of men and wild beasts changed from themselves

(*continued*)

A feat special to heroes, to spare their servants any occasion for being offended or wounded, and later, with the same shield, he changed into a high mountain Atlas, king of Mauritania, who out of fear that he would take from him the golden apples of the Hesperides, denied him the public right of hospitality, which signifies how the heroes, busy with the glory of great undertakings, do not look for others' riches nor seek to despoil their owners of them, and longed only to travel many parts of the world, in order to leave in them the fame of their virtues, which, once known by the envious, cowardly, and greedy, become hardened into stone by force of their admiration. The same saying, idem, legend 17.

Hospes, ait Perseus illi, seu Gloria tangit
Te generis magni . . . .
Sive es mirator rerum; mirabere nostras.
Hospitium requiemque peto <widely spaced dots to end of line>
Id metuens, solidis pomaria clauserat Atlas
Mœnibus, & vasto dederat servanda draconi;
Arcebatque suis externos finibus omnes.
. . . .
Quantus erat, mons factus Atlas.[276]

And although with the same shield he freed Andromeda, who was tied to a reef in danger of being devoured by the sea monster, in order to celebrate a most happy marriage with her; which is the same as saying how Andromeda waited very patiently until she was presented with marriage to an individual of the greatest endowments, and pressed by some lowly man who might be one of the monsters, of whom I spoke in section 3, number 12, she always rejected him and finally succeeded in giving her chaste love to a hero as renowned as Perseus,

---

into stone, having seen the Medusa. However, he had looked on the form of the horrible Medusa reflected on the bronze of the round shield that he carried on his left arm. And while a deep sleep held her and the serpents, he struck her head from her neck." [Lines 778–84.]

276. "Stranger, Perseus says to him, if the glory of high birth touches you . . . or you are an admirer of affairs, look on ours. I ask for hospitality and rest. . . . Fearing this, Atlas had enclosed the orchard with strong walls, and had it guarded by a large dragon, and drove away all strangers from his borders . . . Atlas was turned into a mountain, as big as he was." [Lines 639–42, 646–48, 657.]

who did not consider Andromeda's dowry but the beauty of her virtues. The same poet, loc. cit., legend 19.

Protinus Andromedam & tanti præmia facti
Indotata rapit. Tædas Hymenæus Amorque
Præcutiunt: largis satiantur odoribus ignes:
Sertaque dependent tectis: lotique,[277] *lyræque,*
Tibiaque, & cantus, animi felicia læti
Argumenta sonant.[278]

5 Another heroic military symbol, but from the third age, is represented in Gemelli Careri's picture, the original of which I have in my archive and which can be seen inserted in the previously cited volume 6, page 86. It is mistakenly attributed to *Axayaca*, king of *Mexico*, but it is actually *Netzahualcoyotl*,[279] king of *Tezcoco*, who because of troubles that he had with the said *Axayaca*, his relative, armed himself to the utmost and with the *macana* in his right hand and his shield in his left, on which he had ordered painted the sexual organs of a woman; he went to the gates of *Mexico* [City] and challenged the said king *Axayaca*, treating him as a coward and effeminate if he would not come out to fight a duel. The history of the third age is full of these heroic deeds executed in war by the same kings and principal captains, in which I will point out the heroic symbols of the plumes and golden jewels; the ceremonies of piercing the lip and other parts of the face and of arming knights for the principal lords and other famous captains with the requirements, deeds, and penances necessary.

277. *Sic* for *ubique.*

278. "Thereupon he forcibly takes away Andromeda without a dowry and the rewards of such a great deed; Hymen and Amor shake the torches of pine wood; the fires are filled with strong scents; and garlands hang in the ceilings; and everywhere the lyres and flutes and songs resound with the happy evidence of a joyful spirit." [Lines 757–62.]

279. *Sic* for *Nezahualcoyotl.*

Heroic Political Symbols

§. XIV

1 The same symbolic language that in the previous paragraphs was shown to be the language of arms was also the language of government, with which our Indians kept an account of the lands that they had inhabited over a long period, likewise bearing them painted on their shields and very vividly symbolized, whether for the rare fruits and flowers they produced, or for some particular effort they made in clearing vegetation from them and reducing them to cultivation.

2 And I even observe that in giving and painting the names of the cities and towns they were so ingenious that it is enough to know the said names in order to understand immediately the special properties of one or the others; for example, *Toltecatl* means *Toltec Indian*, that is, *artisan* and *wise*, because those of this nation were that, for they worked precious and common stones, they built sumptuous temples and palaces, and they wove such fine cotton cloth that they could again arouse the jealousy of Minerva. A vestment of the high priest *Achcauhquitlenamacani*[280] was sent to Rome at the time of the conquest, which left that court astonished, and the silversmiths of Madrid, seeing some pieces and armbands of gold with which the Indian kings and captains armed themselves in war, admitted that they could not

280. This seems to be a combination of *Achauhtli*, "high priest," and *namacani*, "vendor, seller." What is *quitle?* According to Siméon this was the name of a Chichimeca king.

be imitated in Europe. *Chichimecatl*, which means *he who sucks*,[281] gives us to understand that the ancient Chichimecas lived by hunting alone, and after having shot the animals and birds with an arrow, they sucked their hot blood, which was the greatest gift to this nation. With regard to the cities and towns, *Tlaxcala, the place of bread*, explains the fertile fields of maize that it has in its four valleys; *Huexotzinco* implies that it is *the city located next to the willow*, and it was that in pagan times, and I have seen it painted on the maps of the said city; *Quetlaxcoapan*[282] means *the place where the intestines were washed*, which was on a level field where the event took place and where Puebla de los Angeles was later built; *Cuauhtitlan*, the town of the grove;[283] *Cuauhtepec*, [on the] hill of the eagle; *Chicomoztoc*, [in] the seven caves; *Epcohuac*, burning serpent;[284] *Tolpetlac*, town where they weave mats; *Chapultepec*, [on the] hill of the locusts; *Tenochtitlan*, city of the prickly pear cactus; all of which they explain with political symbols from nature.

3 With the same artistry, they drew the names they would give to their kings and each person in the town, both when they were born and when they carried out great endeavors and suffered extraordinary labors. They called the captain general of the Chichimecas, who came to populate New Spain, *Xolotl, eye*, because of the vigilance and prudence with which he governed his nation,[285] and another of his lineage *Netzalhualcoyotl*,[286] which means *Fasting Coyote*,[287] not only because he

---

281. Karttunen hypothesizes that it may be related to the verb meaning "to suckle." She adds that "used as a modifier this has both a negative 'barbarous' sense and a positive 'noble savages' sense." *Dictionary*, s.v. Chichimecatl.

282. *Sic* for *Cuetlaxcohuapan.* Perhaps a combination of *Cuetlaxcolli*, "intestines," and *-hua*, passive suffix, and *-pan*, "on, above." Usually, only a transitive verb would have the passive suffix (Sullivan, *Compendium*, 73).

283. More correctly, "in the place of the trees." It should be noted that Boturini does not translate the locatives in any of these place names.

284. *Culebra, que arde. Cohua* is clearly from *coatl*, "serpent." What is the meaning of ep- ? *Eptli* means a seashell. Under *arder* and *quemar*, Molina has no word that resembles it (Spanish/Nahuatl).

285. This seems to be another mistranslation. *Xolotl* means "servant, page, slave." The ordinary word for eye is *ixtli.* There is, however, a form *ixtelolotli*, that means "eye" (Molina, Siméon).

286. *Sic* for *Nezahualcoyotl.*

287. Footnote in the text: A third species between a wolf and vixen.

had been despoiled of his kingdom and persecuted during the lifetime of *Maxtlaton*,[288] tyrant of A*tzcapotzalco*, he was obliged to escape through the woods and mountain ranges and flee like a *coyote* from dogs, but also because this monarch during the height of his kingdom was accustomed to fast forty continuous days in honor of the god, the creator of all things, and thus he did so when the Chalcos[289] rebelled against him and he overcame them (I think that this fast came down to the Indians through the ancient tradition and teaching of the Glorious Apostle Saint Thomas). They also called him *Acolmiztli*, which means *the lion's arm*,[290] because he laid waste to the enemy city of *Atzcapotzalco* and defeated all his enemies. This famous emperor inwardly abhorred idolatry and only pretended in order not to upset his vassals, while he remained most devoted to God, Creator of Heaven and Earth, to whose glory he ordered to be built in *Tezcoco* a nine-story tower, symbol of the nine heavens, and on top of it a dark peak, painted on the inside with the finest blue and decorated with gold cornices, dedicated to God the Creator, whom in the Indian language he called *Tloque Nahuaque*,[291] wishing to have it understood that this one and only powerful and most merciful god had his dwelling above the heavens. In praise of him he composed sixty songs which also may have perished in the incendiary hands of ignorant persons.[292] In the said tower there were sentinels whose duty it was to ring out four times a day on a fine metal sheet. At the sound, the emperor would kneel down and make a fervent prayer to God the Creator, lifting his eyes to heaven and asking his help for good government of his subjects, for whom he prescribed eighty fundamental laws that were the basis of all justice, carrying out great things that will be recounted in the Historia General. And so it is that in order to specify *Xolotl*, the Indians add to the figure an *eye*,

288. Usurper of the throne of Tezcoco. For a full account of him, see Durán, *History*, 84–88, 90–92, 100–102.

289. *Sic* for *Chalcas.*

290. A combination of *acolli*, "shoulder," and *miztli*, "lion."

291. A standard religious name for the all-powerful God, a combination of *Tloc*, "near" + possessive -*e*, "the possessor of the near," and *Nahuaque, Nahuac*, "next to," + possessive -*e*, "the possessive of the adjacent." It can be translated in a number of ways.

292. This may be a reference to some of the early, overly zealous missionaries.

and in order to distinguish *Nezahualcoyotl* they paint as his symbol a *coyote's head*, or *an arm of a lion*, and they do the same with the others with different symbols; and if Gemelli had understood this symbolic political language, he would have added the proper name to his publication, page 85, that is, *Tzontecomama*, which means *head-carrier*, and this labor alone of interpreting the names of the figures exhausts all the attention of a historian.

4 The symbols for the names given to women are easier because, generally speaking, they were of the brightest flowers that those lands produce, such as *Miahuaxochitl*, *Cacaloxochitl*, *Azcaxochitl*,[293] and in the early days of Christianity, *Caxtillanxochitl*, which means *Rose of Castile*,[294] and this custom of universal names causes no little confusion in taking the baptismal certifications from the parish records, as happened to me when looking for that of the blessed Indian Diego Lázaro, to whom the glorious Archangel Saint Michael appeared in the jurisdiction of the town of *Nativitas*, which is commonly called del Milagro.[295]

5 All in all, the principal symbols of this age involved matters of lands, which the Indians cultivated in the great extent of their wanderings, being known from Toltec history, as the people of this nation carried with them the seeds of maize, peppers, and beans, and when they reached a place, the elders fortified their huts and the young men set fire to the woods to clear them, and sowed the land, going out beforehand to ascertain when there would be an opportunity for them to raise camp, and this was the way they would travel from the confusion of tongues until their arrival in New Spain. And although the epoch of agriculture was found from the first dark time in the eighth deity, *Tlatocaocelotl*,[296] nevertheless in this second age, who can contemplate so many lands that were cultivated, so many woods that were devastated

---

293. "Maize flower?," "Frangipanni" or "Raven Flower," "Ant Flower."

294. More accurately, "Castilian flowers. Though this usually meant roses, it could apply to any flowers.

295. Relatively little has been written about this devotion. Taylor says that in 1644 a principal witness for the apparitions was Diego Lázaro's grandmother, who brought two pictures of the event given to her by her grandson (Taylor, *Shrines and Miraculous Images*, 210n6). The town was then called San Miguel del Milagro.

296. "Jaguar ruler."

on such widespread roads? In Indian history there are thousands of Hercules who, with the lion that belches fire from its mouth, burn the forests; who, even in the cradle at a tender age, that is, *in nascent heroism*, tear the serpents of the land into pieces; who cut off the head of the hydra, *symbolically of the land*, which, deprived of its head that are the trees, brings back from their roots multiple new ones; who obtain the golden apples in the Hesperides gardens, that is, *wheat and seeds*; Belerophontes by the thousands who kill an infinity of chimeras, composed of different kinds of animals. *All are symbols of agriculture*: the Bacchi who tame serpents, *fields that snake their way through the shoulders of the mountains*; the Cyclopses, which have only one eye in their forehead, *more than one land apiece which they cultivate for the meager support of their family*; the Aeneas, who with the allegorical branch of gold, *with the bundle of sheaves of maize*, found in the darkest woods and valleys, *where the forests were set on fire*, which cannot be uprooted except with the permission of the gods, *because the impious vagabonds, lacking religion and auguries, cannot obtain it*, they go down to the underworld, *to the graves of their ancestors*, and see their forebears, *the heroes whom the vagabonds cannot see because they do not have the custom of burying the dead*; they present him to Dis, goddess of treasures, *whom Hercules found with agriculture.*[297] Vergil, *Aeneid*, book 6, verse 136, et seq.

latet arbore opaca
Aureus & foliis, & lento vimine ramus
Junoni infernæ dictus sacer: hunc tegit omnis
Lucus, & obscures[298] *claudunt convallibus umbræ.*

Also verse 146, et seq.

Carpe manu; namque ipse volens facilisque sequetur
Si te fata vocant; aliter non viribus ullis

---

297. The Hesperides were nymphs who tended a blissful garden where golden apples grew that conferred immortality. Bellerophon was a Greek mythological hero who slew the monster Chimera. The Bacchae were female followers of Dionysus who engaged in ritualistic, uncontrolled behavior. The Cyclops, according to Homer, the *Odyssey*, were sons of Poseidon, of immense size and strength, and only one eye. Dis was Pluto, god of the underworld. Boturini seems to be mistaken in identifying this deity as female.

298. *Sic* for *obscuris.*

Vincere, nec duro poteris convellere ferro.
Præterea jacet exanimum tibi corpus amici,
Heu nescis! Totamque incestat funere classem
Dum consulta petis, nostroque in limini pendes.
Sedibus hanc refer ante suis, & conde sepulcro.

And book 5, verse 731, et seq.

Ditis tamen ante
Infernas accede domus, & Averna per alta
Congressus pete, nate meos.[299]

Nor do I doubt that the ancient shields[300] of the Indians made up the greater part of their symbols while authenticating the great exploits that the heroes, together with their relatives and followers, performed in opening for themselves the rough road of their daily wandering and cultivating the land. For this reason what still remains for me to explain about the said shields is called *field*, which most appropriately was that of cultivated lands, after arms and lodging, because not only did the thieving vagabonds kill each other in these same *fields*, but also they defended themselves against entire nations that presumed to insult them; and here come to mind so many animals painted on the said shields, some gold, others green, and others black, which, because similar colors are perhaps not found in nature, it is with difficulty that any civil history describes them, and they are usually elegantly explained in the matter of the lands of the heroes, which they occupied with the blessings of heaven, and handed over to their clients for cultivating, because they were of three colors: black for the sowing, green for the first shoots of wheat, and gold for the harvest. In addition to the said shields and fields, there is much to discuss concerning the metals, colors,

---

299. "The branch said to be sacred to Juno of the underworld lies hidden in a dark tree, golden both in its leaves and its stiff twig; every grove covers it; and the shadows enclosed the dark valleys . . . Seize it in your hand; for it will follow willingly and easily, if the fates call you; otherwise you will not be able to conquer with any forces nor tear it with the hard steel. Besides, the dead body of your friend lies by you, alas, you do not know! And it pollutes the entire fleet with a corpse while you seek counsel and hang about on our threshold. Take him beforehand to his dwellings and bury him in his tomb."

300. Or: coats of arms.

arms, crowns, mantles, and other ornaments that compose the iconography of this symbolic science, which ordinarily carries with it symbols of lordship, of auguries, of government, and an infinity of learned things.

6 But Homer does describe on the shield of Achilles, which Vulcan forged for him, the histories of times past. Book 18, *Iliad*, near the end.

Fecit autem primum clypeum magnumque gravemque,
Undique varians: circum autem circulum jecit lucidum,
Tripicem, splendentem: extra autem argenteum lorum;
Quinque autem ipsius erant Clypei plicæ, sed in ipso
Fecit varia doctis artibus.
In quidem terram effinxit, in autem cœlum, in autem mare. &c.[301]

Why can I not read on the shields of the Indians the histories of two dark and legendary times?

7 Finally, I conclude with a heroic political symbol of the third age, which Gemelli Careri cites without explanation in the *Estampa* 4, volume 6, page 86, of *Giro del Mundo*, taken from the original, which I have in my *Museo histórico*, and it concerns the Emperor *Nezahualpiltzintli*, who while he was in the criminal court called *Teotlatolli*, which means, *tribunal of god*,[302] seated on his place of honor with an arrow in his hand and having in view the symbols of something like a *sword*, which is in my opinion a fish's spine, and two things like the joined images of *land* and *water*, demonstrated the eagerness and zeal that he had in having the laws of the kingdom observed and having the delinquents punished (in which he did not even pardon those of imperial blood), and the high sovereign law that he represented over the life and death of his vassals, both on earth and on water.

---

301. "However, he first made the shield large and heavy, varying it everywhere: roundabout he threw a bright, threefold, splendid circle; on the outside, however, a silver leather thong; Five, however, were the layers of the shield itself, but in it he made different things with learned art. In certain ones he depicted the earth, and heaven and the sea, etc." This translation is of Boturini's Latin, not the original Greek.

302. Literally "divine words." Molina, Siméon, and Karttunen all give this meaning. None glosses it as "tribunal."

On the Knots

And Songs, Both Historical and Poetic

§. XV

1 Similarly, there arose in this age a new way of preserving history, and it was with long cords, in which were interwoven other thin ones that hung from the principal cord with knots of different colors. In the kingdoms of Peru these cable histories were called *quipu* and in those of New Spain *nepohualtzitzin*, deriving their names from the adverb *nepohualli*, which means *eighty*, or as if we would say *cord of counting and number*, in which are recorded and enumerated things worth remembering, both divine and human.

2 In both the kingdoms of Peru and New Spain, I observed that for their histories the Indians made use of cords as well as figures, characters, and hieroglyphs, but with this difference, that the pictures among the Peruvians were in the beginning unrefined, of little learning, and in a short time their use was ended. The *quipus*, on the contrary, reached greater excellence, and they endured until the conquest with such a great height of artistry and skill that the Inca emperors used them to register their innumerable vassals; [and] to keep a record of the growth of their armies, since the situation of the knots supplied a strange arithmetic of some things, such as columns of tens, hundreds, thousands, and so on, and recounted the battles and accomplishments of their monarchs and explained everything that we communicate with writing. With the help of these *quipu*, which were the most ancient monuments of that empire and were to be found in the archives of the imperial city of *Cuzco*; and among the Incas who were blood relatives of the emperors, the most noble historian Garcilaso Inca de la

Vega was able to establish the history of his illustrious fatherland.[303] And because, even after the conquest, the Peruvian Indians could not easily adapt to the European alphabet and forget the former custom of the *quipu*, they continued to use them for some time in all their business transactions and necessities of life; and Father Acosta recounts that he saw a woman come to church with a bunch of cords and knots[304] with which she opened the doors of her conscience to her confessor.

3 In the kingdoms of New Spain the opposite occurred, because cords were scarce and barely lasted into the last period of this second age, as proven by the prodigious accumulations of pictures that remain in my archive, without my having been able to get hold of even one of the said historic cords, for the one that I discovered in the province of *Tlaxcala* in the possession of an Indian nobleman was so worm-eaten with age that he was able only to instruct me in what there once was of them, although scant, for which reason we see that all that was precious was contained in the pictures. Notwithstanding that from the said word *nepohualtzitzin*, that of *nepohualco* was derived, which means *countable*, and so that was the name given to the place where *Xolotl* drew up a survey of his peoples, commanding them all that in his presence in passing they toss a small stone into a heap, which eventually formed a measureless body of small stones, which can still be seen nowadays and shows the multitude of people with which New Spain was populated, and in the same way that of *nepohualtlatolli*, which means *tribunal of eighty days*,[305] and it was established in *Tezcoco*, perhaps in imitation of the eighty fundamental laws, of the most distinguished individuals of all the subject provinces of the empire, in order that in the fixed term of the said eighty days he might know by way of appeal all the cases that the ordinary judges had dispatched in the first instance, and that he might discharge feudal matters and the most serious [matters] that he had in his charge.

---

303. El Inca, Garcilaso de la Vega (1539–1616) was the illegitimate son of a Spanish conquistador and a Peruvian noblewoman. He received an excellent education in Spain, where he became a noted historian. His most important work was *Comentarios reales de los Incas* (1609).

304. The printed text has *nados* for *nudos*.

305. Again, Boturini translates *tlatolli* as "tribunal."

4 There is another fertile garden of learning in the *songs*, which, because of having been the works of poet heroes, they took care to preserve, not only the origin and workings of the gods of both times, but also the political and military achievements of the rest of the heroes of the second age.

5 Whoever applies himself to reflecting on them attentively will find in them some most refined legends woven with lofty figures of speech and allegories and which in the same way as with the other nations are composed in heroic verse, born in this age on a level with the spoken language and with phraseology proper to heroism, from its beginning of uncertain meter, not by art but by nature, according to the concept that was offered to the poets to explain, because as Genebrardo[306] and other chronologists note, before the eleventh century no book, whether French or Italian, had been written, and despite that, the Provençal poets in France and the Sicilians in Italy flourished long before, convincing me that all languages began as verse, since I saw, both among the country people of Silesia and among the plebeians of Venice, that all are born with the spirit of a poet, and we have two very clear proofs of this: the first, in the book of Job, which is the most ancient of the histories that Moses wrote, and that Saint Jerome acknowledges is woven together in heroic verses; the second, in the Laws of the Twelve Tables which have an indefinable air of heroic verse, as the first two laws make clear, which are two measured heroic verses.

Divos caste adeunto,
Pietatem adhibendo[307]

And if there were no custom of speaking naturally in verse, it would have been noteworthy if poetry were used in a matter as serious as that of promulgating laws. But experience teaches us that when those who are almost mute pronounce the vowels they sing, and stammerers do the same when they untie their tongues completely and finish their words, which they cannot easily articulate in common prose, and since poetry is in the proper sense song (as was said of the Arcades that

306. Gilbert Genebrard (1535–97) was a French Benedictine exegete and orientalist.

307. "Approach the gods with purity—appear before them in the spirit of devotion." This quotation is not from the Twelve Tables but from Cicero's *De legibus*, book 2.

they were born singers, and it may be that *Carmenta*, the mother of Evandro Arcade,[308] was so called from the word *carmen*), and easier for nature than prose, is proved by the fact that heroic verse proceeded more from the necessities of nature than for the pleasure of the art, and that it is as a consequence the language of heroism is the most ancient articulate language, with which it gave laws to its clients, since the Latins signified with the word *carmina* not only the verses but also the solemn forms of the laws.

6 In heroic verse, which was also called Pythian having been used to celebrate Apollo's feat of killing the Python, Ovid, *Metamorphoses*, book 1, legend 9.

Neve operis famam possit delere vetustas;
Instituit sacros celebri certamine ludos;
Pythia de domita serpentis nomine dictos[309]

Or Saturnine, because most of this poetry must have been employed in exalting the deeds of the ancestral peoples in removing the woods and cultivating the land. The fauns sang of what happened to the Greeks in the age of Saturn, as is evident from the fragments of Ennius.[310] The lyric poets, ancient authors of hymns and praises to the gods, wove together their works, for example, the hymns of Homer among the Greeks and those attributed to Orpheus, and the dithyrambs of Amphion[311] with the chorus of satyrs; and among the Latins the Sallarian verses that the priests of the idols called *Sallii*;[312] before all of these the Indian poets flourished; they composed some hymns to their gods at the beginning of [the age of] heroism, to the extent that the

308. Evander of Arcadia was a mythological Greek cultural hero who brought the Greek alphabet and writing to primitive Italy.

309. "Neither can antiquity erase the fame of the work, he founded the sacred games, celebrated by contests, called Pythian from the name of the serpent he had conquered." [Lines 445–47.]

310. Ennius was an early Latin writer of satire.

311. The dithyramb was an ancient Greek hymn sung and danced in honor of Dionysus, the god of wine and fertility. Amphyon was a hero, the son of Zeus, who had a gift of playing the lyre. He built the walls of Thebes by making the stones move to the sound of his lyre. His name was often associated with that of Orpheus.

312. *Salii* were priests of Mars, and *saliarii* were hymns they were obliged to sing.

language advanced, which they sang at their feasts, having continued this custom without interruption during the entire third pagan age; and even after the conquest the sixty songs that the emperor *Nezahualcoyotl* composed in praise of the creator of heaven and earth were famous; and it is known that on the second day of the month of *panquetzaliztli* on a solemn feast the greatness of the god *Huitzilopochtli* was sung, and in the patio of his temple a man and woman directed the singing, and that on the tenth of the other month *Itzcalli*, on the great feast of the god *Xiuhteuctli*, the king would dance with all the lords, and he himself intoned the song in praise of the idol, the one they called *Noteuhccuicaliztli*, which means the *song of the lords*,[313] while the others responded, In addition, the Mexican histories relate that when a great monarch of the state of the Culhuas had won an important battle on the day Ce Xochitl, One Flower, he ordered that a great feast should be celebrated to this demigod, which was the fifth moveable day of their ritual calendar and was celebrated with royal pomp, and that for the same day new songs were composed, in which no concept of the old ones was to be mingled under pain that the singer would be deprived of his office. Likewise, after the conquest the Christian Indians were very careful to celebrate in songs the new law of the gospel and with them to praise Our Lord Jesus Christ, his most holy mother, and the angels and saints; and when Our Lady of Guadalupe appeared, which was in the year 1531, and offered to place her blessed image in the first chapel of Guadalupe, don Francisco Plácido, lord of *Atzcapotzalco*, attended its placement with his entire Tepanec people, and in front of the image, sang of the apparition of the most lovable queen, something that continued a century later with other tender songs that recounted the sweet conversations that her majesty had with the blessed Juan Diego, and he with the Most Holy Lady.[314]

7 In the same heroic meter are found many songs that recount the illustrious deeds of the heroes of the second and third ages. I have in my archive the song that applauds the victory of *Moquihuix*, king of *Tlatelolco*, which he won against those of *Cuetlaxtla*.

---

313. This is a bit confusing. If *no-* is the possessive adjective, then the form should be *Noteuhccuicaliz*, and the meaning would be "song of my lord."

314. On the question of Francisco Plácido, see Poole, *Our Lady of Guadalupe*, 46–47.

8 Also composed in heroic verse was ancient tragedy, in other words, satire, which has the eternal characteristic of speaking evil and piling up insults, and Tespi used in the time of the grape harvest,[315] accompanying it with a chorus of satyrs, that is, of men dressed in goatskins on their chest and feet and their faces dyed with the musk of grapes and with horns on their heads, so that with such a mask and dress they would have greater license and freedom to be slanderers, and so it was also among our Indians, especially active and ardent among both the Mexican and Tlaxcaltecan nations, among the Mexicans and Tlatelolcos themselves. The reason was that because in ancient times the two cities *Mexico* and *Tlatelolco* were separated only by walls, and the women of one and the other population would peer over the said walls and because of ancient ill feelings, would hurl insults at each other, and the men and boys from time to time would play at war by throwing stones, and I still saw [the stone throwing] in the Indies between those of one barrio with another, and finally it was brought to an end by the vigilance of Your Majesty's justice.

9 The Indians still used to say that those born under the symbol Ce Quauhtli, One Eagle, if they were men, would be satirical, conceited, glib, and mocking; if they were women, shameless gossips who made fun of everyone and mistreated other women in words and actions. Even the old women, on the occasion in the month called *ochpaniztli*[316] when they would celebrate the festival of the goddess *Toci*, which means *our grandmother*, and they participated in the dance which was done without accompaniment or song, and were divided into groups and with yellow roses of *cempohualxochitl*, or *pachtli*, or white balls of *tollin*,[317] they would hit each other in the face: and the same priests of the idols (who did not cut a figure inferior to that of the choruses of satyrs of Amphyon or Tespi) in the month *tititl*,[318] would celebrate

315. Tespi (566 BC – ?) was a semi-legendary Greek poet and dramatist.

316. Literally, "sweeping."

317. Siméon glosses *pachtli* as a parasitic plant that was used to decorate temples. *Tollin*, tule, is glossed by Siméon as "gladiolus," and by Molina as *juncia*, or sedge.

318. Seventeenth month of the year, the word means contraction or withdrawal (Siméon).

in honor of the goddess *Ilamanteuctli*, or by another name *Cozcamiahuatl*,[319] the feast of sacks.[320] They would begin it with skirmishes, with some intervening ceremonies and with some small sacks of *pachtli*, of chicken feathers, or *popoxtli*,[321] which resembles cotton, they struck each other with blows of the sacks, and everybody else watching them. Afterward they would go through the streets with this uproar and they would give blows of the sacks to all the women they encountered, and these would insult them and the feast would end with the children.

10 And because after the heroic verse, among nations there commonly followed the iambic, similarly of uncertain measure in its beginnings, as are the verses of Plautus and Terrence,[322] especially those of Plautus, not by art but by nature, because the first writers of prose were continually on guard that the iamb would not fall into [prose], which disfigured it so much, and because art would not have imitated nature in the middle tragedy and ancient comedy, which were written from their beginning in iambic verses, if men had not naturally spoken in such verses. And iambic verse was truly suitable for tragedy because it is appropriate for expressing anger, and with it Archilochus unleashed his [anger] against Lymcambes, who refused him his daughter as a wife, which he was often to regret.[323] From this stems that monster[324] of poetic art that the same violent and angry verse is equally suited to tragedy, which is a grave and serious poem esteemed by Plato, even more than the heroic, as to comedy, which by its nature is delicate and tender, while tragic verse, full of indignation and of a rapid and fast

319. Also spelled *Ilamateuctli*, "goddess of old women." *Cozcamiahuatl* seems to be a combination of *cozcatl*, "jewel," and *miahuatl*, "maize blossom."

320. *Talegos.* The first meaning is "sacks"; by extension it means a person with a paunch.

321. Meaning uncertain. Ordinarily popoxtli means "energetic," *Popochtli* means perfume or incense. Perhaps Boturini is mistaken about the term.

322. Titus Maccius Plautus (c. 254 BC–AD 184) and Publius Terentius Afer (c. 195/185 BC–159 BC) were early Roman playwrights.

323. Archilochus (c. 680 BC–c. 645 BC) was an early Greek poet. Little is known about him. According to an ancient tradition, Lycambes is said to have betrothed his daughter to Archilochus but repudiated the agreement. The poet retaliated with such abuse and libelous accusations that Lycambes and his daughter committed suicide.

324. *Monstruo*, which can also mean prodigy.

meter, very appropriate for disgorging it, should also be apt for receiving tender loves, concealment, and flirtations, with which comedy is clothed in sweetness and pleasantry. And just as Aeschylus changed the ancient tragedy, that is, satire, into the middle tragedy with human masks, transforming the dithyramb of Amphyon, which was a chorus of satyrs, into a chorus of men, and the same middle tragedy was the beginning of ancient comedy, in which great personages made their entrances, for all of which a chorus was appropriate; so it was that our Indians went from heroic verse to iambic at the time that prose was about to be perfected, and all those songs of pagan times, which are closest to it, are by their nature iambic verse, as will be shown in the General History and in a tragic song of the emperor *Nezahualcoyotl* who, after having killed the tyrant *Maxtlaton* and having razed the enemy city of *Atzcapotzalco*, began to consider and sing of the end of the greatness of this mortal life in the person of *Huehue-Tezozomoctli*,[325] who like a tree grown strong had set down his deep roots in so many provinces and spread his branches, giving shade to the lands of the empire; but finally he fell to the ground eaten away, without hope of being able to return to his first bloom. I have the said song, translated into our Spanish by don Fernando de Alba *Ixtlilxochitl*, a descendant of the aforementioned emperor. And with regard to the chorus, the Indians portrayed it in the same way with artificial masks, and commonly with themselves uncovered, and they are still accustomed to that today, and I have seen it in *Tlaxcala* on the occasion when the duke of the conquest[326] made his entrance into the said city, and other feasts, and it is carried out in this way: in the public square they erect a stall or shade, and in the middle of it they place their musical instruments *teponaztli* and *tlapahuehuetl*. Then the singer begins to intone his poem in which he refers either to the accomplishments of the lords in pagan times or the great benefit that God gave them in sending them the law of the gospel, and with this they celebrate in a high degree the great captain, don Fernando Cortés, and the first Spaniards and spiritual fathers who taught them Christian doctrine; or they sing sweet praises to the Most Holy Virgin and other patron saints, while all the others who surround him respond in great unison and at leisure, and around

325. "Old Tezozomoc," a reference to a long-reigning emperor of Azcapotzalco.

326. Apparently a reference to a descendant of Fernando Cortés.

everybody, the tenant farmers of the chiefs dance in the form of a wheel, each one carrying the insignia of his chief; and this is one form of feudal obligation, whereby they are obliged to participate in the said dance at the appointed times and bring fruit and some few coins to their noble lords, who ordered that the said tenants be adorned with the best clothing, giving them the insignias for the said dance and hosting them in their houses for as long as the function lasts.

11 Returning to the order of poetry, which is the total of the two ages, the divine and heroic, I go on, noting that after the ancient comedy came Sophocles and Euripides, who left us the ultimate tragedy, and Aristophanes put an end to the ancient comedy because of the scandal that occurred in the person of Socrates, because of which Menander composed the new comedy about fictitious persons, without the participation of a chorus, which was a public that did not speak of other matters that were not public. The Indians were excellent even in these new comedies and composed various of them in their language. Among others I have two in my archive about the apparitions of my Mother and Lady of Guadalupe; I cannot even explain how delicate are the voices with which the Virgin speaks to the simple *neophyte*, and how the obedience of this most fortunate ambassador [Juan Diego] is correspondingly humble.[327]

12 There is no language that can equal this one in courtliness, polish, tenderness; or in the highlighting of its figures of speech, as it was refined by dint of poetry during the progress of the two ages, divine and heroic, by a nation as brilliant and scientific as the Toltecs; a reason why the Chichimeca, Mexican, and Teochichimeca nations and many others rejected their native languages in order to adorn themselves with *Nahuatl*,[328] which in a short time became common and the language of the Indian courts; and so that the marvel of its sentences, the tenderness of its poetry may be seen, it is enough to relate a case that happened in *Tezcoco.* A certain emperor had condemned to death one of his vassals for a corresponding crime. The fatal sentence approached,

327. Only two Guadalupan dramas are known today, *The Wonder of Mexico*, dating from either the late sixteenth century or early seventeenth century, and *Dialogue on the Apparition of the Virgin Saint Mary of Guadalupe.* See *Our Lady of Guadalupe*, ed. Sell, Burkhart, and Poole.

328. It is interesting that Boturini uses this term instead of the earlier *Mexicano.*

and the guilty person, who was a noted poet, in the brief timc of life that was left to him, composed a song of farewell so sweet and clothed with such living emotions that the singers in the palace, who were his friends, resolved to sing it surreptitiously to the monarch, who could only take pity on the delinquent and spare his life, which is a rare case in the histories of the Acolhuas, in which are found only examples of the most severe justice, even with royal persons.

13 The said songs are divided into two classes: some are for the most part historic, although perhaps mixed with divine legends; others are purely poetic. The former deal with the greatness of the gods and of the deeds of the heroes; the latter with the reproductions of heroic legends. They make known the customs of the heroic time, and I am in admiration on seeing that the aforesaid divine and heroic legends have all the requirements for the very best poetry, because they are first, *impossible [and] believable; impossible* in giving consciousness and a rational soul to bodies that do not have it, or in perverting the order of nature. Vergil, *Bucolic Eclogues*, 5, on the death of Daphnis.

Daphni, tuum pœnos etiam ingemuisse leones
Interitum, montesque feri[329] *silvæque loquuntur.*[330]

And Sincero, Eclogue 5, on that of Andrageos:

Pianser le sante dive
La tua spietata morte,
I fiumi il sanno & le spelonche e I Faggi
Pianser le Verdi rive
L'herbe pallide, et smorte
El sol piu giorni non mostro suoi raggi
Ne gli animai selvaggi
Usciro in algun prato.
Ne greggi andar per monti
Ne guastaro herbe o fonti:
Tanto dolse a ciascun l'acerbo fato;

---

329. *Sic* for *fere?*

330. "To Daphnis, even the Carthaginian lions mourn your passing, and the mountains and woods almost speak."

Tal che al chiaro, & al fosco.
Androgeo, Androgeo risonava il bosco.[331]

Ovid, book 1, *Tristia*, Elegy 8.

In caput alta suum labentur ab æquore retro
Flumina; conversis solque recurret equis,
Terra feret stellas; cælum findetur aratro;
Unda dabit flammas, & dabit ignis aquas.[332]

And the previously cited Sincero, Eclogue 4.

Gli ignudi pesci andran per secchi campi,
El mar sia duro, and liquefatti i sassi
Ergasto vincera Titiro en rime;
La notte vedra el sol, le stelle il giorno;
Pria che gli Abeti, i Faggi desta valle
Odan de la mia bocca altro che pianto.[333]

Believable, because the same persons who fabricated them were the first to believe them, examples can be found in §. XII, which deals with transformations. Second, *Marvelous and disturbing*, because in believing that *Tlaloc* was the secretary of providence and that in his name the laws were written with lightning and that he published them with thunder, the first men did not dare to use the immoral Venus, giving preference to heaven, and they abducted certain women in to use them

331. Sincero [Sincerus] was the pen name of Jacopo Sannazaro (1458–1530), an Italian lyric poet. "The holy goddesses wept over your pitiless death, the rivers know it, and the caves, and the beech trees, the green shores, the pale and wan grasses wept, and the sun did not show its rays for many days, nor did the wild animals come forth from any meadow, nor the flocks wander through the mountains, nor did they lay waste to the grass or springs; how painful to each one the bitter fate; such that in the light or dark, the wood echoed, 'Androgeo, Androgeo.'"

332. Ovid, *Tragic Elegies*, book 1, elegy 8. "The deep rivers will glide slowly back from the sea to their source, and the sun [Apollo], having turned around his horses, will turn around. The earth will carry the stars; heaven will be cut by the plow; a wave will give up flames and the fire will give up water."

333. "The naked fish will walk through dry fields, the sea becomes hard, and the rocks liquid, Ergastus will overcome Tytirus in rhymes, the night will see the sun, the stars the day; before the low places and the beech trees of this valley hear from my mouth anything but weeping."

with a chaste exercise of eternal marriage. Third, *sublime in the highest degree*, as is verified in *Tezcatlipoca, god of providence*, and in *Tlaloc*, who thunders and commands men with his bolts so that they may give up their scattered and vagabond life. Fourth, *born to teach the common people*, as was seen in the hieroglyphics of the thirteen gods of the pagan ancestors and in some symbols of heroism.

Origin of the Indians

of New Spain

§. XVI

1 Many notable historians have worn themselves out in investigating the origin of our Indians, and some have dedicated entire books to this matter, such as Father Bishop-elect Gregorio García,[334] a Dominican whose studies and efforts, although they are worthy of the greatest praise and esteem, nonetheless were never able to satisfy my limited understanding, which could never be satisfied in that sea of conjectures, where the question is still in flux; and as is often said, *adhuc lis sub judice pendet*,[335] and so many and such diverse opinions have been published about this matter that the more that is written, the more obscure it becomes. But as the conjectures of the authors cited are ordinarily based on three principal arguments; the first, in comparing some words in the *Nahuatl* language to others of different

334. Gregorio García is a relatively obscure figure who was probably born in 1554 and died in 1627. He published a book, *Origen de los Indios del Nuevo Mundo e Indias Occidentales*, in 1607. He believed that the Indians were the descendants of the Ten Lost Tribes of Israel, together with a mixture of Greek and Roman blood.

335. "The case is still under judgment."

nations; the second, in observing the similarity that there is between Indian civil laws and those of the rest of the world; the third, in comparing the customs of the Indians with other ancient idolatry to argue the origins of these peoples; so I deem it appropriate to show before all else that the said arguments are not adequate to the intent, and afterward I will deal with their origin according to the same monuments of the Indians that they left us in their histories.

2 As weak and feeble as the first conjecture is, of comparing however many words there are in the Indian languages with Hebrew, Egyptian, Chaldean, and so on, in order to imply that the Indians are descended from this or that nation, it proves as an indisputable foundation that each language arises from natural necessity in its respective family, with the result that in the first age no other language was used among all the pagan nations but that of the gods, which language was almost totally mute and mental, that is, by means of mute and religious acts or divine ceremonies, very characteristic of this simple time, in which men had little in the way of articulate speech; it was more important to religion to be respected than reasoned, and so most of the said mute language was explained with hieroglyphs and divine characters, which I have interpreted in section 3, and they were like some divine fantastic genres to which they would reduce all their private matters; for example, to *Tezcatlipoca*, everything that concerned providence; to *Tlaloc*, respect for divine laws and the modesty of chaste marriages; to *Macuilxochiquetzalli*, ceremonies of solemn marriages; to *Pilzinteuctli*, the civilized beauty of children; to *Tlatocaocelotl*, agriculture; to *Mictlanteuctli*, the pious act of burying the dead; and to others their particular concerns.

3 The same thing occurred in the second age because, even though in it the articulate speech was spreading, nonetheless each people or nation worked within its own [language], without a connection or dependence on the other languages, and it still had not reached its level of perfection, for in order to explain the year, the Indians had to avail themselves of the word *xihuitl*, which means *grass*, having measured the course of the sun from one year to another with the reappearance of the new grass in the fields, in which the Latins with little difference of ideas numbered the years by the harvests, which shows the poverty of words and concepts that there was at that time, and the same thing is read in 2 Kings, chapter 21, no. 9, *Et ceciderunt hi septem simul occissi in diebus messis primis, incipiente messione bordei.*[336] In addition, there remained in this age another language more usual and common in public affairs, which was the symbolic, that is, with silent heroic symbols which were at the same time fantastic genera, to which they reduced the various species of heroic affairs; for example, to the fathers of families, all the dependents of their children and servants; to their Hercules (so to speak) all agriculture; to their Ulysses, all military skill, because it is known that each nation had its own, *not with regard to office but with regard to persons*, and in this way should be interpreted the opinion of those who believed that the Greek Ulysses founded colonies in Germany, Tacitus, *de moribus germanorum. Aram quin etiam Ulyxi consecratam, adjecto Lærte patris nomine, eodem locl olim repertam: monumentaque, & tumulos quosdam Græcis liteis inscriptos in confinio Germaniæ Rhætiæque adhuc extare. . . . Herculem, ac Martem concessis animalibus placant,*[337] because these names, after some nations had met others and the characteristics of their heroes were known reciprocally, came to signify the government of the persons and not the individuals, in which some Patricians in remote nations, led astray solely by the Greek names, thought to gain much by fabricating Greek monuments and inscriptions, stripping all the glory from national heroes and ignorantly transferring it to foreigners, whose lies did not even deserve that the said author occupy himself with refuting them, *quæ neque confirmare argumentis, neque refellere in animo est: ex ingenio suo quisque demat, vel addat fidem. Ipse eorum opinionibus accedo, qui Germaniæ populos & sinceram, & tantum sui similem gentem extitisse arbitrantur,*[338] which is the same as I feel about the Indian peoples and nations.

---

336. *Bordei, sic* for *hordei.* "The seven fell at the one time; they were put to death during the first days of the harvest, that is, at the beginning of the barley harvest" (2 Kings 21:9). The second book of Kings is now commonly called 2 Samuel.

337. "In fact an altar consecrated to Ulysses was formerly found in the same place, with the name of his father Laertes added, and monuments and certain burial mounds inscribed with Greek letters still exist within the borders of Germany and Rhaetia. . . . they placate Hercules and Mars with offerings of animals" (Tacitus, *De moribus et situ Germanorum*).

338. "I do not have the heart to confirm or reject the arguments; each one according to his ability may remove or add belief. I am close to the opinion of those who believe that the peoples of Germany existed as a real and unique people without any mixture because of any other marriages with other nations."

4 With regard to historical times, the Indians were so far from imitating the nations of the rest of the world in their languages that they did not even have knowledge of them; for that reason all the words that in the course of the three ages arose in the Indies are wrongly compared with those of other remote nations, and it is purely accidental that some Indian terms resemble others of foreign languages, and for this reason they cannot be used as proof of the origin of one nation with another.

5 Nor am I convinced by Indian laws, which some compare with those of foreigners, seeking reasons of origin, because speaking of the first age, the entire everyday wisdom of the pagan fathers breathes nothing but idolatry, solemn marriages, child rearing, cultivation of the land, and burial of corpses, since the said wisdom is not only peculiar to the Indians but also to all the other nations, as based on the natural law of the pagan ancestors, by reason of the fact that the government of this age was called divine, insofar as the said founders of pagan humankind in all things explored what was acceptable to the gods by means of auguries, and enacted it with sacrifices, and up to this point everything is common to everyone, and it neither takes away nor adds anything with regard to the origin of the Indians. Speaking of the second age, for in it the heroes alone gave laws to their households, composed of children and servants, with the mute and symbolic language of arms, those who compare would have plenty to distill their understanding, if they wished to show that the heroes of one or another remote nation had agreed on some of the same symbols to express the same ideas. But if these diligent examiners of antiquity should have recourse to the third [age], they must teach me: what interchange the Americans had with the other nations to accept or imitate their laws? What ambassadors did they send to or receive from them? What writers say that the [the Americans] were either discovered or conquered before Spanish arms subjected them to the mild rule of the Catholic Monarchs? Because whether in pictures or in songs or in manuscripts I have not found that any other nation has set foot in the New World, with the exception of the blessed Saint Thomas, who in both the kingdoms of Peru and New Spain preached the gospel, whose history I have a true desire to write, and by means of the great monuments that I discovered, and one of them is the Most Holy Cross, which I found painted in the form of *tau*[339] in the color blue and the size of a forearm in an inaccessible flank of the mountain *Tianguistepetl*,[340] near the ancient town of *Meztitlan*, to the immense joy of Spaniards and Indians.[341]

6 To better undeceive the said authors, it is not inapropos to refute the legendary origin that Titus Livy and Dionysius of Halicarnassus[342] attribute to the Laws of the Twelve Tables, claiming that they had been brought to Rome from Athens by ambassadors appointed for this purpose in order to calm the Plebeians who had risen against the nobles, in which [the Plebeians] were followed by many others, and Accurcius[343] swallowed the same lie when, as I said of America, the Romans were far distant from the Greeks; there was no interchange of languages except after they offered each other wars and alliances, which were followed by negotiations and agreements; and it is not known how Solon's[344] reputation for wisdom flew to Rome, nor how the Romans at a particular point were acquainted with the total context of the Athenian laws in order to judge them adequate for pacifying the Roman plebeians; even less so, what envoys were those who were charged with such a tumultuous mission;[345] because 172 years later, those they sent to Taranto, which was within the bounds of Italy, were upset with the people of Taranto, who gave as an excuse that they did not know them because this was the first occasion that the two nations, Greek and Roman, dealt with each other; and if Cicero, who was consul and had a deep knowledge of the laws of Rome, denies the foreign origin of the Law of the Twelve Tables, how could a private

---

339. The Greek letter *T.*

340. Literally, the mountain of the marketplace.

341. On Meztitlan, see Gerhard, *Historical Geography*, 183–87.

342. Titus Livius Patavinus (59 BC–AD 17) of Padua was a well-known Roman historian. Dionysius of Harlicarnassus (c. 60 BC–after 7 BC) was a Greek historian and rhetorician who spent his adult years in Rome and wrote a history of the empire.

343. Accursius (Accorso di Bagnolo, c. 1182—1263) was an Italian jurist.

344. Solon (c. 638 BC–558 BC) was an Athenian statesman and lawmaker.

345. According to Livy, the Law of the Twelve Tables was originally kept secret. Pressure from the plebeians eventually forced them to be made public. In this semilegendary account, Roman envoys went to Greece to study its legal systems, but it seems more likely that they consulted Greek colonies in Italy.

gentleman of Padua and a Greek historian, entranced with giving greater glory to their fatherland, dare to foist on posterity such an absurd fiction, which Accurcius adopted in order to lengthen his ever growing glosses?

7 And although with the passage of time there was no lack of persons who would say that the said laws were translated by Hermodorus the Greek,[346] who was in Rome in exile from his fatherland; and to give more color to the legend, others did not resist inventing a letter in which Heraclitus[347] writes to Hermodorus that he had dreamed one night that all the laws of the world came to adore theirs, something that has been proven to be false, because none of them smacks of anything Greek, as Diodorus Siculus[348] admits, and the single word *auctoritas* is so proper to the Latin language and the wisdom of the *Decemviri* that there is no word like it in the entire Greek language that can explain it better; and even more, because the said letter would be unworthy of a Heraclitus, who was such a great philosopher that he could not have bestowed the glory of a lawgiver on someone who had been a mere translator of the laws referred to, nor would Hermodorus himself have ever consented to such shameless adoration, because his gifts were so precise and worthy of such great respect that Heraclitus himself admitted that the people of Ephesus who cooperated in his expulsion and exile were strangled one by one.

8 Still less will it suit the similarities of origin to compare the customs of one nation with the other, because, since it is certain that these derive their principle characteristics from laws, I repeat what I said before with regard to the laws themselves. And it is infallible that if we should take the laws of all the nations, we could with the utmost security say that we had the general history of the customs of the nations, according to Marcion in *Law* 2, paragraphs *de legibus. Lex est communis sponsio civitatis ad cujus præscriptum omnes, qui in ea republica sunt, vitam instituere debent.*[349]

---

346. A Greek writer of the fourth century BC about whom little is known.

347. Heraclitus of Ephesus (c. 535 BC–c. 475 BC) was a pre-Socratic Greek philosopher, a native of the Greek city Ephesus, Ionia, on the coast of Asia Minor.

348. Diodorus Siculus ("the Sicilian") was a Greco-Roman historian of the first century BC, about whom little is known. He wrote a monumental work called *Bibliotheca Historica* (Library of History).

349. "Law is the common bond of the city, to whose prescriptions all who are in that republic should regulate their lives." The first part is usually attributed to the jurist Papinian. The Marcion mentioned here is obscure, perhaps an early heretic who separated the law of the gospel from civil law.

9 In addition, it is well known that customs arise from the people themselves and that [customs] are altered to the degree that the government is disturbed or changed. We saw in the first age, when the government was theocratic, that the first founders of pagan humanity were virtuous and religious by means of auguries and idolatry, and they did not demand anything of their subjects that was not believed to be agreeable to the gods; that their customs were founded on parsimony and sobriety, for example, that they cared only for what was necessary for sustaining life, and that these [people] should be considered to be natural philosophers who reigned in an age that was happy, simple, and free of all malice, all ambition, which Ovid depicts; *Metamorphoses, book* 1, legend 3.

> *Aurea prima sata est ætas, qua vindice nullo,*
> *Sponte sua sine lege fidem rectumque colebat.*
> *Pœna metusque aberant, nec verba minacia fixo*
> *Ære legebantur.*[350]

We saw in this second age that the entire natural law of the heroic peoples consisted in occupying lands for cultivation, seeking open highways, and subjecting nations that were opposed to their just purposes; that the heroes and others following their example paid no attention to any crimes, rather, if they placed all their ambition in showing great force and valor with arms, and from this came the beginnings of the Olympic Games of the Greeks, of the agriculture of the Romans, of the tournaments and other knightly games of barbarian European times,[351] of the challenges, even continued into the third age among our Indians in those heroic and well-ordered wars, which the two eternally opposed nations, Mexico and Tlatelolco, carried out solely for the sake of military vainglory, whose customs appear to have arisen among the Indian heroes themselves, who, because they alone held the law of auguries, boasted their divine origin, not only because they had been born of solemn marriages but also because they aspired to divine honors by means

350. "The first golden age was harvests, in which without a protector, without law, voluntarily cultivated what was faithful and right; pain and fear were absent; nor were threatening words read that were set in bronze."

351. Apparently a reference to the Middle Ages.

of transformations, and their servants thought that the great deeds that they accomplished came from the increased strength that the gods communicated to them. The said heroes were the ones who divided the year into four seasons, foretelling in each one of them the influences that they could have: those who first observed the *wandering* stars, then the *fixed* ones; those who arranged the astronomical and chronological calendars and gave a precise beginning to the ritual one; and those who multiplied agriculture in all those innumerable places through which they passed, rested, and left the elderly behind to settle; the said poet almost expresses it, loc. cit., legend 4.

Postquam, Saturno tenebrosa in Tartara misso,
Sub Jove mundus erat; subiit argentea proles,
Auro deterior, fulvo pretiosior ære.
Jupiter antiqui contraxit tempora veris:
Perque hyems æstusque, & inæquales autumnos
Et breve ver, spatiisque exegit quatuor annum.
Tum primum siccis aër fervoribus ustus
Canduit: & ventis glacies adstricta pependit.
Tum primum subire[352] *domos, domus antra fuerunt,*
Et densa frutices, & vincta cortice virgae,
Semina tum primum longis Cerealia sulcis
Obruta sunt, pressique jugo gemuere juvenci.[353]

All of which they did by themselves, as divine providence thus arranged it, without imitating any nation.

10 And even after the yoke of heroism was shaken off, at which time the servants began to become human and to know that their nature was not of such a lower order as the heroes had convinced them, the

352. *Sic* for *subiere*?

353. "After Saturn was sent to the darkness of the underworld, the world was under Jupiter, the silver offspring arose, inferior to the gold, more valuable than yellow bronze. Jupiter shortened the time of the former springtime and turned the year into four sections: winter, and summer, and unequal autumns and a brief springtime; then the dry air, burned by the raging heat, was first turned white, and the ice hung attached by the winds. Then they first went down into their homes, their homes were caves and dense shrubs or branches fastened with bark. The seeds of cereal grains were first buried in long furrows, and the young bullocks, burdened with the yoke, groaned."

propagation of whom they had just discovered was not of divine origin, after which the multitude wanted to know the internal nature of laws and that they be communicated in an understandable language and not hidden in heroic symbols, and that [the multitude] be governed with justice; because the aristocratic government of the heroes fell and the monarchical [government] came in. Even at this time and in the entire time that continued up to the conquest, the customs of the Indians had no connection whatsoever with those of other nations, and no basis can be argued from [their customs] on the topic of origin, for each kingdom established its own laws and customs, its rites and ceremonies, and so among the Indians themselves there is a great variety of customs, since those in the hot lands are weak, languid, and defenseless, those in the cold lands are robust, strong, and endure great labors; those of the temperate [lands] share in both; those in the Mediterranean areas have one talent, those of the maritime coasts have another, and even the scientific systems are different; for example, the Toltec calendar, which divides the years into eighteen months of twenty days each, and adds five intercalary days, as I explained previously; that of the Indians of the diocese of Oaxaca, which counts its year in thirteen months, with an equal number of figures of gods; and others of other provinces of the same diocese, which number the days of the years by means of winds and serpents.

11 Given this, I found no other light, no other calm, no other port than in the histories of the Indians themselves, and among them I searched for the most ancient Toltecs. I have already said of this nation that they were outstanding in mechanical arts, above, section 14, number 2; here I add the easy method of separating metals (whose secret I have investigated for a long time for public usefulness). The only thing remaining is to recount their excellence in astronomic science and the leap year in section 20, number 2, and section 27, number 2, and as far as history is concerned in section 21, number 1, where it will be seen how careful they were to preserve for posterity the memories of ancient matters with pictorial documents painted in figures, symbols, characters, and hieroglyphs. One of these (which was probably taken from the *Teoamoxtli*,[354] don Fernando de Alba *Ixtlilxochitl* had in his possession, with

354. Literally, "divine book."

many others of the Chichimeca nations, as is clear from his will, which I have seen, and the original ended up in the possession of the chiefs of his lineage, and the said author admits that with their help he was able to write both the Toltec and Chichimeca histories that I have in my archive. He says, then, that in the aforesaid original Toltec pictorial document many ancient memories are in evidence, and in particular the confusion of tongues at the Tower of Babel, which occurred, according to the Toltec calendar, in the year Ce Telpatl,[355] One Flint, on which occasion seven Toltecs, who were helping with the building of the said tower, seeing that they did not understand the others, departed with their women and children, and after having wandered in Asia, some elders, whom they called *huehuetiliztles*,[356] finally reached the lands of New Spain, which was then called *Anahuac*,[357] and they went inland until arriving at Tula, where they set up their court and the capital of their empire.

12 In my opinion one could not wish for a more complete or clearer notice, especially because it is accompanied by the successive wandering and arrival in New Spain, with complete specification of things and years in which they occurred, according to the order of the characters in their calendar, which I in the General History will compare with our European years. But if it causes difficulty for someone not versed in the use of Indian pictorial documents to consider that there were only seven of these Toltec Indians, who separated from the other peoples on the plain of Sennaar,[358] and the growth of innumerable colonies that spread out from them, both in Asia and in America; they [the readers] are advised that it was the custom of the Indians to use very few figures in the pictorial documents, under whose shadow were numerous towns and peoples; and so the said seven Toltecs whose names the foresaid don Fernando lists are understood to have been seven principal heads of the widespread lineages that were hidden under the names of their leaders. What has been said is confirmed with another pictorial document of the Chichimeca empire in which is seen painted

355. *Sic* for *tecpatl.*

356. *Sic* for *huehuetiliztli*, meaning golden age (Siméon).

357. Literally, "next to the water."

358. The settlement at Sennaar or Shinar (Genesis 11:2) is preliminary to the story of the Tower of Babel.

the arrival of the upstart kings who asked the Emperor *Xolotl*[359] for lands to settle in, without one's finding any other figure for their captains and vassals; and the same can be seen in many pictorial documents of the Mexican nation, where the new districts or new nations that entered the continent of New Spain are shown with only nine captains, and each one of them carries on his shield the insignia of the nations. Even in the conquest, when there was an opportunity to write the history of the arrival of the Spaniards at Veracruz, a ship is painted and nothing else; if the expeditions were by land, either Cortés alone was depicted or another European soldier, and as a rule the figures that are painted are few, and many of them are implied, for example, in the battles and other public actions, because with this concise and abbreviated style, vassals are confused with the persons of their kings, soldiers with those of their captains, in the same way that children and slaves are hidden under the names of their parents and masters; and not only are the Indians' pictorial documents studied with this understanding, but also those ancient European histories are rendered credible, which were reputed to be legendary and exaggerated, for example, when they relate the comparable strength of the knights of France and of the Guiscards in Naples,[360] who singlehandedly destroyed entire armies of Saracens, because as in other times it was aptly said that only heroes made war, just as today it is commonly said that only monarchs do so.

13 The Indians likewise celebrated their aforesaid origin in ancient songs, and they had such a living memory of the Tower of Babel that they wanted to imitate it in America with various imposing buildings. One of them was the famous hill that can still be seen (although damaged with time) in the city of *Tollan Chollolan*, built by hand by the Toltec Indians, mostly with adobe and mud, divided into four levels, which in former times were beautified with whitewash and mortar of sturdy composition, leaving on each of the four levels ample space to circle around it. Its peak was reached by a highly polished, zigzagging path, as can be seen on the pictorial document on paper of *metl* that I have in my archive, which on one side depicts the punishment that don Fernando Cortés inflicted on the Cholulans,[361] the taking of the city

359. On Xolotl, see Clavigero, *Historia*, 52–53.

360. The Guiscards were a Norman-French dynasty that ruled southern Italy in the Middle Ages.

361. Actually, the massacre of the Cholulans.

with sword in hand, its pacification and submission, the baptism of the queen doña Maria *Ylamanteuctli*[362] by the hand of don Gerónimo de Aguilar[363] on August 6, 1521, in which don Fernando himself was godfather; and on the other side it depicts the building of the said hill, which in older times was called *Tultecatl Chalchihuatl on azia Ecatepetl*, which means *Monument or precious stone of the Toltec nation which goes with the back of its neck, seeking the region of air*,[364] and the Indian historian has placed some notes in the national language at the foot of the picture of the said hill, as if he were speaking to his Cholulan compatriots, telling them, *Nobles and lords, here are your papers, the mirror of your ancient days, the history of your ancestors, who, moved by the fear of the flood, built this refuge, this asylum, in case you should again be attacked by a similar calamity*, which was the same motive for which the ancestors of these Indians built the Tower of Babel in Asia. Flavius Josephus, *Jewish Antiquities*, book 1, chapter 9, *Ulciscique sese timentes Deum putabant interminantem inferre diluviam terræ. Ob quam rem turrim ædificandam altiorem suadebat*, (meaning Nimrod) *ubi aqua non posset ascendere.*[365] Likewise he [the Indian historian] gives an account of the Most Holy Virgin of the said hill who appeared to a Franciscan Father in Rome at the beginning of the conquest, ordering him to go to the Spanish Indies where he would find a hill built by hand of adobe and mud, and there to construct a building which would be the propiciatorio[366] for all those peoples.

14 The final proof of the certain origin of our Indians is what we owe to the pen of don Francisco Núñez de la Vega, bishop of Ciudad Real de Chiapas and Soconusco,[367] who on the occasion of the

---

362. *Ilamanteuctli* (literally, "ruler of the old women") was queen of Cholula, baptized in 1521 (Siméon).

363. This may be the same person who had been a prisoner of the Mayas and after his liberation had acted as Cortés's interpreter together with doña Marina.

364. Boturini's translation is a bit eccentric. The phrase actually seems to mean, "the Toltec precious stone that reaches over there to the hill of the wind."

365. *Sic* for book 1, chapter 4. "and those who feared God thought that they would be avenged when he would again send a threatening flood on the earth. For which reason he [Nimrod] persuaded them to build a higher tower that the water could not reach."

366. Ordinarily this means a chapel or church built as an expiation for sins.

367. Núñez de la Vega, a Dominican, was appointed bishop in 1682 and died in 1689. He was noted for his campaign against neo-idolatry among the natives. Soconusco was in the area of Chiapas.

visitation that he made of his diocese in the year 1691, seems to have collected among the Indians some antique calendars of theirs, and likewise a very ancient historical notebook written in the language of those ancient people of the nation, which he acknowledged ended up in his possession. He says, then, in the preamble to the diocesan constitutions of the said bishopric, number 54, section 30, *Votan is the third pagan who is placed in the calendar, and in the historic notebook written in the Indian language he names all the places and towns where he had been, and up until the present time in that of Teopixca there has been a generation that they call of Votantes*; he says moreover, *that he is the lord of Palo Hueco (which they call Tepanaguaste),*[368] *who saw the great wall (which is the Tower of Babel), which by order of Noah, his grandfather, was raised up from the earth, even to heaven, and who is the first man whom God sent to divide and separate this land of the Indies, and that there, where the great wall was seen, each people was given its different language.*

15 The items in the said notebook seemed to me very special and individual, and with the intention of subjecting them to a good critique on the touchstone of its original, I asked the present bishop, don fray Manuel Cuberos, of the Mercedarian order, if he would please provide me with it together with the rest of the calendars. With the noble affection that he has for learning, having made the search, he answered that they had not turned up and that it would be difficult nowadays to find them in the possession of the Indians who, because of the latest epidemic, had been notably diminished in their towns. In the meantime a brief digression is worthy of pardon, which gives me the opportunity to clarify some points pertaining to Indian history, which the said bishop don fray Francisco Núñez de la Vega points out in the cited preamble.

16 But before getting to it, I should note that the bishop, in his desire to know both the meaning of the pictures, as well as the contents of the historical notebook in the native language, must have consulted Indian interpreters who gave the said bishop many mistaken and apocryphal reports, together with some good ones, and they did the same with me at the beginning of my historical endeavors, filling me with so many wild ideas that they had me confused until I was able to

368. *Tepanaguaste* is a slit drum, similar to the Nahuatl *teponaztli.*

penetrate things little by little and ground myself in the Indians' most ancient pictorial documents and manuscripts, because those of the present time do not understand a word of the histories nor do they penetrate the sense of the figures, and much less the obscurities of the hieroglyphs and the divine heroic symbols or the beautiful structure of the characters of their years and calendars. In vain I traveled through various provinces in search of some Indians who had the reputation of knowing matters of pagan times, for I found them devoid of any historical truth and full of errors with which, under the guise of elders, they deceive European historians, who excessively trust their gray hairs, when it is certain that even a century before there was no one who knew tolerably well how to explain a historical pictorial document of simple figures, as don Fernando de Alba *Ixtlilxochitl* admits in the introduction to his *General History of New Spain*, which I have in my archive.

17 Therefore I do not wonder at what the said bishop writes in number 32, section 28, of the same preamble, that *they have seven small black persons painted in their accounts or calendars in order to do divinations and predictions corresponding to the seven days of the week, the pagans beginning to count them, for example, by the seven planets,* because such small black people were the principal lords of this nation, who, having the ministry of priesthood together with aristocratic rulers in the heroic age, distinguished themselves from the rest of the heroes by painting their faces with the color black, and I even have in my archive a pictorial document from the third age, in which the priest is seen with his face painted black, for it is certain that in the entire period of paganism, no Ethiopeans[369] at all came to these parts, just that it was the custom among the priests for their faces to be blackened, because in this way they imitated their god of the underworld *Mictlanteuctli* or *Teotlamacazqui*, black and ugly, and from this they were generally called *Tlamacazque*; and the bishop goes on to say that *the one they called Coslabuntox (who is the demon, according to what the Indians say, with thirteen powers) they depict on a chair and with spears on his head, like a butcher*, when the said *Coslabuntox* should be corrected to *Ymos* or *Mox*, and he is not listed in the calendar as a demon but as head of the twenty lords, symbols of the days of the year, and so it would be the first symbol

369. In the language of the time, this meant any black person.

of them and brings with it a triadecaterida of days, which out of ignorance they interpreted as the thirteen powers; and from what I have seen in this number and in 33–34, and 35, the calendrical system of Chiapas and Soconusco agrees with the Toltec, which I have explained above, because in place of the four characters Tecpatl, Calli, Tochtli, Acatl, those of Chiapas make use of four figures of lords, *Votan, Lambat, Been, and Chinax; and the other twenty figures, whose names are: Mox, Ygh, VOTAN, Ghanan, Abagh, Tox, Moxic, LAMBAT, Mola,* (*in others Mulu*), *Elab, Batz, Enob, BEEN, Hix, Tziquin, Chabin, Chic, CHINAX, Cahogb, Aghual,* take the place of the twenty symbols: *Cipactli, Ehecatl, CALLI, Cuetzpallin, Cohuatl, Miquiztli, Mazatl, TOCHTLI, Atl, Ytzcuintli, Ozomatli, Malinalli, ACATL, Ocelotl, Quauhtli, Temetlatl, Ollin, TECPATL, Quiahuitl, Xochitl,* to form the count for the days of the year. Neither do I know how they made out horns on the said *Cozlabuntox*, when in that multitude of figures that I have in my pictorial documents, I have not seen even one with horns; but the mistake consists of the manner with which the lords dressed their hair. See figure 3 in Gemelli Careri, volume 6, page 86, with strange loops, and 2, ibidem, which is that of *Nezahualcoyotl*, and no doubt, anyone would say he has two round horns with tassels, and they are nothing more than the ears of a *coyote*, the emperor's symbol, which is used to distinguish the person, and ladies and noble women wore a hairdo that divided the hair into two parts, lifting it up like two peaks, and it would be ridiculous to say that they are all demons with horns. The bishop goes on to say that the Indians *are very much afraid of the black man because they still have a memory of one of their primitive ancestors of the Ethiopian color who was a great warrior and extremely cruel—whom the people of Ochuc and other towns on the planes greatly venerated as one they call Yalaban, which means Black Leader or Lord of the Blacks.* The explanation, as previously, is that the said blacks were priests deliberately painted with the color black, and who also went on campaigns, and *Yalaban* must have been their great priest, that is, *Lord of the Priests*, as was *Moteucçoma Xocoyotl* of the Mexicans before they chose him as monarch, and he always retained an excessive superstition regarding idols. Finally, this prelate thinks that the Indians of Chiapas and Soconusco are of the lineage of Cham,[370] *and that written in their*

370. The form of the name as found in the Vulgate; most modern bibles have the form Ham.

language they have the animal, bird, heavenly body, or element through which each one adored the demon, and those primitive pagans were sorted by days to designate them with their animals as angels, who they say are the guardians of the little ones who are born.[371] Good heavens, what interpreters of little reflection! The animal, bird, heavenly body, or element signifies nothing more than the name of the figure where it is appended, and by means of the said ciphers I have been able to discover and interpret their history. See Gemelli Careri's pictorial document inserted in volume 6, chapter 4, page 42, where all the figures of the Indians bear their distinctive ciphers, by means of which one arrives at a full knowledge of the history.

18 But in number 33, section 29, the bishop says *that Ninus*[372] *is placed as a heading in a primitive calendar in the Latin language, and that nowadays in the more modern calendars the Latin name of Nino is corrupted into Ymos*; but I believe the opposite, and I infer it from the rest of the names of lords, which indicate the days of the year and have no connection whatever with the lineage of Nino; and with regard to what is recounted here, that the Indians censed the ceiba tree, I do not doubt it, and this was a purely political act with which they signified that that place was (as the Roman laws on cities' walls say) holy and inviolable, because it was there that the selection of judges took place, a custom derived from the times of their paganism, in which, when they had occasion to go out to receive some ambassador, they carried small braziers and censers, and with them they would introduce him at court as a sign that his person could not be mistreated; rather, on the contrary, he was worthy of all respect and compliance. The rest is the ignorance of interpreters.

19 The historical note referred to in number 34, section 30, about the Tower of Babel, I will explain in detail when the said notebook may appear. I am only sorry that the small statues of the twenty lords were burned in the square of *Huehuetan*, which could have been kept in the diocesan archive in case God should awaken the understanding of some person capable of deciphering them. These fires have been frequent and very unfortunate in New Spain. The Indians and learned Spaniards bemoan them, and I lament them because it is clear to me

371. This sentence is confusing.

372. King of Assyria and husband of Semiramis.

that in the ancient pictorial documents there are individual accounts not only of great literary treasures but also of some immense riches kept in [the time of] their paganism and hidden at the time of the conquest, and I do not despair of performing, one day or another, a great and notable service for Your Majesty.

20 I am not disposed to add anything else to number 33, section 31, except that all of its notices are purely chronological, and having studied these calendrical systems, I have found both the four characters of the years and the symbols of the days listed in complete order, and I learned that their structure was determined in this second age.

21 Returning, then, to the origin of the Indians, I think it appropriate to clarify the year of the confusion of the tongues in Babylonia because in this way they were separated from the rest of the peoples. The Venerable Bede, *De ratione temporum*, chapter 18,[373] following the Hebrew calculation, says that the Tower of Babel began to be built at the time when Phaleg[374] was born, about 101 years after the flood, and it is natural that the confusion should have occurred many years after the tower was raised to its prodigious height, as Flavius Josephus admits, *Jewish Antiquities*, book 1, chapter 9. *Sumebat ergo altitudo facilitatem, & plusquam sperare quis posset, multis manibus utique fabricata crescebat. Latitudo tamen ita erat fortissima, ut prope eam respicientibus longitudo videretur imminui. Ædificabatur autem ex latere cocto colligato bitumine, ne forte penetraretur, ac dissolveretur aquis.*[375] For this reason the Abbot Ludovico Morery[376] believed, in his great historical dictionary at the word *Babel*, that it had occurred 146 years after the flood, and the most

---

373. The Venerable Bede (672/673–735) was an English monk, theologian, historian, and polymath. His most famous work was the *Ecclesiastical History of the English People.* His work *De temporum ratione* dealt mainly with the reckoning of the date of Easter.

374. See Genesis 11:16–19.

375. "Therefore the height made it easy, and more than anyone could hope, it grew, built by the multitude of hands. The thickness of it was so great, however, that for that reason its great height seemed to those looking up close to be diminished. It was built of burnt brick, cemented together with mortar, made of bitumen, so that it would not be penetrated and be destroyed by water."

376. Louis Morery was the author of the *Grand Dicionnaire Historique* published at Amsterdam in 1702. Little is known about him.

learned Father Dionysius Petavio,[377] *Rationarium temporum*, part 2, book 2, chapter 3, page 83, gives us to understand that it should be reckoned forward after 150 years, and even the incomparable Father Athanasius Kircher[378] in his work titled *Turris Babel*, book 2, chapter 12, extends it to 275 years, but I, who do not stray far (although by another route) from the opinion of the great Kircher and go through the histories of the Toltec nation and their calendrical systems, have found that the said confusion [of tongues] is recounted in the year *Ce Tecpatl, One Flint*, and that when the Indians count by this number *ce, one*, for example, *Ce Tecpatl, One Flint*, it means once every four cycles, because at that time, they were speaking of the initial characters of each cycle, and thus, according to the device of their painted wheels, *Ce Tecpatl* comes in only once at the beginning of the four cycles because the first cycle begins with the character *Ce Tecpatl*, the second cycle begins with *Ce Calli*, the third with *Ce Tochtli*, and the fourth with *Ce Acatl*; for that reason, when any of these initial characters is placed in the history, four Indian cycles of fifty-two years each necessarily have to pass, which amounts to 208 before [the same combination] can occur in the future, because in this way the count is not by the characters that are in the body of the four cycles, and although the same characters *Ce Tecpatl, Ce Calli, Ce Tochtli, Ce Acatl*, are found in them, they do not make the case, especially when the ancient histories depict the character of something notable after the manner of an epoch and which did not occur in their times, in which case the count is by the initial characters, because it is not the historian's intention to follow the context of the history. And moreover I point out that in order to calculate years by the Indian calendars, one must also add to the aforesaid 208 years those that are found previous to the situation of the four cycles after the manner of fractions. I explain myself by

377. Denis Petau (1583–1652), French Jesuit theologian. His most famous work was *Dogmata theologica*.

378. Athanasius Kircher (1601/1602–80) was a German Jesuit scholar and polymath who delved into oriental studies, geology, and medicine, among others. Though his interpretation of ancient hieroglyphics was basically flawed, he is often considered the Father of Egyptology. The Latin name for the Jesuits is *Societas Jesu*, in English *Society of Jesus*, in Spanish the *Compañía de Jesús*. The *Turris Babel* was published in 1679.

carefully searching for the year of the confusion of tongues, and in order to find it one must investigate that of the universal flood, on whose implied [date] I register the histories of the Indians, and finding it in trustworthy pictorial documents or in the manuscripts of native authors who make note of it, taken faithfully from the pictorial documents from pagan times, without having wearied themselves with our European calculations, I guide myself by the calendars and I cannot mistake the count, but if the said historians do not mention it, I have recourse to the years of the flood, which are gathered from the lives of the first patriarchs in the Holy Bible, and I look for the same year in my Indian tables; I then count the years which I call partial fractions to complete the four cycles, and to these I add the 208, and I find my character *Ce Tecpatl*, and with it the years of aforementioned confusion of tongues, as follows.[379]

Years of the flood, according to the Hebrews and Latins . . . 1656	*Years of the flood, according to the Interpreters and the Septuagint . . . 2242*
I find the said year in the fifty-second cycle at the character 5 Tochtli *and I have no more than fractions left, or to complete the four cycles, than years 9*	*I find the said year in the forty-fourth cycle at the character* 6 Tecpatl, *and I have no more than fractions left, or to complete the four cycles, than years 47*
Added to arrive at Ce Tecpatl *years 208*	*Added to arrival at* Ce Tacpatl *years 208*
1873	*2497*
I say, according to this opinion, that the confusion of tongues was in the year 1873, that is, 217 years after the flood.	I say, according to this opinion, that the confusion of tongues was in the year 2497, that is, 255 years after the flood.

379. On the whole this last part is not very clear.

And the opinion of the Septuagint backs me up more, because it is followed by Flavius Josephus, Philo, Eusebius, and the African,[380] and many others, and by this Indian system one obtains the number of years from the flood to the confusion of tongues that is provided by the multitude of people who were necessary for a construction as arrogant as Babel, and with their multiplication, which was enough to populate part of Asia and all of America without weakening the considerable forces of the ancient kingdom of the Assyrians, which serious authors believe was very flourishing from the beginning of the said tower and the city of Babylonia. Finally, I point out that the Toltecs put at the head of their calendar the character *Ce Tecpatl*, the Mexicans that of *Ce Tochtli*, and it is possible that some begin it with *Ce Calli*, others with *Ce Acatl*, from which has arisen such great confusion, even among the Indians themselves. I will consider all of them at leisure in the General History, in which the most notable epochs and the common tables of the said calendars will be given for a full understanding of the Indian chronology.

22 Having seen the clear origin of the Indians, it becomes easier to learn from which branch they descend of those who were present at the construction of the said tower. The late professor of mathematics at the University of Mexico, don Carlos de Sigüenza y Góngora, and the celebrated Mother Sor Juana Inés de la Cruz,[381] noble gift to the Mexican nation, were of the opinion that thy were descendants of *Nephetuim* or *Nephtuhim*, son of *Mefraim* and grandson of *Cham*,[382] although I am inclined to believe that they were also descendants of the other brothers *Ludim*, *Amanim*, *Phetusim*, and *Capthorim* for two reasons: the first because Nicholas of Lyra, on chapter 10 of Genesis, says that the stopping place of these peoples is not known, *Hæc omnia ignorantur, vel quia deleta sunt gente, bello Æthiopico, vel quia ignoratur quæ nomina nunc habeant*,[383] and Flavius Josephus, *The Antiquities of the Jews*, book 1,

---

380. Eusebius of Caesarea (AD 263–AD 339) was a historian, often called the Father of Church History. The African may have been Augustine of Hippo (AD 354–AD 430), a theologian and Father of the Church.

381. Sor Juana (1651–96) was a Hieronymite nun in seventeenth-century Mexico who was outstanding as a scholar, poet, polymath, and advocate of women's rights.

382. See Genesis 10:13. These names are all in the form found in the Latin Vulgate.

383. "All these things are unknown, either because the people have been destroyed or because it is not known what name they may have now."

chapter 12. *Ex aliis autem, id est, Ludim, & Anamim, & Lahabim, solus Lahabim a se provinciam Libyam nominavit. Nephtuim autem & Phetrusim, Chaslohim, Capthorim ultra nomina nihil scimus. Bello enim Æthiopico, de quo postea declarabimus, eorum civitates eversa sunt.*[384] The second [reason] because there is no evidence up to the present that our Indians are descended individually from just the *Nephetuim*, and even those seven Toltec heads from widespread lineages, which I explained in this same section, number 12, permit us a favorable conjecture that they were from various branches of *Mesraim*[385] because the authors cited did not know their stopping place and their peoples had passed to the New World, a fact that remained unknown to all the nations of Asia, Africa, and Europe until the Spanish conquest, and it was the reason why Flavius Josephus and others thought that their cities had been destroyed in the Ethiopian war, although in Flavius's chapter 10 of book 2, which deals with it, there is no trace of the said cities and peoples.

23 Having departed, then, from the land and plain of *Senaar* with their increased descendants and guided by Divine Providence, as the above-quoted Flavius writes, book 1, chapter 10, *Divisi sunt itaque diversitate linguarum, migrationes agentes ubique, & terram aprehendentes unusquisque felicem, & ad quam eos Deus adduceret,*[386] they dispersed over the great forest of the earth, and all those things happened which I have pointed out in the first age until in the second, when lineages had increased with the new addition of servants, and increased in number, they wandered for a long time in Asia (in the General History, it will be told in great detail), passing from one place to another, taking their seeds with them, particularly maize, chili, and beans, and at each stop they cleared the forests, sowed fields, and perhaps leaving behind the old and exhausted to settle those lands, and so much did they travel that the first and last, at different times, were approaching America, and finally they entered and set foot on their continent, as will be told next.

---

384. "Of the others, however, that is, the Ludim and Anamim and Lahabim, only the Lahabim named the province of Libya after themselves. We know nothing, however, of the Nephtuim and Phetrusim, Chaslohim, Capthorim beyond the names. For in the Ethiopian war, which we will describe later, their cities were overthrown." Josephus's listing is based on Genesis 10. Boturini's reference to book 1, chapter 12, seems to be erroneous. It is actually chapter 6.

385. Mizrahim was a name for Egypt.

386. "And so they were separated by the diversity of languages, undertaking migrations everywhere, and each one taking a pleasant land, and to which God would lead them." This is from chapter 4, not chapter 10.

On the Passage and Crossing

that the Indians of New Spain Took to Arrive There

§. XVII

1 Another most obscure question was the long wished-for investigation of by which lands or seas our Indians came to America. The authors who were mistaken about their origin suffered the same error about their passage. For now I will point out in summary some arguments that prove that the Indians came to the continent of America through the straits of California, reserving to myself in the General History to finish the matter with all care.

2 The first argument is the itinerary that the Toltec nation took in order to reach Tula, which was later their capital and the residence of their monarchs, because of which it will be shown that their passage was from California to the continent.

3 The second [is] because in all the pictorial documents of the Mexican nation and others that accompany them, which I have in my archive, their first arrival is depicted at the town of *Culhuacan*, which means *the town of the serpent*, which is the first [town] on the continent and is situated in front of the said California in perspective almost to the end of the peninsula itself, only separated from it by a branch of the South Sea.[387] The Mexicans crossed this strait with eight other nations in boats with platforms, called *acalles*, that is, *water houses*,[388] and that is how they depict it on their pictorial documents, nor, in my opinion, is it possible to have a better proof.

---

387. The Pacific Ocean.

388. The literal meaning of *acalli*, though it means canoes.

4 The third is that in the wanderings from Asia to America there remained in those left behind the memory of those who gone on, and they preserved it in their songs, and thus with the passage of time they all kept coming by the same path, and it was the cause of the heroic wars because in the course of long centuries they no longer recognized each other, and the wandering of the first left behind undoubted signs of their defeat.

5 The fourth consists in my not having been able in the ancient histories of the Indians (because neither those of Europeans nor of the modern Indians can be relied on in such matters) up to now to discover any trace that the Indians had come from other parts; I am speaking of the beginnings, because later on transmigrations were frequent, and are not pertinent.

6 The fifth consists in the fact that California is a peninsula, and in order to prove it I have various curious notices from the celebrated mathematician Father Kino of the Sacred Company [of Jesus],[389] former apostolic missionary in that land, who went up to the Colorado River in sight of the Sea of California and discovered a tongue of land that extended farther and was alongside the shores of the said sea.

7 The sixth is that the seven principal nations of California did not communicate with those further north, nor vice versa, even though it is known that the former land was populated with people, and I found that in the histories of Muscovy and Japan those parts were depicted as a continent in the most ancient geographical maps on wood, so that with the historic monuments of these three nations, Indian, Muscovite, and Japanese, I flatter myself that I can write based on these, which may supply a human truth, subject nevertheless to the obscurity and confusion of time, something that only an enlightened genius could supply, as was the venerable ecstatic gentleman Gregorio López,

389. Eusebio Francisco Kino (August 10, 1645–March 15, 1711) was an Italian Jesuit who became famous in what is now northwestern Mexico and the southwestern United States. He is known for his exploration of the region and for his work to Christianize the indigenous Native American population. He proved that Baja California was not an island by leading an overland expedition there from Arizona. He established twenty-four missions and visitas ("country chapels" or visiting stations) and was known for his ability to create relationships between indigenous peoples and the religious institutions he represented.

celebrated anchorite of the Indies, who wrote a book on the location of all the nations of the world, the levels they have attained, their rites and customs, the lack of which [book] I have not ceased to lament many times.[390]

8 In my archive there are still many very ancient papers and entire volumes in the Indian language; those that have been translated and added to other material that I do not possess could augment and adorn the present draft still more.

9 I do not despair of the subtle geniuses of Peru who, having exercised for their part the same diligence in South America that I did for the North, advance a similar historical approach, and that they may corroborate it with important researches, and I will be glad that this short work of mine benefits them in some way.

390. Gregorio López (1542–96) was a well-known hermit and holy man, known most from the biography written by Francisco Losa. López's book is now unknown.

Giants

§. XVIII

1 Not only does the Holy Bible recount that before the universal flood there were giants with huge bodies, unimaginable strength, perverse customs, likewise born solely with habits of carnal concupiscence from forbidden marriages between the sons of God, who were the descendants of Seth, instructed in the worship of the true God, and the curious and dissolute daughters of men from the accursed race of Cain, Genesis:6, *number 2, Videntes filii Dei filias hominum, quod esset*[391] *pulchræ acceperunt sibi uxores ex omnibus quas elegerant;* & n. 4. *Gigantes autem errant super terram in diebus illis. Postquam enim ingressi sunt filii Dei ad filias hominum, illaque genuerunt; isti sunt potentes a sæculo viri famosi;*[392] but also after the flood, such as *Nimrod* and many others. The Ordinary Gloss,[393] on chapter 10. *Nemrod secundum Josephum nova regni cupiditate tyranidem arripuit, & auctor ædificandæ turris quæ tangeret cœlum, ipse cœpit esse potens, vel gigans secundum alios.*[394] Numbers 13, at the end. *Populus quem aspeximus*

391. *Sic* for *essent.*

392. "When the sons of God saw that the daughters of men were beautiful, they took them to themselves as wives from all those whom they had chosen . . . There were giants on the earth in those days. For after the sons of God had relations with the daughters of men and they had given birth, these are the powerful ones from the beginning, the famous men." Genesis 6:4. These verses are obscure.

393. The Ordinary Gloss consisted of commentaries that were inserted into the margins of the Latin Vulgate Bible.

394. "According to Josephus, Nimrod, out of greed for a new kingdom, seized the tyranny by force and was responsible for the building of the tower which would reach to heaven, began to be powerful or, according to others, a giant."

proceræ staturæ est. Ibi vidimus monstra quædam filiorum Enac de genere giganteo, quibus comparati quasi locustæ videbamur.[395] Deuteronomii 2:10. *Emim primi fuerent habitatores ejus. Populus magnus & validus & tam excelsus ut de Enacim stirpe, quasi gigantes crederentur, & essent similes filiorum Enacim.* & n. 20, *Terra gigantum reputata est, & in ipsa olim habitaverunt gigantes quos Ammonitæ vocant Zomzommim. Populus magnus & multus & proceræ longitudinis sicut Enacim,* ibid., chapter 3, number 11, *Solus monstratur lectus ejus ferrens, qui est in Rabbath filiorum Ammon novem cubitos habens longitudinis & quatuor latitudinis ad mensuram cubitis virilis magnus*, & n. 13. *Cunctaque Basan vocatur terra gigantum,* 2 Kings:21, n. 18, *Tunc percussit Sabochai de Husati, Saph de stripe arapha de genere gigantum.*[396] And from this comes the opportunity to ponder the physical reasons for the said giants, for which two historical texts are worth noting with regard to the ancient Germans, cited by Julius Caesar, *Commentary on the Gallic War*, book 4, at the beginning. *Neque multum frumento, sed maximum partem lacte atque pecore vivunt, multamque sunt in venationibus, quæ res & cibi genere, & quotidiana exercitatione, & libertate vitæ (quod a pueris nullo officio aut disciplina assuefacti, nihil omnino contra voluntatem faciant) & vires alit, & immani corporum magnitudine hominess efficit,*[397] and by Caius

---

395. "The people whom we saw were of great stature. There we saw certain monsters of the sons of Enac [*sic* for Anakim] or the race of giants, compared to whom we seemed like locusts."

396. "The Emim were its first inhabitants. A people great and strong and so tall that it could be believed that they were of the stock of Anakim, like giants, and they would be similar to the sons of Anakim." And number 20, "It was reputed to be a land of giants, and in it in former times lived giants whom the Ammonites called Zonzommim, a people great and numerous and of great stature, like the Anakim." Ibid., chapter 3, number 11. 'Indeed only Og, the king of Bashan, remained of the lineage of giants. His iron bed is displayed, which is in Rabbath of the sons of Ammon and has a length of nine cubits and a width of four according to the cubit measure of a man's hand." And number 13, "and all Bashan is called the land of giants." 2 Kings, chapter 21, number 18, 'Then Sabochai [Sibbochai] of Hufati [Hisha] struck Saph of the Arapha lineage of the race of giants.'"

397. "They do not live much on grain but live for the most part on milk and meat and are much given to hunting, which both by the nature of their food and by their daily exercise and the freedom of their life (for having from boyhood been accustomed to no employment or discipline, they do nothing at all against their will), both promote their strength and render them men of vast stature of body.

Cornelius Tacitus, *de situ, moribus, & populis Germaniae. In omni domo nudi ac sordidi in hos artus, in hæc corpora quæ Miramar excrescunt. Sua quemque uberibus alit, nec ancillis ac nutricibus delegantur. Dominum ac servum nullis educationis delitiis dignoscas. Inter eadem pecora, in eadem humo degunt, donec ætas separet ingenuos, virtus agnoscat.*[398] From them it is clear how the said Germans, children of lords and slaves alike, being raised with a loose and idle education, and allowing them to sleep on manure-covered earth among the sheep, the tender bodies of the infants, fortified with the nitrates of the earth and the strengthening powers of salinity[399] of manure, cannot but grow to that height that the two histories mention; having affected giants the most, who as one passed on to a bestial freedom.

2 Under this hypothesis, some giants of the lineage of Ham and Japheth spread throughout the world after the confusion of tongues and because of the monstrous stature of their bodies were better able to cross vast lands and with greater speed than others. It is known that those from the second lineage were the founders of the Greek nation, and thus their history brings us very close to the flood, to Prometheus, the giant son of Japheth, and to Deucalion, grandson of the same Japheth and father of Helenos, who founded the Greeks who were named *Hellene*[400] after him, and from here on, through the history of the Greeks, secular and sacred history is joined in perpetuity, and because of this it is believed that the poets, with the legend of the giants who sought to make war on heaven, Ovid, *Metamorphoses*, book 1, legend 6,

---

398. "In all their homes [the children] grow up naked and dirty into these limbs, into these bodies which we wonder at. Their mother feeds each one at her breasts, nor are they given to servants or wet nurses. You cannot tell the lord from the slave by delicacy of their upbringing. They live among the same cattle, in the same dirt, until age separates the free-born [and] makes their strength clear."

399. *Fomentos salitrosos*, translation conjectural. It seems to refer to the strengthening powers of nitrate or saltpeter.

400. Boturini confuses Greek mythology and Old Testament history. Deucalion, son of Promethus, survived the flood unleashed by Zeus on the world. He was not the grandson of Japheth.

Neve foret terris securior arduus Æther,
Affectatus fuerunt[401] *regnum cœleste Gigantas.*
Altaque congestos stuxisse[402] *ad sidera montes*[403]

wanted to preserve the history of the gigantic building of the Tower of Babel, Simon Mayolo, *Dog Days*, volume 2, dialogue 1, *On the origin, worship, and oracles of the pagan gods*, page 313, column 2, number 60, *Fabulam de gigantibus aggestione & cumulatione montium, extructuris aditum ad cœlos, & Jovem inde turbaturis, videtur peperisse mentio gigantum in Genesi, & historia de impedita divinitus ex edificatione turris Babyloniæ, & idem significant vox Titanes, quod gigantes.*[404]

3 On the other hand, the giants from the lineage of Ham took the route through Phoenicia, Egypt, and Africa, and some of them through America, and they were the first inhabitants of the interior of New Spain, because they must have come quite directly without a long stay in any place in their travels. The Indians had noteworthy memories of them, and they say that they were called *Quinametin hueytlacame*, that is, *great and deformed men.*[405] And since the epochs were all drawn either from the kingdoms or from the most notable events that took place in them, so the Indians formed the epoch of the third period of the world in the same year as the destruction of the giants in America, and they say it was that of *Ce Tecpatl*,[406] One Flint, which I will explain in the General History, although the said destruction was not so universal that some did not escape. Their descendants oppressed the Indian settlers who came afterward, compelling

401. *Sic* for *ferunt.*

402. *Sic* for *struxisse.*

403. "Nor was the lofty firmament more secure than the earth, they say that the giants eagerly desired the heavenly kingdom, and raised the abundant mountains to the high stars."

404. "The mention of giants in Genesis seems to have given rise to the legend of the giants about to build an approach to the heavens by heaping up and piling mountains, and thereby about to upset Jupiter, and the history of the divine stopping of the building of the Tower of Babylon [*sic*], and the word Titans has the same meaning as giants." Simon Mayolo was an obscure figure who lived at the beginning of the sixteenth century.

405. Literally, "giants, great peoples."

406. A typographical error for *tecpatl.*

them to provide large meals for them, because of which they took counsel together and decided to destroy them at a banquet they gave them with that purpose, where, drunk with *pulque*,[407] they killed them all.

4 In many parts of New Spain are found bones, fragments, teeth, and molars of the said giants, particularly in the highlands of Santa Fe and in the territories of Puebla and Tlaxcala, and I have in my archive various fragments of the said bones [and] two teeth, and in addition I brought with me a molar which, compared with ours, could make a hundred of them, equal to what Saint Augustine saw in *Udine del Friuli* and Vives in Valencia, as Mayolo mentions in the said place, volume 1, dialogue 2, *On man*, page 25, column 2, number 60.

407. A liquor fermented from the agave.

DIVISION OF THE KINGDOMS OF NEW SPAIN

The Olmec and Xicalanco Indians

§. XIX

This was either a single nation later divided into Olmecs and Xicalancos,[408] as the Mexican one was divided into Tlatelolca and Mexica, or they were two different nations, but friendly and allied. It is certain that both lived in the basin of the Atoyac River, between *Tlaxcala* and *Quetlaxcoapan*, today Puebla de los Angeles, and that they abandoned the land, perhaps going to the kingdoms of Peru and the other windward islands, and although scant notice is found of these Indians, second settlers of New Spain, as happens in both Greek and Roman histories, which are weak, diminished, and dubious in their beginnings, and one has but to read Thucydides, a historian of the greatest reputation and truth among the Greeks, who naively admits that the most educated of his nation and time up to the age of the fathers knew nothing of its antiquities, and Titus Livius, who did not dare set himself up as guaranteeing the histories [of the Romans]; notwithstanding that songs had been of greater duration than pictorial

408. A district on the shore of the Gulf Coast (Siméon). See Gerhard, *Historical Geography*, 392.

documents, such as passed from fathers to sons through the long stretch of the centuries, and [the songs] of the Indian neophytes were reduced to writing in the times immediately after the conquest, I do not despair of discovering through this route some historic traces, since diligence is accompanied by laurels and victories, according to Seneca, *Letters*, book 4, letter 29, *Spargenda est manus; non potest fieri, ut non aliquando succedat, multa tentanti.*[409]

The Toltec Indians

§. XX

1 Nevertheless, we have the Toltec history, which with abundant artistry gives us an account of the confusion of tongues, as I said in section 16, number 21, even specifying the names of those first parents who separated from the other peoples, as well as of the Senios[410] who wandered into Asia, and how they arrived at the continent and went inland as far as *Huehuetlapallan*,[411] the first city in New Spain, which they beautified with sumptuous buildings.

2 And once there, the learned men were convoked one hundred and so many years before the birth of Christ, our Life, and seeing that the civil year was inconsistent with the astronomical one and that the equinoxes did not agree, they decided to add one more day every four years that would bring together the hours which were being wasted, which I suppose they carried out by counting twice one of the symbols

409. "A hand must be spread out. It cannot happen that sometimes it does not turn out well for the one who attempts many things."

410. A word of uncertain meaning. Perhaps it has the meaning of "ancestors."

411. According to tradition, the point of departure of the Toltecs.

of the last month of the year, after the manner of the Romans, who called one and another day, February 24 and 25, *bisexto kalendas Martias*,[412] from the use of which the leap year was named, without disturbing the order of the said symbols, since anything whatever that might be added to them or removed would destroy their perpetual system, and in this way they combined the beginning of the civil years with the vernal equinox, which was the principal and dominant part of the years, as will be shown in the General History, where I will have the opportunity to deal with the *natural year.* With this beginning of the leap year I will put to rest many difficulties regarding the day on which the civil year began, and I will leave it for the end of the third age to describe another kind of intercalation concerning the *year and ritual calendar*, which was the occasion that many became confused, because they wanted to derive universal consequences from the rituals that were not applicable to other materials. In the meantime I point out that although the extra day that was added did not have a home of its own in the symbols of the days of the year, and took up lodging in another's, nonetheless it gave its name to the leap year and reserved to itself in the last month very solemn feasts, which even in the third age were considered special to the emperor or king of those provinces, and they were held in honor of the god *Xiuhteuctli*, *lord of the year*, with great display of food and sumptuous dances in which only the lords sang and danced, and for this reason it is called *song and dance of the lords.* Likewise only in the leap year was the solemn ceremony held of piercing the ears of girls and boys, and it was a right reserved only to the high priest, *achcautlitlenamacani*,[413] and the act was carried out with godfathers and godmothers.

412. "The sixth day before the calends of March." *Bisextus* meant intercalary.

413. *Achcauhtli*, senior priest; *tlenamacani*, present agentive of *tlenamactli*, the incense that was burned in honor of the gods. As usual, Boturini has joined an independent form with another word.

Third Age

§. XXI

1 So then, during the reign of *Yxtlilcuexahuac*[414] in Tula around the year 660 after the Incarnation of Christ, *Huematzin*, a noted Toltec astronomer, called a meeting of all the learned men, and with the pictorial documents they possessed and with the agreement of the monarch, that great book was painted which they called *Teoamoxtli*, that is, *Divine Book*, in which an account was given of the origin of the Indians with different figures of when their peoples were divided in the confusion of tongues, of their wanderings in Asia, of the first cities and towns that they had in America, of the founding of the empire of Tula, of their advances up to that time; of their monarchs, laws, and customs; of the systems of their ancient calendars; of the characters for the years and symbols for the months and days, of the signs and planets, cycles, and *senios*,[415] of the new moons; of transformations, which included moral philosophy; and, finally, of the mysteries of popular wisdom hidden among the hieroglyphs of the gods, with everything concerning religion, rites, and ceremonies, for which reason this book was called *Divine Book for the Greater Analogue*, and that is what the Indians call the Holy Bible, *Teoamoxtli*, in other words, *Divine History*, and in imitation of the said *Teoamoxtli*, each one of the historians kept in his home the particular pictorial document of items he would be noting in his times.

---

414. The name is also spelled *Ixtlilcuechahuac* or *Yxtlalcuexahuac* (Clavigero, *Historia*, 49, 50).

415. *Senios*, translation conjectured as "signs."

2 In the said year of 660, strictly speaking, the third age, or rather historic time, came upon our Indians, and thus it is made manifest that my literary labors, extending from the confusion of tongues, which was in the year 2497, which I calculated previously based on the opinion of the Septuagint, up until 660 of the Incarnation, which was 5859 [years] from the creation of the world, according to the aforesaid Septuagint, reckon the history at 3362 years, which not having been introduced by any other pen, is therefore mine alone, and with such pleasure and usefulness for the public that in vain will ignorance busy itself in discrediting it.

3 Although if someone curious about Indian antiquities should want to undertake the topic, not of the nations in general but of any other specific one, he will be able to determine its historic period from the moment that he finds a foundation for it equal to the Toltec.

4 I have a manuscript book of this history in the *Nahuatl* language, assembled with very beautiful figures, characters, and symbols, and another in the Castilian language, which I cited in section 16, number 12, and the task of working on the songs in order to make it more beautiful still lies before me.

The Chichimeca Indians

§. XXII

1 With the end of the Toltec empire due to various accidents of famine and war, the few remaining survivors resolved to abandon the land to see if by a change of climate they could also change their fortune. Some set out for *Quauhtemallan*,[416] others for *Campech*,[417] in search of less unfavorable lands, and only a few stopped in New Spain, enabling them to say that their settlements had flourished there in former times. At that time *Xolotl*, captain general of the settled Chichimeca nation (as distinguished from the nomadic[418] Chichimecas who nowadays live in the mountainous areas and make continuous raids against peaceful Indians and Spaniards and eat the human flesh of their enemies), for whom there was no room in the ancestral territory because of its large numbers, set out from the remote areas toward *Michoacan* and penetrated the lands of the Toltecs, which he found empty of people, and taking possession of them by means of his son *Nopaltzin*,[419] founded the most noble

---

416. A province against which the Mexican rulers often made war (Siméon). This apparently is modern Guatemala. The name may mean something like "land of the tree sap."

417. Modern Campeche?

418. Spaniards at that time made a distinction between living *bárbaramente* and *políticamente*. The former meant to live a nomadic life; the latter meant living in settled urban areas, with the laws and accoutrements of urban life and society.

419. "Revered Prickly Pear Cactus." King of Acolhuacan, son of Xolotl (Clavigero, *Historia*, 57–59).

Chichimeca empire, not only for his own lineage but also for that of many kings who came afterward to seek lands to settle in, and in a few years it happened that *Xolotl* would see his daughters married and the whole land divided, in which he and his successors dominated, in part as property owners, in part as monarchs who had supreme rule in it. Later this empire grew to such magnificence that more than sixty crowned kings attended the burial of *Texotlalatzin*,[420] not counting the lords, whose number was enormous. After his body was burned, his ashes were placed and buried in an emerald chest, covered with a sheet of gold. He had severe criminal laws that were administered irrevocably, and very human civil ones, all of them included in the number of eighty fundamental ones. In the beginning the court was in *Tenayuca*, and later it was transferred to *Tezcoco*, where in pagan times a famous university of all the sciences and humane letters flourished, and the lords of the land sent their sons in order to learn the most polished *Nahuatl* language, poetry, moral philosophy, pagan theology, astronomy, medicine, and history, as well as the style of courtly speech which they had to practice on the occasion of embassies and to treat with the court and the rest of the nobles, which are printed in the Indian language and which I have in my archive. And here, in addition to the imperial residence of such sublime and wise monarchs as *Nezahualcoyotl*, who composed sixty songs in praise of the creator of all things, who, he said, dwelt above the nine rows of heaven, mentioned in section 14, number 3, and *Nezahualpiltzintli*, his son, who was the celebrated poet, historian, and astronomer, there was the great council of the eighty judges, which I mentioned in section 15, number 3, and the criminal chamber that they called *teotlatolli*, that is, *tribunal of God*, of which I spoke in section 14, number 7. And in this tribunal the criminal trials depicted in pictorial documents and the law that the accused had broken were presented to the emperor, and the monarch pronounced sentence by making a line of death over the person of the delinquent. I have the complete material of this history both in pictorial documents as well as in manuscripts, and the Chichimeca monarchy lasted until the Spanish conquest.

---

420. Usually spelled Techotlalatzin, a major ruler of Tezcoco before it joined the Triple Alliance.

The Tepanec Indians

§. XXIII

1 The Tepanec kingdom, whose capital was *Atzcapotzalco*, was given by the emperor *Xolotl* as a fiefdom to King *Aculuhatl*, one of the upstarts who married [Xolotl's] elder daughter, of which marriage was born *Huehuetezozomoc*, who after the death of the legitimate emperor *Ixtlilxochitl Ometochtli*, tyrannized the Chichimeca empire, and his son *Maxtlaton* did the same, who following in his father's depraved footsteps, on various occasions sent assassins to take the life of *Nezahualcoyotl*, son of *Ixtlilxochitl*, to whom the kingdom lawfully belonged, but saving [his life] through events and very strange adventures, [Nezahualcoyotl] arranged his affairs so well that he eventually killed *Maxtlaton* and, having recovered the throne of his grandfathers, he destroyed the enemy city of *Atzcapotzalco*, which he ordered should be thereafter, as a sign of infamy, a slave market. However, since the kings of *Tlacopan*, though of Tepanec lineage, always abstained from involvement with the designs of the principal house of *Atzcapotzalco* or of committing treason against the empire, in this way they merited being favored by the other monarchs and adopted into the Triple Alliance of *Tezcoco*, *Mexico*, and *Tlacopan*, which in the final times represented the majesty and greatness of the empire. This royal house of *Tlacopan* lasted until the Spanish conquest, and even its descendants have the privilege from the Catholic Monarchs[421] of being buried with royal pomp. And I attended some honors for a lady of this royal lineage

421. Fernando and Isabel.

and saw all the ceremonies that were performed at the funeral. I have the history of this nation scattered among the manuscripts and pictorial documents of my archive.

The Mexican Indians

§. XXIV

1 It was during the reign of *Quinatzin* over the Chichimecas that another warlike and glory-seeking nation reached the lake of *Chapultepec*, which let it be known through its military efforts that within a brief time it would rule the others. It was divided between Mexicans and Tlatelolcans and other renowned nations that took their places in New Spain, although the Mexican was the one that displayed the most heroism and was the best of all, for when they had helped *Coxcox*, the king of *Culhuacan*, in his wars, that monarch wanted to know the measure of Mexican valor and asked his vassals how the newcomers had behaved during the war. They wanted to disparage them and answered that it was very badly and that as proof of this his majesty could ask the slaves that had been taken in combat. The king did not delay in ordering the Mexican captains to show the prisoners of war, and they took from inside their cloaks some small sacks full of ears that they had cut off from the same prisoners, not caring to bring the persons, deliberately leaving them for the *Culhuas*, and they showed them to the king, telling him that the slaves whom

his vassals had brought had previously been their prisoners, as he could see from the ears, and that if he wanted greater proof, he should order those to be counted who would be found to be without them [ears]. This the king did and having seen the reality of the matter, he so esteemed this brave nation that afterward he married his daughter and only heir to *Acamapich*,[422] first king of Mexico-Tenochtitlan, through which the succession to the kingdom of *Culhuacan* came to him.

2 So it was that with the passage of time [Acampich] gained so many advantages over his neighbors that he not only became related to the highest-born of the land but also by the valor of his arms conquered many more kingdoms, provinces, and dominions, and the greatness that Emperor *Moteuczoma Xocoyotl* had, in whose time the Spaniards arrived in North America, is well known.

3 I have a large number of pictorial documents and manuscripts for this history of the Mexicans and even for that of Culhuacan, which for great and undeniable reasons should be joined, because the said kingdom of Culhuacan was very ancient and was established on the remnants of the Toltecs and had a long series of kings whom our historians overlook.

4 At this point I would happily undertake the task of rescuing from the very many errors about this history that Samuel Purchas, an Englishman,[423] published in his work on the description of the world, and especially the explanation that was previously made in the *Nahuatl* language and later translated into Castilian, English, and French, of the eighty Indian pictorial documents that in the times immediately after the conquest the viceroy of New Spain sent to Emperor Charles V, and they fell into a foreign power (like my papers), passing from the hands of the heirs of Thevet[424] to those of Hakluyt,[425] at that time the

---

422. Usually given as *Acamapichtli.*

423. Samuel Purchas (1575/77–1626) was an English travel writer and Anglican clergyman. He published a series of travel works called *Purchas's Pilgrimages*, beginning in 1613. His works have been criticized for a lack of accuracy and a misuse of sources.

424. André de Thevet (1516–90) was a French Franciscan and travel writer, noted for a visit to and description of Brazil. He was the author of *Singularitez de la France Antarctique* (1557), of which his authorship has been disputed. His works were not always accurate.

425. Richard Hakluyt (1552/53–1616) promoted English settlement of North America. A clergyman, he was chaplain to Sir Edward Stafford, English ambassador

almsgiver to the English ambassador, who out of a desire to know what those strange figures contained, urged in the same direction by Walter Raleigh, ordered a translation by someone named Loke of the explanation of them from the Castilian language to the English, until Henry Speelman[426] obliged Purchas to copy the said pictorial documents into color plates, which I found in Your Majesty's library, *dans les Relacions de divers Voyages, Curieux qui n'ont point eté publié, ou qui ont eté traduit d'Hacluyt, de Purchas, & d'autres Voyageurs Anglois, Hollandois, Portugais, Alemands, Espaüols, Troisieme partie,*[427] printed at Paris by Sebastien *Mabre Cramoisy*[428] in the year 1666 with the title *Histoire de* [*sic*] *Mexicains*, and with its aforesaid explanation in French. And while it is true that the first twelve pictorial documents deal with the imperial city of *Mexico* and its monarchs from *Acamapixh*[429] to *Moteuczoma Xocoyotl*, with the years that each one of them reigned, of the provinces they conquered, and other memorable things, nevertheless they have no more authority than that of one particular author, and it is necessary to compare them with other annals of different authors that I have in my archive since, besides purging them of any slanted interpretation, it is necessary to pay attention to other historians, both in pictures and in manuscripts, and with the most solid rules of criticism, to establish the truth of each thing in itself, something that will have more space in the General History.

5 I also observe that Purchas's other pictorial documents from numbers 13 to 49 are taken from a schedule of tributes that the vassals of that land paid to their kings, of which I have the original in my archive, and what I can say for now is that the said pictorial documents [of Purchas] are missing many things that are found in the original, such

---

to the French court (served 1583–88). His best-known work was the *Voyages.* In 1587 he published an edition of Peter Martyr d'Anghiera's *Decadas.*

426. Henry Spelman (correct spelling) (c. 1562–1641), was an English antiquarian and collector of documents.

427. "In the accounts of diverse curious voyages which have not been published or which have been translated by Hakluyt, Purchas, and other English, Dutch, Portuguese, German, Spanish explorers, Part 3."

428. Sebastien Mabre Cramoisy (1585–1669) was a French printer and bookseller, best known for his religious publications.

429. Misspelling of Acamapichtli.

as the number of cities and towns that paid the aforementioned tributes, from which it is known that the Indian who copied it did not list it faithfully. As for what concerns those from numbers 9 to 63, it should be noted that they deal with various matters without following the thread of history, some of them pertaining to childrearing, others to wars, and others to different things, and the viceroy must have gathered them from various persons and ordered them translated for forwarding to his imperial majesty as something strange and as monuments of Indian history.

6 The incomparable Father Athanasius Kircher of the Sacred Company, who with such skill penetrated the Egyptian sciences and made its pyramids speak, when he saw in Purchas the said Indian pictorial documents with his explanation, and the rest of what the said author writes in his work on the description of the world, which Kircher considered trustworthy, he gave to the public in his hieroglyphic survey, *Oedpius Aegyptiacus*, volume 3, chapter 4, the first triadecaterida of the Toltec calendar, which begins with *Ce Tecpatl*, and he erred in his explanation of the characters for the years from top to bottom; and he also explains the symbols for the months and days, which it is necessary to correct, and on page 32, he brings forth the first of Purchas's pictorial documents; on 33, the second; on 34, document 49, explaining them in the same way as Purchas. For that reason I am not bothered that in the place cited he should write that the Indian paintings are unpolished and of rough artifice, devoid of any hieroglyphic and scientific secrets, because all those of Purchas do not contain anything that would make his case, and because they belong to the third age they deal with historic matters that are plain and common. On the contrary, those of the first and second age, and even some from the third, comprise the most noble secrets of popular wisdom and symbolic science, and the exalted matters of pagan theology, from whose treasures I have given enough brush strokes in this, my *Idea of a History*, reserving to myself to enliven them with more brilliant colors in the General History.

The Teochichimeca Indians

§. XXV

1 With the Mexican nation came the Teochichimeca also, and after it had passed through the edges of the hills of *Tezcoco*, it was to take its seat in *Texcallan*; it fortified the neighboring *Texcalticpac* mountain, and had an aristocratic government, its territory divided into four principal parts that even today are called *Ocoteluico*, *Tepetlicpac*,[430] *Quiahuiztlan*, and *Tizatlan*. This is that unconquered Tlaxcalan republic whose fame will always remain immortal because it shared so much in the conquest of *Mexico* and did so much to spread the gospel throughout all that widespread region. The exploits that it carried out in the time of its paganism, and more in the conquest, deserve to be written with letters of gold. They are narrated in its copious history, which I have in pictorial documents and manuscripts.

430. Again, Boturini does not use the combining form.

Conquest

by the Spaniards

§. XXVI

1 Knowing the solid foundations of the pagan history of the said empire, the glorious conquest commences and takes place, which the Spaniards achieved under the command of the celebrated don Fernando Cortés, who can never be praised enough; and although many Europeans have written [the history of the conquest] despite their having been unaware of most of the said pagan history, they have not been able to adorn it with the requirements that it needs, and even in the individual descriptions of places and other circumstances, it is notably lacking, because it is not humanly possible to write in full detail any histories without having examined the contemporary materials from the same land where the events occurred, and because the historians were at no less a distance than from one world to another. I have that which don Domingo de San Antón Muñón *Chimalpahin*, an Indian noble, wrote in a manuscript volume in folio, and the other of don Fernando de Alva *Ixtlilxochitl.* In addition many manuscript fragments in both the Indian and Castilian languages, with many other pictorial documents that depict it according to the topic of each matter and time. Also a pictorial document on cotton cloth, as large as a sheet, on which are depicted in different quarters the general conquest, the four parts of the territory of Tlaxcala, the Spanish governors who there were in the same city and province of *Tlaxcala* up to the time in which the historian lived, the arms of the Catholic monarchs and below them those of the said city, and what captivates me the most, the blessed image of Our Lady and Patroness of Guadalupe with the background of her first chapel of ease.[431] This ancient work of art will have a worthy place in the histories both of Guadalupe and the conquest, and I will explain it with the greatest care because it is important and because the malevolent and envious continually accuse Spanish historians of being prejudiced, and they seek at every step to tarnish the glorious deeds of the conquest. I will be able to shut their mouths with the Indian authors themselves who, despite having been the aggrieved ones, admit sincerely everything that happened in it.

Observations

on What Has Been Said

§. XXVII

1 Previously I said, in section II, number 3, that the ritual calendar was completed in this third age, in which, after the nations had been intermingled through the ambition of some to dominate the others, and the rites and ceremonies having been multiplied on this occasion, it was necessary that the number of gods be increased. In addition there were certain other deities in this age fabricated for the purpose by command of the sovereigns and confirmed by the foolish consent of the common people, which were likewise inserted into the catalog of moveable feasts in the said calendar. One of these was the wife of a certain monarch of the *Culhuas*, whose husband commanded she be worshipped as a goddess because she died in childbirth,

431. *Ermita*, chapel of ease, a shrine or chapel without a resident pastor or parish status.

and in imitation of her, the people deified all the rest who died because of the complications of childbirth, calling them *Cihuapipiltin*[432] and considering them as intercessors that they might safeguard pregnant women, and the third moveable feast was dedicated to them. In the same way, one of the said monarchs, having become drunk in public, to gild over the disgrace of the drunkenness, instituted a feast day which was the fourth mobile one, in honor of the gods of wine, with a special devotion to the drunken god *Yzquitecatl*,[433] who supposedly was the one who invented the method of extracting the juice from the *magueyes*, which was converted into wine, and on the said day a general permission was given to everyone to be able to get drunk.

2 I also pointed out in section 20, number 2, that the Toltec sages, beginning in the second age, put the leap year in order by adjusting the civil year with the vernal equinox, and that in the third age there was another method for the intercalary days with regard to the ritual calendar. And so it was that in order not to disturb the perpetual order of the fixed feasts and of the sixteen moveable feasts that rotated in the symbols of the days of the year, on the occasion that the symbol of the last month of the leap year was counted twice, in which they must have detected some absurdity and the anger of the gods on the issue of rites and ceremonies (since I have read that in the ancient times of the kingdom of *Culhuacan*, when the moveable feast of *Huitzilopochtli* had overlapped with the fixed feast of *Tezcatlipoca* [shown on] the table, they preferred the moveable one to the fixed one, without caring that once the first one was finished, the second would immediately be celebrated, for which reason, they say, the god *Tezcatlipoca* was angry with the Culhuas to such an extent that, unable to hide his anger, he made known to them how the kingdom of *Culhuacan* would be lost in later times, in which the rites of their former gods would come to an end and they would be subject to those of a single God, neither seen nor known, and under the command of some remote foreigners, whose existence having been known by the Mexican emperors, by public edict ordered that when a moveable feast, whose quality might be preferred to the fixed one, when the solemnity of the first one was

---

432. "Noblewomen."

433. It may be translated as "He of the toasted maize" (Durán, *History*, 23n1).

finished, immediately on the following day they were to assist at the transferred one), they thought it best to avoid all these difficulties and confusion by reserving the thirteen leap days for the end of the cycle of fifty-two years, which they distinguished in the wheels or tables with thirteen zeros in cerulean blue or another color, and they did not belong to any month or year nor did they have their own symbols like the other days. [The intercalary days] were passed over as if there were no such days, nor were they applied to any of their gods because they considered them to be bad luck. All of this *triadecaterida* was given over to penance and fasting out of fear that the world would come to an end; nothing hot was eaten because fires were extinguished throughout the land until the next cycle began, which brought with it the aforementioned *New Fire.* And being that all the aforesaid concerned only the rites and sacrifices, then this method of intercalary days could not be extended to the tropical years, because that would have notably changed the solstices and equinoxes and the start of the years; and the proof is evident, because these thirteen days did not have any symbols of those that belonged to the days of the year, and the ritual calendar considered them to be leap days at the decline of each cycle, imitating with a different order the leap day of the civil year, more proper to the government of public affairs.

3 I also called this, my work, *Idea of a General History*, not because it supplies at the present time all the information about the nations that there were in New Spain, but because it supplies the majority of them, dealing with the Olmec, and Xicanlanca, Toltec, Chichimeca, Tepanec, Mexican, and Teochichimeca, who were the most principal nations, although there were in addition to the republic of *Tlaxcala* another two, that is, the *Matlaltzinca Huejotzinco*, and the kingdom of *Michoacan*, and some other provinces that were not subject to the kingdom and were governed by their own independent laws. I even have a great deal of information on all these in the monuments in my archive, and at the same time that I write about these nations, I will make an effort to gather the material about the others that I lack, in order to leave the history entirely complete.

4 Nor is the ecclesiastical history after the conquest of lesser importance, such as the spread of the Holy Gospel throughout that New World, in which the Catholic Monarchs worked wonders, and Your Majesty does every day by aiding from your royal treasury so many apostolic men who go to raise the Most Holy Cross in the most remote parts and distribute the bread of the angels to so many hungry peoples buried in the horrible night of idolatry. In the valuable *Historical Museum* that I have put together are found, both in pictures and manuscripts, ancient monuments of the preaching of the gospel by the glorious apostle Saint Thomas, whom the Indians called *Quetzalcohuatl*, which means *serpent clothed in rich feathers*.[434] The original standard under which Mexico was won, which has on one side a very beautiful image of the Immaculate Conception, adorned with stars and with a gold crown, with her hands together, with some resemblance to that which appeared later as Guadalupe, and on the other Your Majesty's arms, also with a gold crown because the Virgin's crown is the most firm basis for Your Majesty's crown. There are many pictorial documents that depict the first apostolic men who planted the faith; the history that I discovered of Our Lady of the Hill of *Cholula*; some traces of the apparition of Our Lady of *Ocotlan* in *Tlaxcala*; various papers and proofs of the apparition of the glorious Archangel Saint Michael (which today is called del Milagro) to Diego Lázaro, a Tlaxcalan Indian leader, his will and baptismal record; the published history of the three Tlaxcalan boys Juanico, Cristobalico, and Antoñico, who, because they reproached their fathers for the idolatries that they secretly practiced, suffered martyrdom while preaching to them in their torments the great benefit that God had granted them in sending them the Holy Law, and the constancy with which they should follow it. There is a great deal of material about the appearances of my Mother and Lady of Guadalupe. The original will of a relative of the blessed Juan Diego on *metl* paper and in the Indian language in which the said appearances are mentioned in these words: *Sapa omonextitzino itlazocihuapilli Santa Maria, inoque cayotilique in itlazoteopixque Guadalope*, that is, *On Saturday the very beloved Lady Saint Mary appeared, and news of it was given of it to the dear pastor of Guadalupe*, and one reads of a bequest of three plots of land, which the said relative and native ruler left to the most holy lady, with the expression *To axcatzin*,

434. A more common translation is "plumed serpent." Was Boturini one of the first to claim that Christianity had first been brought to New Spain by the Apostle Thomas? In the early nineteenth century this idea was popularized by fray Servando Teresa de Mier, who had been influenced by a lawyer named Ignacio Borunda. See Poole, *Guadalupan Controversies*, 16–18.

which means, *that the virgin belongs to us Indians*;[435] and with good reason, because the miraculous hand of the Most High painted it on Juan Diego's tilma,[436] although it was necessary to unfold it, with the base material of the cloak giving way to the precious nature of the picture.[437] There is also found an account of the purity and chastity in which Juan Diego lived during his marriage with María Lucía, who *omomiquili in Ychpochtli*, meaning *she died* a virgin, and *relativorum eadem est ratio*,[438] and the same is proven from the history of the said apparitions printed in the Indian language.[439] I have the original portrait, of exquisite artistry, of Juan Diego himself, on his knees at the side of the well of Guadalupe, and looking at the peak of Tepeyecac hill,[440] where the Great Lady appeared to him; many instruments that prove how the handing over of the miraculous *ayatl*,[441] in other words, the blessed image of Guadalupe, took place in the archbishop's home, which still exists today, to the first archbishop, don fray Juan de Zumárraga.[442] There are many precious memories of when the most holy image was brought to Mexico [City] and saved the said imperial city from the great flood of the years 1629 and 1630, whose rewards, both ecclesiastical and secular, are fully justified in the acts that are pending before Your Majesty in this, your Council of the Indies, and from them it is clear that my archive contains a thousand things for the service of God, of my mother, the Virgin of Guadalupe, and Your Majesty, and finally the history itself of the Divine Lady, which I began to write in the Latin language, who will always be the object of my desires and my love.[443]

---

435. Boturini is the only source for this information. This will is now presumed lost. On this and the other wills of Cuauhtitlan, see Poole, *Our Lady of Guadalupe*, 195–96.

436. From the Nahuatl *tilmahtli*, "cloak."

437. This is not clear. Boturini seems to be implying that the tilma was somehow changed. It is possible that he was referring to some early retouchings of the picture.

438. An axiom of scholastic philosophy which says that the same idea or meaning applies to related matters.

439. This may be a reference to Laso de la Vega's *Huei tlamahuiçoltica* (1649).

440. Usually given in the shorter form *Tepeyac*, meaning "on the nose of the hill."

441. Another word for cloak.

442. Actually, he was only a bishop-elect in 1531.

443. Seemingly, this work was never finished or published.

The Usefulness

That This Work Can Produce

§. Final

1 First of all, it will conclude the explanation of the common wisdom about the lineages of the first age, which until the present day has been concealed between divine hieroglyphs and obscure legends, and it will show the beginnings of the natural law of the ancestors, which they derived from a sense common to all of them, not fully noted during that time, pondered later, but always linked to religion and human needs.

2 There will be an extensive treatment of the heroism of the Indian peoples and the strength of those under their protection.[444] The aristocratic government of the said heroes will be seen, and the makeup of the natural heroic law of the second age.

3 Likewise, the beginnings of the sciences, of which Divine Providence was the architect and human understanding the artisan, will be explained in a more lively fashion. In its transformations philosophers will understand the morality of these times, in its songs poets will drink the nectar from the Indian Parnassus, and in its symbols philologists will find the languages and the stuff of heroism.

4 The much-disputed origin of these Indians will be clarified with the greatest care in order to remove from future writers the pain of complicating their understanding so much.

5 A clear and individual account will be given of the places through which these nations traveled to the continent of New Spain.

444. *Clientelas*, meaning unclear.

6 There will be speculation about the ways in which these nations were obliged by Providence to join together in families, sustain themselves in cities, spread through provinces and kingdoms, and defend themselves, not only with their own strength but also with those of their neighbors by means of alliances, inviolably keeping their human faith, bound together by the powerful bonds of religion and law.

7 Furthermore, a general history of the empire, kingdoms, and republics that were founded in North America will be woven together, not abridged but complete, and will proceed in the greatest possible coordination joined with and expanded with sacred history.

8 And since the new historian is more attracted to the wheat than to the chaff, he will set his *meticulous* attention to searching out the civil law of each nation and illustrating it with their respective histories and customs, in order, after having examined it in its parts, to reduce it to a whole, as I make clear in a separate volume, in which the interpretation that each nation gave to the natural law of human peoples is specified, which is a matter particular to the third age, in which, after people had mastered the languages that previously were in the power of the ancestors and heroes alone, cloaked in the darkness of divine hieroglyphs and heroic symbols, and because the multitude wanted to be governed with justice, it craved monarchical government more than any other, and that intelligible, truly human laws be promulgated, not created with blows of the infinitely outsized hammer of heroism, but tempered with a natural equity, which is what Ulpian[445] wanted to make clear, in book 1, section *Jus gentium, ff. de Just*[*itia*] *&* *jur*[*e*], ibid.: *Jus gentium est quo gentes humanæ utuntur*;[446] and Emperor Justinian[447] in section *Jus, autem, Instit*[*uta*] *tit*[*ulo*] *de Jure natur*[*ali*] *gen*[*tium*] *&* *civil*[*i*], ibid.: *Jus gentium omni humano generi commune est* (he is speaking of this third age). *Nam usu exigente & humanis necessitatibus gentes humanæ jura quædam sibi constituerunt.*[448]

---

445. Gnaeus Domitius Annius Ulpianus (c. AD 170–AD 223), anglicized as Ulpian, was a Roman jurist and commentator on the law.

446. "The law of peoples is that which human peoples use."

447. Justinian I (AD 483–AD 565) was the Eastern Roman Emperor who sponsored the codification of Roman law, the *Corpus Juris Civilis,* also known as Justinian's Code. The *Instituta* were the textbook for the code.

448. "The law of peoples is common to the entire human race. . . . For by the demands of usage and human needs, human peoples have established laws for themselves."

9 The four calendars mentioned above will be explained, and that of the natural year will be useful for farmers who can be guided (if they wish) by the Indian system in the cultivation of their properties, since the Indians were great observers of the celestial bodies; and speaking of the Toltecs, it is known that more than a century before the birth of Christ they had adjusted the civil year to the vernal equinox, and that the said calendar remained so arranged in the second age.

10 No less useful are the notices of the chronological calendar, because no one can write Indian history with due exactitude without possessing the key to the labyrinth of their characters and symbols, and I have observed that some historians either do not point out the years reduced to the European count, or if they do reduce them, they skip over some five hundred and eight hundred years before or after the event that occurred.

11 With regard to the astronomical calendar, I know that the teachers of this science will not disdain the knowledge of the Indian systems, their signs and planets, and the new moons, with everything that leads us to this material [being] subtle and ingenious, and of seeing the wheels and tables of the Indian cycles appearing in print with what little explanation my limited understanding may achieve, which they could expand on at their pleasure.

12 As for the ritual calendar, I shall be brief because its principal purpose was the individual devotion to the gods, which the Divine Majesty wanted to banish into perpetual oblivion.

13 The roots and figures of speech of the *Nahuatl* language must also be discussed, which, in my opinion, surpass Latin in beauty.

14 There will be an opportunity to contemplate the internal and external justice of the wars that one nation waged against another, on which occasion military law anticipated sending ambassadors three times before starting the war; the first were dispatched to the king or ruler to warn him that he fulfill what was asked of him within a certain time limit, based on some reasons or another; the second [ambassadors] addressed themselves to the nobility, warning them to persuade the king or ruler not to resort to force; the third convoked the people and gave them an account of the motives that their monarchs had for waging war against them; and so great was the eloquence with which they praised the benefits of peace and the evils of war, and one time or another they made such a strong impression, that it resulted in a treaty or agreement. But if the king, the nobility, and the people resisted unanimously by going to war and they were defeated, as if they had contracted a kind of obligation *Nexus mancipique*, graven in the Laws of the Twelve Tables, law 5, table 7, thus the kings and lords lost the supreme rule that they had in their lands; and vassals, like the nobles, the best rule; and the common people the *bonitario*[449] that they had in their lands; and prisoners of war, *ex quasi delicto*,[450] were sentenced to death and to being sacrificed by the conqueror; and for this reason the Romans called their sacrificed or about to be sacrificed enemies *hostes, quasi hostias, victos quasi victimas*, in punishment *victima simul ac pœna*,[451] and from this the increasing sacrifices of prisoners of war spread among the Indians, because they considered them to be consecrated beforehand to the gods. And famous captains, when they were going to be sacrificed, would be tied at the waist with a cord and placed standing on a round rock that had a hole in the center, they would allow them to fight once again and would give them shortened weapons, as I have in my pictures, and attacked by other valiant captains of the victorious nation with long spears and other advantageous weapons, it would happen that they would not only defend themselves but they would also kill some of them until, exhausted now by the long combat, the servant who was below the stone would pull on the cord and hold the prisoners down, for whom the priest in the temple, in the blink of an eye, would begin and end the sad performance, opening their breasts with a very sharp flint knife and, removing the heart, would finish the sacrificial ceremonies, to which the prisoners would consent so willingly that there is no known instance that any of them would have wished for their liberty, perhaps relying on that heroic virtue of paganism, *Dulce est pro patria mori*,[452] which must have come from the second age when the common people and dependents did nothing more than imitate their heroes. And since there were

449. Meaning uncertain.

450. "As if for a crime."

451. "Enemies, at the same time offerings, conquered as if victims. . . . victim as the same time as penalty."

452. "It is a sweet thing to die for one's country." The full form is *Dulce et decorum est pro patria mori*, "It is a sweet and pleasant thing to die for one's country" (Horace, *Odes* 3, 2, verse 13).

among the Romans *curcios*[453] who in the midst of peace threw themselves into fire, and Decians who in a war of two on two immolated themselves for the well-being of their country, so it is said of our Indians in general that they not only fought for [their country] and to preserve their rites and ceremonies, which is per se war *pro aris & socis*,[454] but they also wanted to die for it and for their gods, not to mention the rites of their conquerors, something that was a form of pagan heroism, which the Greeks also practiced, and we have the famous example of that Spartan matron, who while arming her son with his shield, told him, *Aut cum hoc, aut in hoc.*[455]

15 Nor is there any lack of the famous rights of asylum, which some nations practiced with others whenever the weak ones resorted to imploring the strong ones. The republic of *Tlaxcala* was very notable for this, which like a mother in common gave shelter to all the unfortunate, distributing lands within its borders in order that they might defend with their own means the freedom of the senate.

16 It should also be noted of the qualities of Indian nobility that they are altered and elevated with the distinction of various hierarchies, wrongly confused with the word *caciques.*[456]

17 The ancient origin of the domains from the second age will be seen, and continuing into the third. It was said that *Xolotl*, the supreme monarch of the Chichimecas, when he distributed the lands of New Spain to his own people and foreigners, gave them with special feudal conditions to observe, not only total fidelity to the empire, but also to aid with their persons, goods, and vassals whenever someone would rebel against him.

18 It is of no little importance to know how to distinguish the quality of the properties and goods of the Indians, of their entailed estates and *alodia*,[457] for some of these derived from their right of ancient occupation, others from the distribution that families, towns, cities, and

---

453. Word of uncertain meaning.

454. "For altars and hearths."

455. "[Return] either with it or on it."

456. A Caribbean word adopted by the Spanish with the meaning of "chieftain" or "leader."

457. *Alodium*, a possession not held by tenure of a superior lord, free of every burden or seigneurial right.

provinces made among themselves; others were conquered in war, and this land was called *yaotlalli*, that is, *conquered by force of arms*,[458] and they bring with them a different nature and privilege. Others were attached to the palace of kings and lords, which land was called *tecpantlalli*,[459] and it contributed to them many fruits and personal service, and many nobles nowadays hold these lands and tributaries which they cannot alienate, and once the lineages of these feudataries end, they revert to the lord's palace, who can dispose of them as a returned feudal land. Other [properties and goods] belonged to the common lands of the towns, but burdened with tribute, and they were usually distributed among the citizens, and this land they call *altepetlalli, the town's land*, and tribute land, to which all the citizens have a right and are registered in order to be able to cultivate and pay the tributes to Your Majesty, and these Indians can be considered similar to the *Glebæ addictos, adscriptitios* and *censitos* of the Roman people, whom the title of the Code deals with in *de agricolis & censitis.*[460]

19 Of even greater importance will be interpreting the numbers in the measurements of lands and geographical pictorial documents of the Indians, which at every step in their claims and lawsuits they present in Your Majesty's tribunals as authentic titles, and it is the task of the interpreters to explain them, who, because of their profound ignorance have given and give such foolish reports by which they have sadly confused matters, because on a genuine understanding of the said pictorial documents, many acts of possession and property and frequent verdicts depend, *Familiæ erciscundæ, Communi dividundo, & finium regundorum* in the Digest.[461]

20 Last, the unknown will become known, and since I have worked on this matter for about nine years, I flatter myself that Your Majesty will be pleased in a most merciful way to look favorably on so many sleepless nights, so many journeys, so many costs spent in bringing together a prodigious archive of such notable monuments and to recreate,

458. More literally, "enemy land."

459. Literally, "palace lands."

460. I have been unable to locate the meanings and sources of these legal citations. In medieval Latin, *glebae ascriptus* meant a serf attached to the land.

461. The Latin is archaic. The Digest was part of Justinian's Code that contained a summary of what began as legal opinions but came to have the force of law.

with sovereign favor, my long literary tasks, directed to the glory of your imperial crown and the public benefit of Your Majesty's vassals in that New World, having proven that this Idea of a History is *new* in regard to material recently discovered, *new* in the method and its interpretation, *new* in its duration, and *new* in its usefulness, which I have just described.

Laudamus veteres, sed nostris utimur annis.[462]

Ovid, *Fasti, book* 1, verse 225

462. "We praise past times but make use of the present."

CATALOG
OF
THE HISTORIC INDIAN MUSEUM
OF
THE KNIGHT LORENZO BOTURINI BENADUCI, LORD OF LA TORRE AND HONO

who arrived in New Spain in February of the year 1736 and through persistent investigations and immense expenses from his purse, gathered the following literary treasures in different provinces. It is cataloged and divided according to the various affairs of the nations and ancient kingdoms of the Indians and may serve to organize and write the General History of that New World based on the indisputable records of the Indians themselves.

If, during the time of my long stay in the Indies, I always considered my home and historic museum to be open to the public, taking enormous pleasure in the fact that the most distinguished persons in the sciences would frequent it, how much greater will be the satisfaction that today is granted me on the occasion, after writing the preceding Idea, that this Catalog has arrived, to present to the Republic of Letters the new, abundant additions to the history of the Indian nations, in which are found the numerous scientific treasures hidden behind the images of innumerable figures, ciphers, characters, symbols, and hieroglyphs, and the outline for a General History that not only justifies with ample fundamentals what I have dealt with in the Idea of a History, but that also promises a great work that may be written in various volumes, adorned with reproductions of the most precious historical sources, as long as the unconquered and most benign Catholic Monarch may condescend to protect and help my loyal efforts with his sovereign protection.

I will not tire you by recounting the immense labors and expenses that these inestimable trophies of Indian antiquity have cost me. I will only point out emphatically that since the Indians of that vast region had and do have other documents, I had to cover extensive lands, seeking out and inquiring. And although, with evident steadfastness, I never took my hand off the investigations I had undertaken, nevertheless two years passed without my being able to obtain even one pictorial document or see the cover of a manuscript, since it happened to me quite often that I traveled from some places to others for five and six months continuously and returned to the capital city without any gains whatever, until with heaven's favor the way was opened to me, and I not only obtained what is listed in the said catalog but I also learned that much other material could still be hoped for.

Panormitanus, book 4, On the Deeds of Alphonse[2]

This is the only property that I have in the Indies, and so valuable that it will not be exchanged for gold and silver, for diamonds and pearls, and the lord don Alfonso, king of Aragon and Sicily, used to say, *Malle se gemmas, uniones, margaritas suas, quæ quidem essent in toto orbe celeberrima, & preciosissimæ, quam libras qualescumque perditum iri.*[1]

1. "He preferred to lose his gems, natural pearls, and large pearls, which indeed were most famous and precious in the entire world, than any one of his books."

2. Nicolò de'Tudeschi "Panormitanus" (1386–1445) was an Italian Benedictine canonist. Panormitanus is the Latin name for the city of Palermo, Sicily.

INDEX

OF THE SECTIONS IN THIS CATALOG

Toltec History	§. I. Pictorial documents
	§. II. Manuscripts
Chichimeca History	§. III. Pictorial documents
	§. IV. Manuscripts
	§. V. Separate items
Tepanec History	§. VI
Mexican History	§. VII. Pictorial documents
	§. VIII. Manuscripts by Indian authors
	§. IX. Separate items
	§. X. Manuscripts by Spanish authors
Tlatelolco History	§. XI. Pictorial documents
	§. XII. Separate manuscripts
Various Histories	§. XIII
History of Michoacan	§. XIV
Matlaltzinca History	§. XV
History of Huejotzinco	§. XVI
History of Tlaxcala	§. XVII. Pictorial documents
	§. XVIII. Manuscripts by Indian authors
	§. XIX. Separate items
Various Other Historical Sources	§. XX
Pictorial Documents of Tribute	§. XXI
Manuscripts of Tribute	§. XXII

Rare Books	§. XXIII
Learned Manuscripts	§. XXIV
Christian Doctrine in Figures and Ciphers	§. XXV
Books Printed in Nahuatl	§. XXVI
Indian Calendars	
Natural Year	§. XXVII
Chronological Year	§. XXVIII
Astronomical Year	§. XXIX
Ritual Year	§. XXX
History of the Conquest	§. XXXI. Pictorial documents
	§. XXXII. Manuscripts
Ecclesiastical History	§. XXXIII
History of Guadalupe	§. XXXIV. Printed books
	§. XXXV. Manuscripts
	§. XXXVI. Public instruments and other records
Observations	§. Final

INTERROGA GENERATIONEM PRISTINAM, ET DILIGENTER INVESTIGA PATRUM MEMORIAM

Job 8:8[3]

3. "Ask the former generation and learn carefully from the fathers' memory."

Toltec History

Pictorial Documents

§. I

Volume 1 in folio. Originals.

1 Some painted annals and manuscripts in the *Nahuatl* language, fifty leaves and on European paper, embellished with different figures that represent the deeds, wanderings, battles, and lords of this nation, with their characters of the years and symbols of the days on which such things took place. They deal with the coming of the Toltecs to the famous city of *Tula*, which was later the capital of their empire, and they continue until twenty-six years after the Spanish conquest. At the beginning of the said annals there is a pictorial document painted on European paper and bound in Indian [paper]. The author of this history is an anonymous Indian.

Manuscripts

§. II

Volume 2 in folio. Copy.

1 Some historical accounts of the same nation on European folios, which I copied with my own hand on thirteen leaves from their original, their author being don Fernando de Alva *Ixtlilxochitl*, one of the *tlatoques*[4] descended from the Chichimeca emperors of *Tezcoco*. The said accounts were written around the year 1600 and were taken by the said author from the ancient original pictorial that he had in his possession, and as is clear from his testimony, although with all the investigations I did, I was not able to find it.[5]

---

4. Doubled plural of *tlatoani*, ruler.

5. Ixtlilxochitl, a descendant of Nezahualpilli, the last king of Texcoco, was a mestizo, probably born about 1570. This entry may refer to his *Relación de la nación tulteca*, written between 1600 and 1608. See Alva Ixtlilxochitl, *Obras históricas*, ed. Chavero, and Poole, *Our Lady of Guadalupe*, 85–87.

2 Fragments of the same history are also found in other accounts that the said author made for one of the viceroys of New Spain and in his summary account of the Chichimeca kings, which will be mentioned later.

Chichimeca History

Pictorial Documents

§. III

Original. *1* A pictorial document of exquisite quality on Indian paper, rather large-sized, with figures and characters, giving the history of the beginnings of the Chichimeca empire from *Xolotl* to *Nezahualcoyotl*, after he recovered the empire from the power of the tyrant *Maxtlaton.* It has six leaves and ten pages with writing, entirely painted, the first two of which have some lines inserted in the *Nahuatl* language, almost erased with age. The aforementioned don Fernando *Ixtlilxochitl*[6] had this pictorial document in his library, and he used it to write the history of the same empire, as is evident from his testimony.[7]

Original. *2* Another pictorial document on Indian paper, bound like a book in quarto of twenty-five leaves. It begins with the image of the Emperor *Xolotl* and other figures of lords and characters for places, dealing explicitly with the province of *Tepotzotlan*, its first foundations, and churches in Christian times, and it is accompanied by a number of other pages in the *Nahuatl* language, which narrate the same thing.

Original. *3* Another pictorial document on a cured skin on which is depicted the descendants and different relationships of the Chichimeca emperors, from *Tlotzin* to the last king don Fernando Cortés *Ixtlilxochitzin.* It has various interstitial lines in the *Nahuatl* language.

---

6. Ixtlilxochitl, a descendant of Nezahualpilli, the last king of Texcoco, was a mestizo, probably born about 1570. This entry may refer to his *Relación de la nación tulteca*, written between 1600 and 1608. See Alva Ixtlilxochitl, *Obras históricas*, ed. Chavero and Poole, *Our Lady of Guadalupe*, 85–87.

7. This probably refers to his *Historia chichimeca.*

Original, and in addition I had a copy made.

4 Another large pictorial document on Indian paper, extended like a long strip. It divides the figures above and below with the characters of the years, which run through the middle. It represents the succession of the various Chichimeca and Mexican lords and what happened to the two monarchies. From what can be seen, their history begins from the year *3 Flints* and ends in that of *7 Rabbits*,[8] although something is missing at the beginning and the end.

Original.

5 Another pictorial document on Indian paper that has various figures and some numerical ciphers and some lines in the *Nahuatl* language. It deals with the affairs of the Emperor *Nezahualpiltzintli* and his sons. It is longer than a sheet of *papel de marca.*[9]

Original.

6 Another pictorial document on European paper, shaped in the figure of a wheel which deals with the descendants of the Emperor *Nezahualcoyotl.*

Original.

7 Another pictorial document on a quarto sheet of Indian paper on which is seen painted the city of *Tezcoco*, with some ciphers that specify its extent in ancient times.

Original.

8 Another pictorial document on Indian paper which depicts the lake of the said city and its boundary lands that belonged to the estate of doña Isabel *Ixtlilxochitzin.* It has their measurements in ciphers.

Original.

9 Another pictorial document on Indian paper concerning the lawsuit over lands in the jurisdiction of *Tezcoco*, with a verdict at the bottom in the *Nahuatl* language given by a judge of the natives[10] of the said city in the year 1565. It can be of use to the history.

Original.

10 Another pictorial document on European paper of the town of San Lorenzo *Axtopan* and a memorial of the Indians of the ancient San Luis *Huejutla*, poorly painted, and bound in old [papal] bulls.

Original.

11 Another pictorial document of the lands of the towns of *Tepoztlan*, *Panhuacan*, *Ayapanco*, and *Tlanahuac*, in which is made known the method that the ancients had for distinguishing their measurements.

---

8. Ordinarily this would be 3 Flint and 7 Rabbit.

9. Paper that is ordinarily the size of stamped paper, i.e., carries the seal of the nation.

10. This may refer to the Juzgado General de los Indios, the legal system established for the natives by the Spanish Crown toward the end of the sixteenth century.

Original in folio. 12 A book on European paper that must have been about fifty-six leaves and today is missing the first; in it are registered the families and lands of the towns of *Calcantloxiuco*, *Tepotitlan*, *Patlachiuca*, and *Texcalticpac*, with their ciphers of measurements. This book is signed by someone named Vergara.

Manuscripts

§. IV

Copy in folios. 1 A manuscript, its title: *History of the Chichimeca Lords*, in the very hand, which I know, of don Fernando de Alva *Ixtlilxochitl*, and which I copied by hand so as to return the original to its owner. It deals with the affairs of this empire and the ordinances that the great *Nezahualcoyotl* enacted, and it recounts something of the coming of the Spaniards. It is found in volume 2.

Original in folios. 2 Another manuscript on European papers, its title: *Historical Accounts*, which the same author composed for one of the viceroys of New Spain, and they give very full news of Toltec, Chichimeca, and Mexican history. I had the original copied, and it is found in the said volume 2.

Copy in folio. 3 Another manuscript on European paper by the same author, its title: *Summary Account of the Chichimeca Kings.* It deals with them in particular, although it says something about the first Olmec and Xicalanco settlers, about the Toltecs and Mexicans. It was copied from another, not in the author's hand, and is found in the aforementioned volume 2.

Volume 3 in folio. Copy. 4 Another manuscript on European paper by the same author, its title: *General History of New Spain.* It has seventy-six chapters and is not complete. It is a copy.

Copy in folio. 5 Another manuscript by the same author, it is titled: *Historical Compendium of the Kingdom of Tezcoco.* It was copied from another copy on European paper and is found in the said volume 3, and don Carlos de Sigüenza y Góngora recognized it as being by the same author.

Separate Items

§. V

Copy in quarto, no. 1

Another manuscript on European paper that deals with the great many children that the Emperor *Nezahualpizintli* had. It is in the *Nahuatl* language and at the beginning has three figures of kings and at the end another of a prince and twenty leaves with writing without any author's name.

Original in quarto, no. 2.

Another manuscript of twelve leaves with writing on European paper. It contains two songs by Emperor *Nezahualcoyotl*, translated into Castilian from the *Nahuatl* language, rendered into poetry by don Fernando de Alva, from whom I think that there is also a piece on the life history of the aforementioned *Nezahualcoyotl.*

Originals in folio, no. 3.

A bundle of letters written by the counts of Benavente and don Luis de Velasco, viceroy of New Spain, to don Fernando Pimentel, lord of *Tezcoco*,[11] and his response to the said counts with a letter of the bachelor don Antonio de Tovar, [Diego] Cano, *Moteucçoma*, *Ixtlilxochitl*, in which are cited ancient pictorial documents of the descendants of the kings of *Tezcoco.*

Copy in folio.

A fragment on European paper of the lords of *Tezcoco* after Christianization, written on December 13, 1564, in the *Nahuatl* language by don Juan de San Antonio.[12] It is found in volume 4, below.

Copy in folio.

Five bundles and a quarter-sheet of fragments on European paper and in the *Nahuatl* language by unknown authors.

---

11. It is not clear who these people are. The title Count of Benavente was held by numerous members of that family. Luis de Velasco was viceroy of Mexico, 1550–64, and his son, 1590–95.

12. This is in Nahuatl and in English translation in the *Codex Chimalpahin*, 2:207–39.

Tepanec History

§. VI

Cloth, no. 1. *1* I have a lienzo that I had copied from the original pictures which today are on the walls of the Tepanec palaces of *Azcapotzalco*, with the wheel of the domains that this lineage enjoyed. Many lords, both pagan and Christian, are seen in the said pictures, with the ciphers of the years in which they governed.

Cloth, no. 1. *2* The said wheel can also be compared with that which is at the bottom of the pictorial document under no. 1 cited in the Tlatelolco history below, to shed greater light on things so obscure and ancient. The rest is found scattered in the pictorial documents and manuscripts of the two histories, Chichimeca and Mexican.

Mexican History

Pictorial Documents

§. VII

Original. *1* A pictorial document on Indian paper with folds like those of a piece of cloth, and it is stretched out like a strip, we will say that it covers about twenty-three pages. It depicts the departure of the Mexicans from the island of *Aztlan*[13] and their arrival at the continent of New Spain, with the dwellings they constructed in each place, and their years signified with their characters, and at the end, the wars that they waged in the service of *Cocoxtli*, king of *Culhuacan.*

Original. *2* Another ancient pictorial document on Indian paper that contains about fourteen pages, and on them they depict the kings of *Mexico* from *Acamapich*[14] to the great *Moteucçoma*, and it continues to the conquest of *Mexico.* It should be observed that a simple Indian disfigured this history by adding to it some printed figures.

Copy. *3* Another pictorial document on European paper of twenty-five leaves, perhaps translated from another ancient one. It recounts Mexican history: the coming of their peoples to New Spain, the dwellings that they built in places, with the characters of the years and symbols of the days, the arrival of the Spaniards, the preaching of the Holy Gospel, and the rites of our Sacred Religion.

---

13. Aztlan was the semi-legendary homeland of the Mexica (Aztecs) in northern Mexico. Boturini apparently considered it to be an island.

14. There is a space between this name and the following comma, probably because the original intention was to give the full name *Acamapichtli.*

Copy. *4* Another pictorial document on European paper of twenty-one leaves. It deals with the descendants of the kings of *Mexico* and of the lords of *Cuitlahtepec*, *Tepanohuayan*, and *Altepetlac*, the conquest, and the arrival in the Indies of various viceroys and archbishops, and it lists the Indians who were governors in the said town and many other towns, and toward the end it has some lines and memories of things that around the year 1712.

Original. *5* A fragment of a pictorial document on half-rotted Indian paper on which various things are depicted with the characters of the years. It begins in pagan times and reaches to those of the conquest.

Original. *6* Another pictorial document on Indian paper, about as large as a sheet of larger-than-usual paper. It depicts the wanderings of the Mexican nation and their stay in *Chapultepec.*

Original. *7* Another pictorial document on Indian paper of that famous bird with the head of a man that twelve years before the arrival of the Spaniards, the Indians brought to their emperor *Moteucçoma*, and it also depicts something of the conquest.[15]

Original. *8* Another pictorial document on Indian paper on which are depicted, apparently and as far as can be stated at present, some ancestral lands of different lords, beginning with the said Emperor *Moteucçoma* and continuing with others up to Christian times.

Original. *9* A schedule of tributes that were paid to the two kingdoms of *Mexico* and *Tlatelolco* by the respective subject provinces. It is sixteen leaves on Indian paper, although something is missing at the beginning and end, and on it are depicted the tributary locations and the nature of the tributes, which they paid in fruit and other goods.

Original. *10* Another pictorial document on Indian paper that explains the history of three cycles in use in that land which belongs to the kingdoms of *Tezcoco* and *Mexico.* It is curious, being painted in four quarters with the characters of the years, as in the shape of a cross.

Original. *11* Another pictorial document on Indian paper on which is depicted the lake of *Mexico* with its boundary towns.

---

15. This refers to one of the omens that supposedly occurred before the arrival of the Spaniards. However, the original account does not mention one man but a multitude. The account is to be found in Book 12 of Sahagún's *Florentine Codex.* For the text and translation, see Lockhart, ed. and trans., *We People Here*, 54, 56.

Original. *12* Another pictorial document painted on thin, coarse cloth. It contains some notable things that occurred in the year 1522 and the second year of the conquest.

Original. 13 Another pictorial document in book form. It seems to deal with some things about the city of *Iztapalapa*, its wards and neighboring towns, and the first churches that the ancients founded. It has a page written in the *Nahuatl* language at the beginning, and another two complete ones at the end, and various lines on almost all its painted pages. It is bound in Indian paper as large as official documentary paper, and it is somewhat burned on one side.

Copy. *14* A copy of a pictorial document of the imperial city of *Tenochtitlan Mexico*, which was founded (according to what it says) around the year 1327, taken from the pagan original in the year 1631, with an explanation of the letters placed in different parts of the said pictorial document. It is on cloth, painted with oil, in very poor condition, and in it is seen the succession of the first founders, the kings of the said city.

Copy. *15* A pictorial document on Indian paper, as large as a bedsheet. It shows the situation of the said imperial city which (I suppose) was beautified in the reign of *Itzcohuatl*, with royal canals and private ones for each ward and household. It seemed to me that *Mexico* in its pagan times had a layout similar to that of Venice. It is torn in the middle and shows both the pagan kings and the Christian caciques who governed in it.

Original. *16* Another pictorial document on Indian paper, of the size of half a sheet. It pictures the plaza of *Mexico* with its marketplace and the different products that with an orderly policy were sold in their respective shops.

Original. *17* Another pictorial document on nineteen leaves of European paper, of the lands won in war, which King *Itzcohuatl* distributed among the Indian conquerors. On it are depicted the kings of *Mexico* and *Tlatelolco* with the Christian lords who governed at a later period, and an account in the *Nahuatl* language of the war that took place between *Axayaca*, king of *Mexico*, and *Moquihuix*, king of *Tlatelolco*, who died by being sacrificed, as is clear on leaf fifteen, and on the next [leaf] the map of *Xochimilco* is added and they continue to the end with some ciphers of measurements and division of lands.

Original. *18* Another pictorial document on twenty-six leaves of Indian paper; the first six are manuscripts, and the rest painted, to which there are added some lines in the *Nahuatl* language, with the names of the towns that it comprises.

MANUSCRIPTS by Indian Authors

§. VIII

Volume 4 in folio. Copy. *1* A *History of Mexico* written around 1626. I suppose its author to be don Domingo de San Antón Muñón *Chimalpahin.* It deals with the affairs of this nation, the succession of its kings, and what occurred up to the year 1526. It is in the Castilian language and is on European paper.[16]

Copy in folio. *2* *Mexican Chronicle* in the *Nahuatl* language by the same author and on European paper. It begins in the year 1068 and continues to 1597. It can be found in the said volume 4.[17]

Copy in folio. *3* Nine sheets of historic fragments of the same nation and language on European paper. Their author is unknown. They are found in the said volume 4.

Copy in folio. *4* Historical notes of the same nation in the *Nahuatl* language and on European paper, their author don Gabriel de Ayala, a noble of *Tezcoco* and notary of the republic. They begin with the year 1243 and end with 1562. They are to be found in the said volume 4.[18]

Copy in folio. *5* Other notes of the same history in the *Nahuatl* language and European paper by an anonymous author. They begin with the year 1367 and conclude with 1569. They are to be found in the said volume 4.

Copy in folio. *6* Other [notes] in the said language and paper, their author the aforesaid don Domingo *Chimalpahin.* They begin in the year 1064 and continue to 1521. They are to be found in the said volume 4.

Copy in folio. *7* A memorial in the same language and paper of the coming of the Mexicans and what happened afterward, by an unknown author.

16. See *Codex Chimalpahin*, ed. and trans. Anderson and Schroeder.

17. Ibid.

18. Little is known about Ayala. He was a notary of the royal audiencia of Mexico and was the author of *Apuntes de los sucesos de la nación mexicana desde el año 1243 hasta el de 1562*, in Nahuatl. The unedited manuscript is in the Biblioteca Nacional in Madrid.

It begins in the year 1066 and ends in 1316. It is to be found in the said volume 4.

Copy in folio.

8 Nine sheets of historical fragments by various authors in the said language and paper. They are to be found in volume 4.

Copy in folio.

9 A *Historical Chronology of the Ancient Kings of Culhuacan*, who were succeeded by the Mexican kings, written by the lords of *Culhuacan* in the *Nahuatl* language and on European paper. It is found in the said volume 4.

Volume 5 in folio. Original.

10 Some *Historical Annals of the Mexican Nation* on Indian paper, almost the size of official stationery and in the *Nahuatl* language, bound with ixtle cords,[19] which are woven with strands taken from the fleshy leaves of the *maguey*, in sixteen useful pages. It begins in pagan times and continues, touching on something of the conquest, at which time the author must have died. It is an ancient piece and of great value.

Volume 6 in folio. Original.

11 *Mexican Chronicle*, on European papers, written in the Castilian language by don Hernando de Alvarado *Tezozomoc* around the year 1598, and it contains 112 chapters, from pagan times up to the arrival of the invincible don Fernando Cortés in those lands. It is the first part, and the second is missing.[20]

Volume 7 in folio. Original.

12 Different *Original Histories* in the *Nahuatl* language and on European paper, *of the kingdoms of Culhuacan and Mexico and other provinces*; their author was the said don Domingo *Chimalpahin*. They begin in pagan times and reach the year 1591.

Volume 8 in folio. Original.

13 A *History of the Kingdoms of Culhuacan and Mexico* in the *Nahuatl* language and on European paper by an anonymous author, and there is added a *Brief Account of the Gods and Rites of Pagan Times* in the Castilian language, written by the bachelor don Pedro Ponce, an Indian cacique and beneficiado,[21] who was from the district of

19. *Ixtli*, whose second meaning according to Molina (Nahuatl/Spanish) is "ñudo de la caña."

20. Hernando de Alvarado (c. 1525–c. 1610) was a Nahua historian who wrote in both Spanish and Nahuatl. His best-known work is the *Crónica mexicayotl*, which is known entirely from Chimalpahin's work. See Lockhart, *Nahuas after the Conquest*, 389–90.

21. Someone who held an ecclesiastical office to which an income was attached. This person is known only from Boturini's entry.

Tzumpahuacan.[22] It is copied entirely in the hand of don Fernando de Alva, and the first page is missing.

Volume 9 in folio. Original. *14* Another *History of the Mexican Nation*, partly in figures and characters and partly in prose in the *Nahuatl* language, written by an anonymous author in the year 1576 and continuing in the same manner by other Indian authors until the year 1608. At the beginning it contains a painting of the four triadecateridas of the Indian calendar and at the end some figures of Mexican kings and other Christian governors, with the ciphers of the years in which they governed.

SEPARATE ITEMS

§. IX

Original in quarto, no. 1. Another history on European paper of the same nation in the *Nahuatl* language, twenty-eight written leaves. It starts with the founding of the city of Mexico and continues to June 13 of the year 1596.

Original in quarto, no. 2. Another similar [history] in the same language and paper, which has the characters of the years drawn and ciphers of the various places. It depicts the arrival of the Mexicans at the city of *Tollan* in the year 1196 and continues to 1590.

Original in quarto, no. 3. Another in the same language and paper, of forty-one nicely written leaves. It begins with the coming of the Mexicans to *Chapultepec* and continues to the year 1590. The ending is missing.

Originals in folios, no. 4. Eight leaves of historical fragments in the same language and on the same paper, with the corresponding years of the two calendars, Indian and European.

Originals in folios, no. 5. Seven leaves of other fragments in the same language and on the same paper. In them the author narrates the kings of *Mexico*, the conquest, and many things that happened to the Mexican nation from their arrival at the continent of New Spain until the year 1586, although the two leaves six and seven are missing from the historical thread.

Originals in folios, no. 6. A history in the same language and on the same paper, of thirteen leaves, with the Indian and European years. It begins with the coming

---

22. Nahuatl *Tzompahuacan*, modern Zumpaguacan (Zumpahuacán), is in the modern state of Mexico, to the west of Cuernavaca (Gerhard, *Historical Geography*, 170).

of the Mexicans and ends in the year 1596. It should be noted that two leaves are missing, and their contents from the year 1310 to 1361.

Originals in folios, no. 7. Some historical notes in the same language and on the same paper, nine pages. They begin with the year 1507 and end with 1670.

Originals in folios, no. 8. Another history in the same language and paper, twelve leaves. It begins with the coming of the Spaniards to the Indies up to the year 1697. It appears to have been begun by one author and continued by another.

Originals in folios, no. 9. Some historical notes in the same language and on the same paper, four pages, from the year 1519 to 1667.

Originals in folios, no. 10. A leaf of historical notes in the same language and on the same paper from the year 1519 to 1531.

Originals in folios, no. 11. Other notes in the same language and on the same paper, thirteen leaves. They begin with the year 1534 and continue until 1608. Their beginning is missing, although the ending seems complete.

Originals in folios, no. 12. Other similar ones in the same language and on the same paper, five large leaves. They begin with the year 1519 until 1649.

Originals in folios, no. 13. Other similar ones in the same language and on the same paper, twenty leaves, to which are added some crude pictures. They begin with the year 1519 and continue to 1645. Some pages inside and at the end are missing.

Originals in folios, no. 14. Other historical pieces in the same language and on the same paper, which begin with the year 1223 and end with 1546, although they lack continuity of the years. Likewise I have various manuscripts of more modern authors who, having wanted to imitate their ancestors and add the characters of the Indian calendar, have mistaken the count of the years and perhaps some facts, and because I alone am in a position to write the General History, I will be able to critique them and separate the good from the bad.

MANUSCRIPTS *by Spanish Authors*

§. X

Volume 10 in folios. Copy. *1* *A summary account of the lords and of the difference between them in New Spain and of their usages and customs, especially in matters of succession and tributes*; its author was Doctor don

Alonso de Zorita, formerly oidor of the Royal Audiencia of *Mexico.*[23] I copied it from the original.

Volume 11 in quarto. Copy.

2 *Manual for Ministers of the Indians, and Notice of Their Ancient Idolatries*, composed by doctor and pastor don Jacinto de la Serna, Mexican patrician; in part, I copied it and in part, I had it copied by others, from the original.[24]

Volume 12 in quarto. Copy.

3 *Light on the Unknown Land*, which Captain don Juan Mateo Mange[25] composed in the year 1720, and some daily accounts are added by Father Eusebio Kino of the Sacred Company of the discovery of the Río Grande, adjacent to the Sea of California, and of the peaceful state of the provinces of Pimería and Sonora. I have the original.

Volume 13 in quarto. Copy.

4 *Historic Account of the Growth of the Glorious Province of the Holy Gospel of the Observant Order of Saint Francis of the Dioceses of Mexico; the author is Father fray Agustín de Betancurt, chronicler of the said province.*[26]

---

23. That is, a judge of the royal law court or administrative council. Zorita (c. 1512–c. 1585) was a judge, author, and historian, who was noted for his enlightened attitudes toward the indigenous peoples of New Spain. He was the author of the *Breve y sumaria relación.*

24. Serna (d. 1685) was a seventeenth-century criollo priest, known for his learning and for his work that was intended for missionaries among the natives. He was also three times rector of the University of Mexico.

25. Mange, or Manje (1670–1727) was an Aragonese military captain who was active in the northern borders of New Spain. He accompanied Kino on several of his expeditions, especially that of 1707. His *Diario* of 1694 is a valuable source for knowledge of the Apaches and Pimas. The work that Boturini refers to was *Luz de tierra incógnita de la América Septentrional.*

26. Agustín Betancurt or Vetancurt (1620–1700), a Franciscan, was the author of *Teatro mexicano*, a history of New Spain. He was also noted as a scholar of the Nahuatl language. See Poole, *Our Lady of Guadalupe*, 171–72.

Tlatelolco History

Another branch of Mexican history is that of the kingdom of *Tlatelolco*, and although the Indians of one or the other part may have moved away before reaching *Mexico* and built their respective cities with the mere separation of a stone wall.[27] In the same way, each city had its own kings and separate governor; nevertheless they were of the same lineage. And on the occasion when *Axiaca*,[28] king of *Mexico*, overcame *Moquihuix*, king of *Tlatelolco*, the latter's kingdom came under the power of the Mexicans, in whose annals mention is made of this history and even in [that of] the Tepanecs, and I will also point out the separate material I have about it.

PICTORIAL DOCUMENTS

§. XI

Copy. 1 A pictorial document on European paper on which are depicted the kings of *Tlatelolco* and *Mexico*, apparently a copy made from another ancient pictorial document, and it can be compared with the one that I cite in the History of Mexico and its pictorial documents at number seventeen [catalog, section 7, no. 17], and the wheel it has at the end, with which I note as number one in the Tepanec History and its pictorial documents.

---

27. "con la sola división de una albarada." Boturini may mean "albarrada," dry-stacked stone wall.

28. *Sic* for *Axayacatl*?

SEPARATE MANUSCRIPTS

§. XII

Original in folios, no. 1. A history in the *Nahuatl* language of the most memorable events of the Mexican nation and even more of Tlatelolco, twenty-three written leaves and European paper.

Original in folio, no. 2. A historical memoir of when the royal courts of justice were established in *Tlatelolco* and the events that occurred around that time, in five written pages in the *Nahuatl* language and European paper.

Original in folios, no. 3. Some historic fragments of the events of *Tlatelolco*, six written pages, in the same language and on the same paper.

Various Histories

§. XIII

Although the history of the Chichimecas, Tepanecs, and Mexicans can be considered as the general history of the kingdom, since these three nations and royal houses, by reason of the final Triple Alliance, represented the majesty of the empire and subjected by its arms, either its own or with allies, the greater part of the land of *Anahuac*, which today is called *New Spain*, there were many provinces, kingdoms, and republics that observed their own laws and liberty and did not recognize the empire, such as the powerful kingdom of *Michoacan*, the republics of *Matlaltzinco*, of *Huejotzinco*, and *Tlaxcala*, and so I will point out the historical material that I have of the said kingdom and republics.

History of Michoacan

§. XIV

1 In pagan times this kingdom was very powerful. It shared its borders with those of *Mexico* in *Ixtlahuacan*, district of *Toluca*, and from there to the South Sea, extending 150 leagues, and from the province of *Zacatula*,[29] crossing toward the north as far as *Zichu* more than 160 leagues, whose limits included great centers, like the city and province of *Michoacan* and those of *Colima* and *Zacatula* and the towns today called *of Avalos*, and a countless number of others, with an abundance of warlike people. Likewise, in pagan times it succeeded in being independent of the empire and having its own kings, such as were *Tzihuanga* and his son the great *Cazontzin Tangajuan*,[30] he who received the Spaniards in peace in a memorable incident, and it is the following. When the imperial city of *Mexico* found itself confined by a rigorous siege by the Spaniards, the three allied kings of the empire, *Cuauhtemoc* of *Mexico*, *Cohuanacotzin*[31] of *Tezcoco*, and *Tetlepanquetzatzin* of *Tlacopan*,[32] dispatched ambassadors to the great *Cacontzin* to ask his help in their great need, and this powerful king immediately

---

29. A Mixtec land in modern Oaxaca (Thomas, *Conquest*, 318). It was the center of a number of independent states (ibid., 558).

30. Thomas (*Conquest*, 429) gives the name as Zuangua. *Cazonci* meant monarch.

31. Thomas (*Conquest*, 321–22) mentions him as a brother to Cacama. Thomas gives the name as Conacochtzin and says that he also was king of Tezcoco (ibid., 458–59).

32. One of the partners in the Triple Alliance. Tetlepanquetzatzin was ruler at the time of the Spanish conquest. Thomas identifies him as king of Tacuba (ibid., 523).

ordered two hundred thousand combatants from among his most select vassals to come together on two plains, which today are called *of Avalos.* One hundred thousand were Tarascans and some others Teochichimecas; but after a princess, a sister of [Cacontzin], died, at the end of four days which, according to the custom of that land, they kept vigil over her in the room of the principal temple,[33] she revived and ordered the king, her brother, to be summoned, telling him that in no way should he help the Mexicans because the foreigners who were making war on them would become lords of the land and their holy law would rule over it all. And for clearer testimony, the day of the principal feast, he [Cacontzin] would see come in the region of the air from the east a youth with a light in one hand and in the other a sword, which was the weapon that this recently arrived nation used, and passing over the city he would go to stop in the west. And when everything was fulfilled to the letter, the king put complete faith in these and other things that his sister told him and recalled his soldiers and received the Spaniards peacefully into his kingdom.

Original. *2* I have a pictorial document of this kingdom on cotton cloth, and it belongs to the province of San Pablo *Yuririapundaro.* It was painted in the year 1589.

Copy in folios. *3* Plus certain memorials in some acts originating in the Higher Government of *Mexico* by don Constantino *Huitzimengari*, son of don Antonio and grandson of the *Cazontzin*, in which are specified the cities and settlements of this kingdom. They are to be found in volume 4.

Copy in folio. Sheet no. 1. Also, part of a memorial that don Agustín López, the governor of *Yuririapundaro*, drew up, in which many titles of the said town are cited and serve as a history of its founding.

Copy in folios. Sheet no. 2. Also, some four pages of the founding of the convent of the said *Yuririapundaro*, which apparently were taken from the chronicles of Our Father Saint Augustine, because chapter 12 is cited in them.

Copy in folios. Sheet no. 3. Also, a grant of lands made by the Viceroy don Luis de Velasco to different towns in *Michoacan*, and the approval of other lands which the said towns exchanged among each other for the greater convenience of their populations in the year 1586, and it is clear to

33. "Templo mayor," not to be confused with the one in Tenochtitlan.

me that the inhabitants of this kingdom made use of paintings in the days of their paganism, but because I was so busy and exhausted, I was unable to travel to their provinces to do the investigation to obtain them.

Matlaltzinca History[34]

§. XV

1 Another independent republic was that of *Matlaltzinco*, located in the valley of *Toluca*, where in the past there were some large buildings and temples built by the Toltec Indians and later, in Christian times, that famous wall with two gates and a bridge for livestock to enter, as is clear in the two large pictorial documents that are in my archive, one on Indian paper, the other on cotton cloth, in which the entire province and valley are described. It was governed by its usages and customs, and because its boundaries are very short, no notable things were written about it.

---

34. On this see Gerhard, *Historical Geography*, 106, 141–42. Boturini or his printer consistently spells this Matlaltzinca.

History of Huejotzinco

§. XVI

1 Another Indian republic was that of *Huejotzinco.* It was composed of four sections with an aristocratic government, free of all subjection. In wartime it regularly sided with the empire of *Tezcoco,* since its rulers were from the same Chichimeca lineage. The caciques of this province today have some ancient pictures, which I have seen, and the history of their pagan times is found dispersed in the body of the General History of New Spain.

Copies. 2 Of this history I have twenty-two pictorial documents taken from their originals, and [from] Indian paper onto European paper, in which the city of *Huejotzinco* and its districts, wanting to give an account of the tribute that they still owed the Catholic Monarchs, the officials of the republic, with elegant style and numbered ciphers, painted the quantities that they had to pay in money and produce.

Original. 3 Another map on Indian paper in which are shown the allotments of land belonging to some natives of the said city, and the ciphers for their measurements are visible, which, when properly explained, can be of use in understanding the pictorial documents and boundaries of the Indians' towns.

Originals. To be found in a book in folios and European paper. Other figures in an account of tributes that the officials of that republic drew up, registering the tribute payers. It is very useful for interpreting the ciphers of the Indians' surnames and knowing how to distinguish the figures.

History of Tlaxcala

The courageous republic of *Tlaxcala* was and always will be famous in all ages, not just in their pagan times, for having resisted with heroic efforts the arms of the Mexicans, safeguarding their ancient liberty and sheltering as many nations as escaped from the fury of the conquerors, but also helping the Spaniards to conquer Mexico and the other lands. I have no doubt that this glorious city and nation have an eminent place in the history of New Spain, full of laurels and applause, and I will proceed to indicate the historical material that I have gathered together, of this most noble republic.

PICTORIAL DOCUMENTS

§. XVII

Original. *1* A pictorial document on cured skin with the insignias of the four districts of the republic and, as an adornment, the royal arms of Spain, and around them can be seen seated on their chairs ten personages, five on each side, who I suppose must have been the first ten viceroys who governed. In the middle there seems to be depicted in the form of a wheel the principal towns of the province with their distinctive ciphers, which will yield much to do on the occasion of interpreting them, and at the end there are some lines in the Castilian language, marred by time like the pictorial documents, and on the back of the same pictorial document are depicted other towns of the said province.

Originals. 2 Another three genealogical pictorial documents on Indian paper of the descent of various caciques of the aforementioned province.

Originals. 3 Another five genealogical pictorial documents and a piece of another on European paper.

Original. 4 A pictorial document on European paper in which can be seen depictions of Father Martín de Valencia, a Franciscan,[35] and the corregidor of *Tlaxcala*, don Hernando de Saavedra, with many lords and nobles of the republic. It has a speech in the Nahuatl language, with which the said Father Martín makes clear to the leaders that it was necessary to give the proper remuneration to the Spanish notaries in the same way that it was given to the notary painters in pagan times.[36]

Originals. 5 Other fragments of a pictorial document on European paper, of certain divisions and shares of land.

Originals. 6 Two small pictures on a similar number of sheets on European paper, which depict two towns.

Copy. 7 A rough drawing on European paper of the ambassadors whom the invincible don Fernando Cortés sent from *Cempoala* to the four lords of this republic, *Xicotencatl*, *Mazizcatzin*, *Citlalpopocatzin*, and *Tlahuexolotzin*, so that they would receive our Holy Catholic Faith in peace.

Copy. 8 Another on the same paper. It deals with the republic's reception of the said don Fernando [Cortés] in *Tezcacohuac*;[37] and likewise by the house of *Xicotencatl*, where he lodged; by the town of San Esteban, where the first gospel was chanted; and by the town of San Buenaventura, where the brigantines were built to win *Mexico*.

MANUSCRIPTS *by Indian Authors*

§. XVIII

Volume 14 in folio. Original. 1 A large book on European paper. It describes all the towns [and] noble and plebeian houses of the four districts of

35. Martín de Valencia (?–1534) was the leader of the first group of twelve Franciscans who arrived in 1524 to begin the evangelization of New Spain. See Mendieta, *Historia*, 571–605.

36. Actually Valencia, who arrived in New Spain at the age of fifty, did not know Nahuatl. See ibid., 584.

37. Not in Gerhard.

Tlaxcala. It is in the *Nahuatl* language, without [its] beginning or ending.

Volume 15 in folio. Original.

2 Memorials of the notable events and government of the city of Tlaxcala in the *Nahuatl* language and on European paper. They begin in the year 1547 and continue to 1577.

Volume 16 in folio. Original.

3 A very polished history of the said city and republic from its pagan times through a large part of the conquest, in the Castilian language and sixty-four folios on European paper. The beginning and end are missing. It is surmised that the author was don Domingo Muñoz Camargo, a Tlaxcalan mestizo.[38]

Volume 17 in folio. Original.

4 *Chronicle of the Very Noble and Loyal City of Tlaxcala*, written in the *Nahuatl* language and on European paper by don Juan Ventura Zapata y Mendoza, cacique of the section of Quiahuiztlan. It begins with the coming of this nation to New Spain up to the year 1689.

SEPARATE ITEMS

§. XIX

Originals in folios, no. 1.

Some pieces of ancient songs badly written on European paper, and they are the best records of this history, on three pages.

Copy in folios, no. 2.

A history on European paper of the founding of the city of *Tlaxcala* and its four sections, translated from the Castilian language into *Nahuatl* by don Francisco de Loaysa, former interpreter for the city, who told me that its author was a cacique of the first Christians. It has twelve leaves.

Copy in quarto, no. 3.

Two notebooks copied on European paper by the said Loaysa from its original of a history that deals with different things and with the four sections of *Tlaxcala.* It goes as far as chapter 12 and is incomplete.

Copy in quarto, no. 4.

A history in the *Nahuatl* language of the three boys of Tlaxcala, Cristobalito, Antoñico, and Juanico, who died because of their confession of the Catholic faith. It was copied on European paper by the said Loaysa from the one that was printed in the Imperial College of *Tlatelolco* in the year 1601, which I also have in my archive.

Copy in quarto, no. 5.

A book on European paper and in the Castilian language of historical notices that a Spanish citizen of *Tlaxcala* copied and the natives

---

38. Diego Muñoz Camargo (c. 1528–99) was a descendant of a conquistador through an illegitimate line and historian of Tlaxcala. Domingo is an error.

of *Pueblo de la Magdalena* had. It begins with the year 1519, and the Indians continued to write the history in it, one [year] after another, up to the year 1713, and the said citizen continued it until 1722.

Original in quarto, no. 6. A catalog of the ancient and noble families of the sections of *Tlaxcala* on forty-three fojas of European paper and in the *Nahuatl* language.

Original in quarto, no. 7. A small notebook on European paper of happenings in the city *of la Puebla* from the year 1585 until 1677, in thirty-three pages and in the *Nahuatl* language. This manuscript is placed in the history of *Tlaxcala* for two reasons: first, because the said city was founded in its territory, and its bishops were at first called [bishops] of *Tlaxcala*; second, because its author may have been some Tlaxcaltec cacique of those who went on to settle in the wards *of la Puebla.*

Originals in quarto, no. 8. Some historical notes in the *Nahuatl* language, thirteen leaves, on European paper. They begin with the year 1519 and end in 1697.

Originals in quarto, no. 9. Other notes in the same language and on European paper, twenty-eight leaves. At the beginning they have two wheels and the listing of the kings of *Mexico*, and they begin in the year 1519, ending in 1739.

Originals in quarto, no. 10. Others in the same language, twenty-five pages of European paper. They begin with the year 1454 and end in 1737.

Various Other

Historical Sources

§. XX

Original. 1 A large and old torn pictorial document on cotton cloth, five and a half *varas* long and two and a half wide, a little less. It is well painted and represents various wars that took place in pagan times, and the many captives who were taken on the said occasion among the towns *Tonalxochitlan*, *Quauhtepan*, *Ynenechcoyan*, *Tepeyahualco*, *Ohocotlan*, *Tlilalpan*, *Ameyalato* on the one side, and the towns *Huixocotepec* . . . *Huecoyotzi* . . . *Coyoacan*, *Quetzalcohuapan*, *Tlacotlan* . . . *Atlan*, *Quimichocan* . . . *Chipetzinco*, *Quanapa* . . . *Tepeyahualco*, *Yxtlahuaca*, *Ocotzoquauhtla* on the other, and at the end a large church that was built in Christian times, next to these last towns.[39]

Original. 2 Another very large pictorial document in one piece and deteriorated on both sides, on thick Indian paper. It is somewhat more than eight varas in length and two and a quarter wide, and with rough pictures it deals with the cruel wars in pagan times among different towns whose names are *Hecatepec*, *Huyatepec*, *Amoltepec*, *Nientlah*, *Tzatzaqualan*, *Hueymetlan*, *Coltepec*, *Antlacaltepec*, *Tepechalla*, *Xiquipilco*, *Achalalan*, *Zayutepec*, *Teconhuac*, *Totolhuitzocan*, *Yahueyocan*, *Zacatzolah*, *Mazapila*, and after having shown with some rivers of blood both the bloodiness of war and of the sacrificed prisoners, it notes the arrival of the great Cortés and the Fathers of Saint Francis at *Quauhmanco.* It should be noted that this pictorial document and the preceding

39. In margin: "NOTE: *These dots mean the town names are rubbed off and not intelligible.*"

one were buried in a box beneath the ruins of an ancient chapel of ease in the jurisdiction of *Huamantla*, province of *Tlaxcala*, and I had them taken from there and they can only be interpreted as a whole on the occasion when the manuscripts of the General History are consulted.

Original. *3* Another pictorial document on coarse Indian paper, painted on both sides. On the first side is shown the conquest of the city of Cholula, as well as the punishment that Cortés inflicted on the citizens, and of the baptism that doña María Itlamanteuctli and other caciques accepted at the hand of don Gerónimo de Aguilar,[40] August 6, 1521, and in some rough lines in the *Nahuatl* language are specified other notices of the said city in ancient times. Apparently this pictorial document was painted around the year 1586. I also have two copies of the first side, the one done on cloth, and the other on European paper. On the second side, or back, of the said pictorial document is depicted the famous hill that is in the aforementioned city, called *Ecaticpac, Toltecatl, Tlachihuatepec*, made by the hand of the Toltec Indians, and one reads in the same language some historical lines of its very ancient construction and how and when the first chapel of ease to Our Lady was built and her image that appeared was placed in it, relating the case of the said apparition in Rome to a Franciscan Father.

Original. *4* Another pictorial document on a sheet of European paper in which can be seen as prisoners some caciques of the towns of San Pablo and San Andrés (I suppose, from the province of Cholula), to whom Cortés, Marina, and don Andrés de Tapia[41] seem to be communicating the news of our Holy Catholic Faith.

Original. *5* A polished geographical pictorial document on Indian paper in which are drawn the cities and towns of *Tlaxcala* with its mountain range, *Matlalcueye, Puebla, Amozoc, Totomihuacan, Quauhtinchan, Tetela, Napalucan, Tecalco, Tepeyacac, Tecamachalco, Acacinco.*

Original. *6* Another pictorial document on Indian paper. The principal town of *Mizquiahuallan* is shown, together with other adjacent ones.

---

40. This may be the same Gerónimo de Aguilar (1499–1531), a Franciscan, who had been a prisoner of the Mayas and acted as an interpreter together with doña Marina for Cortés.

41. Doña Marina was Cortés's interpreter and mistress, also known as Malinche. Andrés de Tapia (c. 1485–1561) was one of the first conquistadores and closely involved with many events in Cortés's life.

Original. *7* Another on two cured skins, joined at the middle, of the town of *Amatla*, and other towns of its boundaries.

Originals. *8* Two large pictorial documents on European paper from the villa of *Chietla*; on the one is depicted the church of Saint Francis of the said villa and that of Saint Augustine *Xolalpa*, with some lands; and in the other, which is incomplete, the *Tecpan*[42] of the said villa, with many adjacent towns.

Original. *9* A small pictorial document on Indian paper, in which are painted the towns of *Chalma*, *Tlaltecahuaca*, and *Tlaxichco.*

Original. *10* Another pictorial document of the site of San Juan Bautista and adjacent towns on a double sheet of European paper.

Original. *11* A pictorial document of the Indians of *Totolapa*, which was presented to the high government of *Mexico.* It bears news about the temple and patio of the detestable idol *Huitzilopochtli.*

Original. *12* Another drawn on European cardboard, very old and incomplete.

Original. *13* A pictorial document in the shape of a strip on very fine and smooth Indian paper, of the church of Santa Cruz *Tlamapan* and of its *tlapixques* and cantors, of the lords of the said town, justice, foremen and their wives. The structure of this document and the beauty of the paper are admirable.

Original. *14* Another on European paper, although incomplete, of the same town and site of *Tlamapan*, in which the royal audiencia of *Mexico* seems to have commissioned Bernardino del Castillo to take the account of the tributes of the said town, as may be seen in the said pictorial document by different well-placed numerical ciphers and which cannot be easily explained.

Original. *15* Another on European paper like a strip, four and a half *varas* long,[43] and I suppose it to be from the same town, in which the notaries and majordomos of its church are painted from the year 1564 to 1577, with the ciphers of what was paid each year to the said church.

Originals. *16* Six rough genealogical pictorial documents, on European paper, seemingly of the Indians of *Yetla*, with the descent of its caciques from pagan times.

Originals. *17* Another two pictorial documents in the same form. It is not possible to interpret which caciques it deals with.

---

42. Nahuatl for a royal residence.

43. Somewhat over thirteen feet long.

Original. *18* Another on cotton cloth like a bedsheet, on which are depicted different towns in the diocese of *Oaxac*[44] and the succession of their caciques.

Original. *19* Another on some cured skins joined together, which were sent to me from the said diocese, with the pictures of their caciques, who have their surnames painted in characters after the manner of the Toltec calendar.

Original. *20* Another, badly treated, on European paper, of the principal town of *Meztitlan*, and the hill *Metztepetl* can be seen with its demon. It is useful for the history of the Most Holy Cross that I discovered near the precipice of the large hill *Tianguistepetl*, and it is found to be painted by angelic hands from pagan times, according to the account of Father fray Esteban de Salazar, an Augustinian and later a Carthusian monk, in his published book *Discursos sobre el Credo*, and it must belong to the time when the glorious apostle Saint Thomas preached the gospel in that land.

Original. *21* Another of average size on cotton cloth. It depicts some towns and their borders.

Original. *22* Another on European paper, bound with silk, of some towns and surrounding areas of Queretaro.

44. *Sic* for *Oaxaca.*

Pictorial Documents of Tribute

both in money and produce
that the Indians of New Spain
paid to the Catholic Monarchs,
to the Spanish encomenderos,
and to their caciques

§. XXI

Originals. *1* Three pictorial documents on Indian paper like strips. They deal with the tributes that the town of *Mizquiahuallan* paid and in it can be seen the numerical ciphers of each item given by the inhabitants.

Original. *2* Another, longer and of the same material, of the said town.

Original. *3* Another, longer and on the same paper, of the same town.

Original. *4* Another on the same paper and as wide as two sheets, of the town of Santa Inés among the *Otomites* [*sic*].

Original. *5* Another, on the same paper, of the Indians of *Tlatlauca.*

Original. *6* Another on the same paper, of some *Tarascan* and *Otomites* Indians.

Original. *7* Another on European papers, as long as two sheets, well drawn, of the town of Tecpatepec.

Original. *8* Another on cured skin made by Pedro de Santiago *Tequitlato*[45] of the town of *Zapotitlan.*

Originals. *9* Seven pieces of pictorial documents on Indian paper, of the towns of *Tezarco*, *Tlacoapan*, *Coyotepec*, and *Tezontepec.*

45. Tribute collector.

Original. *10* Another on the same paper like a wide strip, more than three *varas* long.[46] Which town is not known.

Original. *11* Another on the same paper, and it depicts a large number of turkeys that were paid as tribute. Which town is not known.

Original. *12* Another of the same paper, as large as two sheets together and with some ciphers. Which town is not known.

46. About eight and a quarter feet.

Manuscripts

of Tribute

§. XXII

Originals in folio. *1* Six and a half leaves on European paper of notices and matters of tributes paid by different towns named on its annexed map to the encomendero don Miguel Deza.

Original in folio. *2* A file of records of tributes on European paper.

Original. *3* A mitigation of tributes that because of mortality among the Indians was ordered to be made in the town of *Tehuacan*, as is evident from the pictorial document on Indian paper and attached deposits.

Originals in folio. *4* Some very ancient accounts on European paper. It is unknown whether they are of tributes or something else.

Original in folio. *5* A double sheet of European paper that shows the tributes paid by I don't know which town.

Original. *6* A remnant of Indian paper, with some small pictures of tributes.

Original in quarto. *7* A small account book of the tributes of the year 1574 in the section of San Pablo *Teocaltitlan* of *Mexico* in twenty-seven written leaves on European papers, although the beginning is missing. It should be noted that here are some original signatures of don Antonio Valeriano,[47] former governor of the Mexican Indians and historian of the apparitions of my Mother and Lady of Guadalupe.

Original in quarto. *8* Another small account book of tributes of the said section for the year 1566, on twenty leaves of European paper.

Originals in folio. *9* Eight leaves of accounts of tributes for the town of San Pablo *Huitznahuatonco* in the years 1567 and 1568. The beginning is missing.

---

47. On Valeriano, see Poole, *Our Lady of Guadalupe*, 83–84, 166–69.

Rare Books

§. XXIII

Original, somewhat longer than in folios. 1 A large book on Indian paper and in the *Nahuatl* language. It consists of sixty-five written leaves, in which the church officials painstakingly listed all those who were baptized in the principal town of *Huitzila.* Good historical notices can be taken from its context.

Original, somewhat longer than in folios. 2 Another similar one of ninety-four written leaves, on the same paper and in the same language, in which there is a description of the principal town of *Teputzla* and the other [towns] annexed to it, namely, *Tlacatecpa, Tlalnepantla, Teycapa, Calitec, Tepetitla, Tlacouca, Acxotla, Amatla, Tepetlapa,* with the number of the houses in each town, of the married Indians and children, all precise. It is possible that the Indians retained this account to distinguish themselves in the schedule of tributes.

Original, the same as the preceding. 3 Another similar one of 119 written pages, on the same paper and language with a complete description of the towns *Molotlan, Atepan, Tenanco, Alacatlan, Tlacatecpan, Texihuaca, Tezcacohuac, Conquechuacan, Totla, Dedepan, Tlacolpa, Zacanco, Tepeyahualco, Panchimalco, Tonallapan,* following the style of the preceding ones.

Other Various

Learned Manuscripts

§. XXIV

Original in folios. *1* A vocabulary or dictionary, as large as a missal, in the *Otomita* [*sic*] language, of 470 leaves on European paper. A valuable work and which cost its author immense labor.

Original in quarto. *2* *Genuine Teacher of the Most Elegant Nahuatl Language*, thirty-six leaves on European paper, that is, the grammar of the said language that don Joseph Antonio Pérez de la Fuente composed.[48] Part of the end is missing.

Original in folios. *3* A small booklet in Mexican and Castilian by the same author, in twelve leaves of European paper.

Originals in folios. *4* Eight double sheets of European paper that contain the principles of Mexican grammar by an anonymous author.

Originals in folios. *5* Various works in the said two languages and on European paper, and some only in the *Nahuatl* language by the said Pérez. They are in a book in folio, nineteen leaves, and they are the following.

I. *Account of the marvelous apparition of Our Lady of Guadalupe in the two languages, Castilian and Mexican.*

II. *Questionnaire for hearing the confessions of Indians in the said two languages.*

III. *Practice of aiding a good death, copied from the Roman Ritual.* It is in the *Nahuatl* language.

---

48. On Pérez de la Fuente, see *Our Lady of Guadalupe*, ed. Sell, Burkhart, and Poole, 23–24. Boturini is our principal source on the works of this author.

IV. *The Wonder of Mexico. Comedy in Mexican verse about the apparition of Our Lady of Guadalupe.*[49]

V. *The Festival Day of the Soul, taken from various authors and translated into the Mexican language.*

VI. *Laudatory Mercury,* that is, twenty poems of praise in Mexican verse for diverse purposes.

VII. *Devotional Drafts.* They contain various prayers of the Most Holy Rosary and many others.

VIII. *Mexican Verses about Our Lady of Guadalupe.*

IX. *Sacred Philomena, which comments in the Mexican language about the mysteries of the Most Holy Rosary.*

X. *A consideration of the Most Holy Trinity in the same language.*

XI. *The schedule with all its prayers in the same language.*

Originals in folio.

6 In addition I have some historical notes about the preaching of the Glorious Apostle Saint Thomas in America. It is in thirty-four leaves of tissue paper, I suppose don Carlos de Sigüenza y Góngora used to write on the same theme in the *Phoenix of the West,*[50] which I have not been able to obtain up to the present because it has been given to the presses; and apropos of things (separating myself briefly from this class of books).

Lienzo no. 2.

I say that with regard to the mentioned preaching of the holy apostle I have a canvas of the Most Holy Cross of the hill *Tianguiztepetl,* of which I spoke previously in section 20, number 20, of this catalog, painted in the form of a *tau* and in size a little more than that of a forearm, on a background of the finest blue color, likewise scattered with some things like white stars, having on its right side a coat-of-arms with an equally blue background, with five white balls in the middle which undoubtedly symbolize the five most precious wounds of the Redeemer, whose records have been preserved from pagan times until our days, without the rain and other inclemencies of the heavens to which they are exposed having been able to dim them in so many centuries. I also have the drawing on canvas of another Holy Cross of wood, which was extracted with a device which was made for the purpose,

Lienzo no. 3.

49. A transcription and translation of this play is in *Our Lady of Guadalupe,* ed. Sell, Burkhart, and Poole.

50. Apparently this is the only known reference to this work.

from an inaccessible cave of the *Mixteca Baja*, and which today is venerated in the conventual church of *Tonala* of the Dominican Fathers, and in the same way it was deposited in the said cave since pagan times and was discovered by angelic music that was played in the said cave every year on the vigil of the glorious apostle. And the aforesaid preaching was so clear in the histories of the Indians that there was a memory of it among the pictorial documents of the *Chontales*, where a most miraculous cross was found, in addition to those that the Spaniards found on the island of *Potonchan* and in the city of *Texcala*, to which the Indians gave adoration, offering them flowers and incense and calling on [the crosses] for the god *Tlaloc*, *the rain god*, since likewise many vestiges of the holy footsteps of the said apostle have remained in different places of New Spain and outside of it, it is a constant in the aforesaid histories that a *white man* preached a Holy Law there; and the forty days' fast which the emperor *Nezahualcoyotl* often practiced during the major ebbs and flows of his monarchy; and they say that he left there once it was prophesied that in the year *Ce Acatl*, *One Reed*, of his calendar his sons would come from the east to preach to them again. One reason why the Indians were bewildered when they learned of the arrival of the Spaniards at a fixed point in the year and character *Ce Acatl*; and when I went through the Indian calendars, I found that the saint's prophecy had been verified to the letter. With the high figures of speech of their language, the Indians called the glorious apostle *Quetzalcoatl*, which means *Bird Serpent*,[51] understanding by *bird* the speed with which he had come from foreign lands to theirs, and by *serpent* the prudent care of the law that he went about preaching, which they regard as very precious feathers from the bird *quetzalli*, which they esteemed in innumerable ways, for example because they made use of them not only as ornaments in war but also in public dances and solemn feasts.

Original in quarto.

17 [*sic*] A book in the *Nahuatl* language and on European paper. It deals with various things and moral explanations and the beginning is missing.

Original in quarto.

18 Dialogues on the gospel on the same paper and in the same language. The beginning is missing.

---

51. More commonly, plumed or feathered serpent. The primary meaning of *quetzal* is of a Central American bird of striking beauty, but it has also taken on other associated meanings.

Original in quarto.

19 Various sermons on the same paper and in the same language. The beginning and end are missing from them.

Originals in quarto.

20 Examples and lives of the saints on the same paper and in the same language. The beginning is missing from them.

Originals in quarto.

21 A book on the same paper and in the same language. It explains some moral examples.

Original in quarto.

22. Another similar one. It contains some sermons in honor of the saints.

Originals in octavo.

23 Some fragments of Our Lord's Passion, on the same paper and in the same language.

Originals in octavo.

24 A book on Indian paper and in the *Nahuatl* language. It deals with various events and songs in praise of the saints. It does not have a beginning or end.

Originals in octavo.

25 Another book on the same paper and in the same language. It contains different prayers and matters of our Holy Faith. It does not have a beginning or end.

26 Other notebooks and fragments of various Christian learning.

Christian Doctrine

in Figures and Ciphers

§. XXV

Originals in quarto.

1 Eleven leaves of the said doctrine on European paper in figures and ciphers, its author is Father fray Bernardino de Sahagún, a Franciscan religious,[52] and it is something to see, very curious, and with it the Indians easily learned the mysteries of our Holy Faith.

Original.

2 Another piece of a pictorial document with figures and ciphers on Indian paper. It depicts part of the said mysteries.

Originals in quarto.

3 Some principles of the said doctrine in four leaves on European paper and not finished. In addition to the figures and ciphers, they have some few lines in the Otomí language.

Original in octavo.

4 A small book on European paper, forty-eight small pages. It explains with rough figures and ciphers the said doctrine.

52. Bernardino de Sahagún (1499–1590) was a Franciscan friar, missionary priest, and pioneering ethnographer, often called the father of ethnohistory. His most famous works, still of great value, are *The General History of the Things of New Spain* and its Nahuatl equivalent, *The Florentine Codex*. See Mendieta, *Historia*, 663–65. It is not clear which work is referred to here.

Printed Books

in the Nahuatl language, which today are scarce and hard to find

§. XXVI

In octavo. *1* *Grammar of the Mixtec Language*; its author is Father fray Antonio de los Reyes, Dominican.[53] Printed in *Mexico* in the year 1593.

In octavo. 2 A manual dictionary of the two languages, Castilian and Mexican; its author is Pedro de Arenas. In *Mexico*, the year 1583.[54]

In quarto. *3* *Confessionario mayor* in the said two languages by Father fray Alonso de Molina, Franciscan. In *Mexico*, the year 1565.[55]

In quarto. *4* The same, in duplicate.

In quarto. *5* *Christian Doctrine* in the said two languages; its author is Father fray Domingo de la Asunción, Dominican. In *Mexico*, the year 1565.

In octavo. 6 *Dialogues in the Mexican language, on Christian peace and tranquility*, its author is Father fray Juan Gaona, Franciscan.[56] In *Mexico*, the year 1583.

---

53. Reyes (c. 1520–1603) was the author of the first grammar of the Mixtec language.

54. This work is *Vocabulario manual de las lenguas castellana y mexicana.* Little is known about Arenas.

55. Alonso de Molina (1513/14–1579/85) was a Franciscan friar, missionary and grammarian whose dictionary of the Castilian and Nahuatl languages (1571) is still an important reference work. The book referred to here is his *Confesionario mayor* (1565). See Mendieta, *Historia*, 551, 685.

56. Fray Juan de Gaona (1507–60) was a Franciscan friar. Born in 1507 in Burgos, Spain, he studied at the University of Paris before journeying to New Spain in 1538. He taught at the College of Santa Cruz de Tlatelolco and was provincial of his order. He was renowned for his knowledge of Nahuatl. Gaona died on

(*continued*)

7 The same in manuscript.

In octavo. 8 Ancient dialogues that Father fray Juan Bautista, Franciscan, corrected and expanded into the most excellent *Nahuatl* language.[57] In *Mexico*, the year 1599, and something is missing from it at the beginning and end.

In quarto. 9 *Misery and brevity of man's life*, a reflection in the said language by the aforementioned Father fray Juan Bautista. In *Mexico*, the year 1604.[58]

In quarto. 10 Book of sermons in the same language by the same author. It is the first part. In *Mexico*, the year 1606.

In quarto. 11 The *Road to Heaven*, composed in the same language by Father fray Martín de León, the year 1611.[59]

September 27, 1560. He had composed a Nahuatl-language text, *Colloquios de la paz, y tranquilidad Christiana* ("Dialogues of peace and Christian tranquility"), which was published in 1582 after his death. See Mendieta, *Historia*, 690.

57. Little is known about Bautista. See Mendieta, *Historia*, 516, 551.

58. On this, see Mendieta, *Historia*, 551.

59. Little is known about León, a native of New Spain, who joined the Dominicans in 1574 and died sometime in the early seventeenth century (Beristáin de Souza, *Biblioteca*, 3:120). See also Poole, *Our Lady of Guadalupe*, 91–92.

INDIAN CALENDARS

Natural Year

First calendar.

1 Once the ancestral Indian peoples had been deprived of all their acquired wisdom in their first simple and pastoral age, and finding themselves notably limited in an articulate language, they gave all their attention to observing the course of the natural year, and as they saw that it made its entrance at the same time as the grass was sprouting in the fields and that it lasted until such time as the land, after having shaken off winter's cold, was returning to its former greenness with new shoots, they called it *xihuitl*, that is, *newborn grass.*[60] What was happening repeatedly from one grass [crop] to another, which meant the same as from one year to another, left no room for speculation nor any mistake whatsoever in the reckonings, because nature itself was that which measured this course of the sun with the greatest perfection.

2 And noting further that in the interim between one grass [crop] and another, the earth was producing four different changes, that is, the first grass emerged in the spring and was crowned with flowers, maturing with the heat of summer, perfecting its seeds in autumn, and finally fading in winter, they divided this natural year into four seasons, equivalent to ours of *spring*, *summer*, *autumn*, and *winter*, with four other divine characters, *Tecpatl*, *Calli*, *Tochtli*, [and] *Acatl*; *Flint*, *House*, *Rabbit*, and *Cane*, hieroglyphs of the four elements and images of another four of the first and most principal deities,

60. This word also means "year."

Xiuhteuctli (or *Huitzilopochtli*, being accompanied by *Teotecpatl*), *Tlatocaocelotl*, *Quetzalcoatl*, and *Chalchiuhcueitl*, of whom I spoke in this, my Idea of a History, at section 3, numbers 13, 14, 15, and 16.

3 This was the first attempt at periods of time, and so meager that for that timespan it did not have a year nor months nor weeks nor symbolic days, but I do believe that when necessity obliged the said ancestral peoples to specify the natural days, they made use of the sun, because in the most ancient histories they called a day *Tonalli*, a word derived from *Tonatiuh*, which meant *the sun*; and it may well be that in the first age they understood[61] that there were as many days as there were suns, until in the second age when [the year] was divided by the chronologists and astronomers into symbolic months, weeks, and days. And moreover the astronomers, speculating on the situation and influence of the planets[62] and signs, without departing from the principal bases of the aforesaid four characters, formed a perpetual wheel with them, dividing them into the four seasons of the same natural year. The result was that as [the natural year] had its beginning in summer, thus the character that signified it must by congruence have fallen in the same season and influenced the entire year with a special prerogative, dominating the others within the narrow confines of the three remaining seasons.

Copy. *4* I have the said wheel on European paper, copied from other ancient ones by the bachelor don Manuel de los Santos y Salazar, formerly pastor of *Quauhpiaztla* and patrician cacique of *Tlaxcala*;[63] and to find out which character corresponds to each season of the year, one may consult what I have written against Gemelli Careri in the *Idea of a History* at section 10, number 5, reserving to myself to give the public my interpretation of the said wheel in the General History for that concerning the characters of the seasons, as well as the symbols of the days.

---

61. *Ender*, seemingly a typographical error for *entender.*

62. *Panetas, sic* for *planetas.*

63. On Santos y Salazar, see *Nahuatl Theater*, ed. Sell and Burkhart, 4:31–33.

Civil Year, That Is,

Chronological

§. XXVIII

Second calendar. *1* With the scant foundations of the natural year and with new things that presented themselves to the heroic peoples in the second age, in which the wandering and fixed stars had now been deciphered and articulate language somewhat more extended, the Indian heroes found themselves compelled to speculate on how to distinguish some years from others. The civil year, or rather the chronological, was invented based not only on the same four divine characters of the first age, who (perhaps in honor of the thirteen principal deities of the ancestral peoples) were distributed into another four triadecateridas, which were woven together with an everlasting exquisite skill and formed a cycle of fifty-two years, which the Indians called *Xiuhmolpia*, in other words, *one who binds the years*, but also divided and augmented with equally divine symbols into months, weeks, and days, as I have said in different places in the Idea of a History, not exceeding the 365 complete days, and it is called chronological insofar as it later helped in being able to coordinate the history.

Originals. *2* With regard to this material, I will explain two wheels of the Indian cycle that I have on European paper, and with them the one that Doctor Serna brings forth in volume 11, cited in this catalog at section 10, number 2, and that of Father fray Diego de Valadés, a Franciscan,[64] that is in his published book on Christian Rhetoric, the one he wrote for the instruction of Indian students of the Imperial College of Santiago *Tlatelolco.*

Original. *3* And concerning the eighteen lunar months of twenty days each, I will finish deciphering their wheel, which I have on European paper, with everything that may be elegant in this matter.

Original. *4* Likewise I will interpret another wheel on European paper, of the symbols for the days, and I will have thirteen pages of twenty symbols each printed on plates, and I will demonstrate their infallible

64. Valadés (1533–82?) was a mestizo, the son of a conquistador and a native woman. He was a noted linguist. His work *Rhetorica Christiana* was written in Latin.

system to be able to learn the symbol for each day of the year that corresponds to that in the Indian calendar, and I will put the weeks in order, imitating the same Indian systems, with the result that it will be possible to specify the events and the time when they occurred in the histories, distinguishing them by their Indian days, weeks, months, and years.

Volume 18 in quarto. Original.

5 [Authors who] deal with this chronology, its characters and symbols, although with very scarce information, are: the anonymous author cited in this catalog in section 8, number 14. Don Fernando de Alva *Ixtlilxochitl* in some fragments added to volume 16, cited in this same catalog at section 18, number 3. Don Domingo de San Antón Muñón *Chimalpahin* at the end of volume 20, which I will cite here in section 32, number 3. And in addition I have a chronological computation of both the Mexican and Tlaxcalan nations; its author is the said bachelor don Manuel de los Santos y Salazar; and it is anticipated that in general, the Indian authors include in their manuscripts both the characters of their years and the Arabic numerals of ours, although many of them make mistakes, others are now confused in their years and perhaps in ours, and it is not possible to ascertain, if the General History does not provide it, and it is still indispensable to draw up complete tables of the years, beginning with the creation of the world and continuing through all the ages, which is necessary for the History. For that reason I have devoted myself to drawing up the said tables first, and I went on to collect about thirteen. And more epochs of the most notable things, adjusted with uniformity by all the historians into their respective years, in order that they would be infallible proof of the tables, and through them writers can follow a sure course without stumbling, and even correct the Indians themselves in what they neglected.

Astronomical Year

§. XXIX

Third calendar.

1 The wise Toltec nation could not but notice that in the preceding civil year almost six hours were lost each year, for which reason the equinoxes were notably altered in the course of so many cycles; but because they found themselves in their painful daily wandering without that repose that such delicate matters require, it was impossible to apply an adequate remedy to this oversight, until,

after their peoples had reached the continent of New Spain and built their first city, *Huehuetapallan*, about one hundred and some years before the birth of Christ, the mathematicians came together in it and fixed the mistake by adding the leap year, as I have pointed out in the Idea of a History at section 20, number 2, and on such occasion the Indians' lunar-solar year reached its maximum perfection.

2 At the same time, the final touch was also given to the natural year after the astronomers had formed that perpetual wheel that I referred to in this catalog at section 27, number 4, by which agriculture was regulated.

3 In the General History I will give a full explanation of the map and wheel that Gemelli Careri has in his work *Giro del Mundo, part* 6, *chapter* 5.

Copy. *4* In the same way I will explain another pictorial document and wheel that I have on European paper *of the nine masters of the night or nine companion lords* who ruled from sunset and [until] it rose again.

Original. *5* Also, I will be given an opportunity to write some curious scholarly observations on another pictorial document that I have, on coarse Indian paper, painted in the form of a wheel, in which its author placed the course of our planets in an Indian cycle and noted some things about the Mexican nation that always occurred in the years of the character *Acatl*, *Reed*, which [the Indian nation] considered favorable, just as the Toltecs considered that of *Tecpatl*, *Flint*, as unlucky, as their histories relate.

6 Of no less importance will be to give the public the heavenly signs of our Indians which, from what I have seen, were twenty, and they are listed here, although not in their strict order.

Principal Deities of the Pagan Indian Ancestors[65]

I. *Tezcatlipoca, god of providence.*
II. *The same,* accompanied by *Teotlamacazqui, god of the priests.*
III. *Macuilxochiquetzalli, goddess of virtuous love, or like the Greeks' Venus Pronuba.*
IV. *Tlazolteotl, shameful Venus.*

65. This is perpendicular in the margin.

V. *Piltzinteuctli, god of children,* accompanied by *Quetzalcoatl, god of the winds.*

VI. *The same,* accompanied by *Tetzauhteotl, frightful god.*

VII. *Teotlacanexquimilli, a dark bundle, or a god without feet or head,* accompanied by *Tlazolteotl, the shameful Venus,* and by *Tlateuctli, vengeful god of adulteries.*

VIII. *Teoyaotlatohua-Huitzilopochtli, the war god,* accompanied by *Teoyaominqui, goddess who* (according to their understanding) *gathered up the souls of the dead.*

IX. *The same,* accompanied by *Teotecpatl, divine flint.*[66]

X. *Tlatocaocelotl, the jaguar king.*[67]

XI. *Quetzalcoatl, god of the winds,* accompanied by *Quetzal-Mállin.*[68]

XII. *Chalchiuhcueitl, she of the skirt of precious stones.*[69]

XIII. *Hahuiatlteotl, god of vagabonds, gamblers, and tricksters.*

XIV. *Mictlanteuctli, god of the underworld,* accompanied by *Teotlamacazqui, god of the priests.*

XV. *Teoiztactlapanqui, he who cleans the saltworks of the gods,* a figure of speech for restraining anger, or *Quetzalhuexoloquauhtli,* which means *an eagle like a turkey with a crest.*

Demigods of the Heroic Peoples[70]

XVI. *Ollin Tonatiuh, movement of the sun*, accompanied by *citlalcueytl, of the Milky Way*, and it is also one of the symbols for the days of the year.

XVII. *Ce Xochitl, One Flower.* It is also one of the symbols for the days of the year.

XVIII. *Ce Quauhtli, One Eagle.* It is also one of the symbols for the days of the year.

XIX. *Ce Ehecatl, One Wind.* A sign dedicated to *Quetzalcoatl, god of the winds.* It is also one of the symbols for the days of the year.

---

66. In margin: *Hieroglyph of* Fire, *first element.*
67. In margin: *Hieroglyph of* Earth, *second element.*
68. In margin: *Hieroglyph of* Wind, *third element.*
69. In margin: *Hieroglyph of* Water, *fourth element.*
70. This is perpendicular in the margin.

XX. *The same*, accompanied by *Chalchiuhcueitl*, *water*. It is also one of the symbols for the days of the year.

And if I should have the good fortune of finding among the histories of the Indians some author who puts the aforesaid signs and even the planets in order, I will shape pictorial documents and wheels of them in the Indian style, following their own systems; and with regard to the signs, I will exercise great care with the pictorial document of the ritual calendar, which I will refer to next in the following section [30] at number 2, in order to ascertain those eighteen figures of the principal gods that it contains on as many pages, and the other two that are missing, because many of [the figures] seem to be positioned there after the manner of signs, as is made clear by the figure on the first page, *Macuilxochiquetzalli*; that of the third page, *Quetzalcoatl*; that of the fourth page, *Quetzalhuexoloquautli*; that of the fifth page, *Chalchiuhcueitl*; that of the seventh page, *Huitzilopochtli*; and that of the eighteenth page, *Tlatocaocelotl*. Nevertheless, I have not been able to interpret them completely, because they will be better digested on the occasion when [the subject of] to whose signs our Indians attributed greater or lesser divinity is dealt with topic by topic and item by item, according to whether they were principal deities or semi-deities, like those enumerated among the divine heroic symbols of the days of the year.

Ritual Year

§. XXX

Fourth calendar.

1 Although it is a constant that in the first age things were explained with hieroglyphs and divine legends, and that from that era divination and sacrifices emerged in the same birth, because it was, strictly speaking, the age of oracles, in which the first founders of pagan humanity explored the good will of the gods beforehand and confirmed it with sacrifices, despite the notable increase in the number of gods in the second age due to so many heroes who were elevated to divine honors, and to the transformations, which they believed to have been almost as many as the events; and adding in the third age some deities made as if for the purpose by order of the sovereigns, and also the year being divided into months, weeks, and days, with the distinction of heroic divine symbols, the priests of the idols distributed (imitating the system of the chronological and astronomical calendars) to each day of the week its gods and rites and ceremonies which they were bound to observe.

Original. 2 I have a very ancient pictorial document of this ritual year on coarse, worm-eaten Indian paper, which in one part has some bird feathers attached, and it is tied together and folded like a piece of cloth, on which the priests of the idols, who were in charge of the rites, spread out the moveable and fixed feasts of their gods in twenty pages or panels, each one of them bearing a triadecaterida of symbols of the days of the year, corresponding to the common system of the year, although missing the two final pages for completing the twenty principal symbols of the days of the year, which are distributed in this pictorial document in a different manner than is seen in the tables of Doctor Serna. The count should begin in reverse, where the *Ce Cipactli* should fall at the end, despite the fact that the same thing happens with regard to the count of the days of the year, whether in the tables of Doctor Serna of thirteen tables of twenty days or in this pictorial document of twenty pages of thirteen days.[71] And it should be noted that page nineteen, which is missing, should begin with the symbol *Ce Ocelotl, One Jaguar*, that corresponds to it, and his triadecaterida should finish at 13 *Miquiztli*, 13 *Deaths*; and page two, which is also missing, should begin with *Ce Cipactli, One Shark*, and end with its triadecaterida on 13 *Acatl*, 13 *Reeds*, with the result that in one way or another, that is, from thirteen tables of twenty days or twenty pages of thirteen days, they result in a count of 260 days and it returns to the beginning, continuing to count up to 100 more days, and it gives 360 in a year, and then they add five intercalary days, with their successive symbols, and the year is completed, and the feasts and ceremonies that correspond to each day were known at a fixed point. On the respective pages of the same pictorial document the feasts of each day of the year are specified by some small sculptures of the gods, and outside of these a large idol is seen depicted which was revered par excellence for that entire triadecaterida, that is, his feast was more solemn,

71. This sentence is rather confused.

and its rites and ceremonies lasted thirteen days, with greater demonstrations, just as when in our ecclesiastical calendars some feasts with an octave[72] are noted.

Original. *3* Likewise consigned to this class is another pictorial document that I have on a cured skin, with a circle of colored[73] beads in the middle that form the numbers of four triadecateridas, accompanied by a head of a *rabbit*, and different figures of very ugly idols are visible in the four corners of this document, which were like guardians and custodians of the cycle, to whom, both at [the cycle's] entrance and exit, great feasts were celebrated, which will be specified in the General History.[74]

Original. *4* From the diocese of *Oaxac*[75] I was sent another pictorial document on Indian paper that is stretched and folded like a piece of cloth. It seems, from what I can say at the present time, that it has the outlines of some calendar of those nations, in agreement with the Toltec system in many ways, but with a variety of characters and symbols. Its interpretation will not fail to give me plenty to do, nor can I be sure if its strange characters and symbols are consistent with rites and ceremonies.[76]

5 To top off this curious material I will explain the feasts, whether fixed and posted or the sixteen moveable ones, which circulate around the entire year with the symbols of the days, keeping in mind the ritual intercalation, which I previewed in the Idea of a History at section 27, number 2.

72. An octave was a period of eight days following a major feast day, during which the feast was still celebrated.

73. *Colorado* can also mean "red."

74. This is Aubin Ms. 20.

75. *Sic* for Oaxaca.

76. This is one of the Humboldt items.

HISTORY
of the Conquest
Pictorial Documents
§. XXXI

Original. 1 I have a pictorial document of the expedition that the celebrated don Fernando Cortés made into *Cempoala* and of the progress of our holy Catholic faith in that province, and of some Franciscan Fathers and of Your Majesty's officials who governed it, some in spiritual matters, others in temporal. It is on Indian paper, long like a strip, and it is something like two spans wide. Its figures are well drawn.

Original. 2 Another pictorial document on cotton cloth, as large as a bedsheet. At the beginning it carries Your Majesty's arms, and they are immediately followed by those of the city of *Tlaxcala* and the first chapel of ease that was built to Our Lady and Patroness of *Guadalupe*, with her most holy image and then a cross. In this upper part of the said pictorial document can be seen painted the four sections of *Tlaxcala*, its first bishop, and something like thirteen Spanish personages on their chairs who, it seems to me, were the corregidores[77] of the said city and province, as I shall explain in the history of the Virgin, when dealing with that same pictorial document. In the lower part, the deeds of the general conquest of New Spain are depicted in order in distinct panels, although it may have a few of them spoiled because of their antiquity. It is an important piece for the history of *Guadalupe* and of the conquest, and the said panels can be copied onto plates and joined with other documents to corroborate it and make it more beautiful.

---

77. Corregidor was a Spanish official in charge of a province or district. He had both judicial and administrative powers.

3 It should be noted that in all the pictorial documents from pagan times and extending into Christian times, there are many painted depictions of the conquest that should be kept in mind so that, when all its fragments have been carefully collected, an entire, completely authentic corpus can be put together.

Original. *4* I was also able to obtain the original standard of red damask that the invincible Cortés gave to the captain general of the Tlaxcalans, I suppose on the second expedition that was made against Emperor *Moteucçoma* and the other allied kings. On the front side of the said standard can be seen a depiction of a most beautiful likeness of Most Holy Mary, crowned with a gold crown, and with hands joined, as if she is praying to her Most Holy Son to protect and strengthen the Spaniards to subjugate the idolatrous empire to the Catholic faith, and in some respects it does not fail to resemble her who appeared later, of *Guadalupe.* On the back likewise can be seen depictions of the royal arms of Castile and León. I reserve for the General History to give the indisputable basis for which the said standard is the sole original still in existence today.

MANUSCRIPTS

§. XXXII

1 The manuscript of an anonymous Indian cited in this catalog at section 8, number 10, and other native authors cited in the manuscript of the said section 8, number 14, deal with the conquest in the *Nahuatl* language, and in the Castilian language don Fernando de Alva *Ixtlilxochitl* at the end of the *History of the Chichimeca Lords*, which I cited here at section 4, number 1. The same author in the historical compendium of the kingdom of *Tezcoco*, which I cited in the said section 4, number 5. Don Diego Muñoz Camargo in the history of *Tlaxcala*, which I cited in this catalog at section 18, number 3. Don Juan Ventura Zapata y Mendoza in the chronicle of *Tlaxcala*, cited in the said section 18, number 4. And it is noteworthy that all the authors who go on to write history in both languages from pagan times to Christian times usually touch on many things in passing that pertain to the said conquest and more to the spread of our Holy Catholic Faith.

Volume 19 in folios. Original.

2 In addition I have a volume by a Spanish author, whose name I do not remember, that deals with the conquest of New Spain and matters pertaining to the kingdoms of Peru.

Volume 20 in folios. Original.

3 Another history of the conquest, its author don Domingo de San Antón Muñón *Chimalpahin.* It is a complete work, well arranged and extensive. Other different native authors have written about this subject, such as don Hernando de Alvarado *Tezozomoc* in the second part of the *Mexican Chronicle*; don Tadeo de Niza, on the district of *Tepeticpac* of *Tlaxcala*, at the express order of the governor in the year 1548, and some thirty Tlaxcalan caciques, who had assisted and commanded the auxiliary troops of the republic in the said conquest, signed his history. There is a judicial report of the first soldiers and conquistadores. There are other manuscripts by Spaniards and many more by Indians, which with the will of God and the approval of Your Majesty, I will not fail to obtain, if my life does not fail me.

Ecclesiastical History

Some Things that Pertain to the Said History

§. XXXIII

1 A printed history of Our Lady of La Defensa, whose sanctuary is located in the province of *Tlaxcala.*[78]

2 Another, printed, of Our Lady of *Tecaxitl*, whose church is located in the province of *Tolocan.*

3 A testimony to the wonders that the Most Holy Image of [Our Lady of] La Defensa has performed, and of some things concerning the venerable Brother Juan Bautista, which I copied from the books and archive of the convent of Saint Francis of *Tlaxcala.*

4 An ancient comedy, in which notices of the Most Holy Virgin of *Ocotlan* are told, which was found, according to ancient tradition, in a pine tree in the town of *Ocotitlan* close by the said city of *Tlaxcala.*[79]

5 Testimony of the baptismal record of the fortunate Indian Diego Lázaro, to whom the glorious Archangel Saint Michael appeared in the site of his sanctuary that today is called San Miguel del Milagro, in the province of *Tlaxcala.*

6 An authentic copy of the testimony of the said Diego Lázaro. It is useful for the history of the said apparition.

---

78. Nuestra Señora de la Defensa was and is one of the principal Marian devotions of Tlaxcala. It originated with a pious Indian named Juan Bautista de Jesús in the mid-seventeenth century. He prepared a written account of the miracles associated with the devotion and shrine for Bishop Juan Palafox y Mendoza. The principal feast of La Defensa is on October 12.

79. Our Lady of Ocotlán is the patron saint of Tlaxcala and Puebla. In some ways her story is similar to that of Guadalupe.

7 Testimony of the investigations that the governor of *Tlaxcala* carried out concerning the spring and water issuing miraculously in the place of the said sanctuary, and the glorious Archangel discovered it. It is useful for the history of the said apparition.

In octavo. *8* A printed history of the said miracle and apparitions of the glorious prince [Saint Michael]. I do not remember the name of the author, but I know that he is a cleric of Puebla.

In quarto. *9* Another history of the said apparitions published by Father Francisco de Florencia of the Sacred Company.

10 Notices of the apparition of Our Lady of the hill of *Cholula* is found on the pictorial document that I cited in this catalog at section 20, number 3.

11 A manuscript history in Castilian verse of the most miraculous image of Our Lady of Remedios, venerated on the hill of *Totoltepec*, close to *Tlacopan*. The imperial city of *Tenochtitlan Mexico*, is the patron of that sanctuary. The author is someone named Betancurt, a Franciscan tertiary,[80] and he was the first to write about this topic before the printed histories of this subject by Fathers Masters fray Luis de Cisneros, of the order of Merced, and Francisco Florencia, of the Sacred Company. Included in the said history are various poems by the same author on other topics.

80. Angel Betancurt was the author of a poem *Historia de la milagrosa imagen de Nuestra Señora de los Remedios*. This poem is in the Archivo General de la Nación in Mexico City. See Poole, *Our Lady of Guadalupe*, 985–96.

HISTORY
of
GUADALUPE

Printed Books

§. XXXIV

In quarto. *1* A printed history in the Castilian language of the apparitions of the great Lady; its author is the licentiate don Miguel Sánchez. It is the first that was published, and it is in a panegyric style.[81]

In quarto. *2* He also published a *Devout Novena*, which I have in incomplete condition.[82]

In quarto. *3* Another printed history in the *Nahuatl* language by the bachelor Luis Laso de la Vega, formerly vicar of the sanctuary of the Divine Lady.[83] This is not nor can it be by the said author, rather it can be strongly argued that it is by don Antonio Valeriano or another Indian alumnus of the Imperial College of Santiago *Tlatelolco*,[84] a contemporary of the miracle of the said apparitions, and I will prove it with solid arguments of my own that I am writing about the Most Holy Lady, and for this purpose I am very much aided by the approbation

---

81. Sánchez, *Imagen*, in the bibliography.

82. This work was *Novenas de la Virgen Maria, Madre de Dios, para sus devotisimos santuarios de los Remedios y Guadalupe*, published in Mexico City in 1665.

83. Laso de la Vega, *Huei tlamahuiçoltica*, in the bibliography.

84. On the subject of the author of the *Nican mopohua*, see Poole, *Our Lady of Guadalupe*, 111–13, 117–18.

that the said bachelor included in the history of the licentiate Sánchez, and what Father Florencia writes in the chapter on manuscripts by Indian authors, and the narrative itself by the said bachelor Laso, in which he deals with the miracles of the holy image and of that which occurred to the Indians of San Juan *Teotihuacan*, who, having regretted the great disrespect that they committed against God and the sacred religious order of the lord Saint Augustine in burning the conventual church of the said city, went to *Azcapotzalco*, and hiding from justice in the homes of relatives and friends, they went by night to visit and ask the appeared Blessed Image of Guadalupe to soften the indignation of the viceroy and the Augustinian Fathers.[85] And this proves that the author was an Indian and from *Azcapotzalco* (as is from San Juan *Teotihuacan* he who left the history of the said disrespect painted on an ancient pictorial document that I have in my archive, in pieces), and also that mentioned in the said *Nahuatl* history is the testament of don Francisco Verdugo *Quetzalmamalitzin*,[86] lord of the said city, and the bequest that he left, that is, that after his death they should go to the sanctuary of Guadalupe to have some masses said for the repose of his soul. I have a copy of that testament in the Castilian language, drawn from the Mexican; and it should be seen that no Spaniard could have had such individual knowledge of these things and of the ancient miracles, as did the contemporary Indians; and if the bachelor Laso had been [its] true historian, he would have made it clear in the approbation he gave to the said history of licentiate Sánchez and not when scarcely six months had passed since the printing, he made known with his name the aforementioned history in the *Nahuatl* language, not citing any authors from whom he took it, and I believe, rather, that by chance he found some ancient manuscript by an Indian author, and he did no more than publish it and put his name on it, quite simply taking away, not only from the natives the honor of having written it, but also the antiquity of the history,

85. For the original account of this story, see Sousa, Poole, Lockhart, eds. and trans., *Story of Guadalupe*, 111.

86. On this will, see Poole, *Our Lady of Guadalupe*, 85–86. Boturini makes a common error that any mention of the shrine at Guadalupe authenticates the story of the apparitions.

something that will be remedied in my defensive[87] prologue where I deal with and do a critique of the manuscripts of the natives.

In quarto. *4* I have the translation of this history in the Castilian language which I caused to be made for this purpose.

In quarto. *5* Another printed history in the Castilian language by licentiate Becerra Tanco.[88] Its author bases it on the Indians' records, but he did not give an individual account of them, nor was he careful to append [the records] to it and leave the originals in a safe place so that they could be examined.

In quarto. *6* Another printed [history], and more extensive, in the Castilian language by the most learned Father Francisco de Florencia of the Sacred Company.[89] It traces the route of the tradition, and there is little of ancient proofs, but it is not possible for religious, subject to obedience, to be able to cover the land as I did, for so many years looking for accounts apropos of the prodigious miracle.

In quarto. *7* Another brief and succinct [history] of the said apparitions in the Castilian language, published by a canon of the cathedral of Puebla, whose name I do not remember.[90]

In octavo. *8* Another printed in Rome in the Italian language by Anastasio Nicoseli, taken from records and investigations that were made in that court about the tradition.[91]

In octavo. *9* Another in Castilian verse by a Father of the Company by the name of Carnero.[92]

---

87. *Galeato*, the defenses and refutations found in a prologue.

88. Luis de Becerra Tanco (1603–72) was a Mexican priest and scholar. It is not clear which work Boturini is referring to. In 1666 Becerra published a pamphlet, *Origen milagroso del santuario de Nuestra Señora de Guadalupe.* See *Testimonios históricos guadalupanos*, 309–33. A revised edition, titled *Felicidad de Mexico*, was published posthumously in 1675.

89. Florencia, *Estrella del norte*, in the bibliography.

90. This probably refers to an abbreviated version of Sánchez's work published by the Jesuit Mateo de la Cruz, 1660, under the patronage of Juan García de Palacios, a canon of the cathedral of Puebla. It was reprinted in 1662 (Vera, *Tesoro guadalupano*, 2:80).

91. Nicoselli, *Relatione Istorica*, in the bibliography. His work was printed in Rome in 1681.

92. Juan Carnero (b. 1660) was a Jesuit who taught in Jesuit colleges and was the author of numerous devotional works (Beristáin de Souza, *Biblioteca*, 2:49–50).

In octavo. *10* Another also in Castilian poetry, its author a cleric whose name and surname I do not remember.

In folio. *11* *Centonicum Virgilianum*, that is, the apparition of the Divine Lady, ingeniously taken from the works of Vergil. Its author is a canon of the cathedral of Valladolid, whose name slips my mind.[93]

In folio. *12* The same apparition in Latin verse with some notes. Its author, if I am not mistaken, was someone by the name of Avilés, a priest. The verses are somewhat tired, but the notes are very erudite.[94]

In octavo. 13 Some Castilian verses about the lovely causeway from this city to the sanctuary that an archbishop of Mexico ordered to be made. They are somewhat mouse-eaten.

Guadalupe

Manuscripts

§. XXXIV

1 The history in the Nahuatl language by the bachelor Luis Laso de la Vega, which I cited in the preceding section, number 3, should be counted among the manuscripts by Indian authors for the reasons that I have touched on in passing and will prove in my defensive prologue.

Original in half folio in length. *2* A manuscript in the *Nahuatl* language. It deals with many things pertaining to the Mexican empire and in a few lines, with a concise style (like the rest) relates that the Most Holy Lady appeared on the hill of *Tepeyacac*. Its author did not give the correct Arabic numbers for the year the apparition occurred, but the history is ancient, trustworthy, and I will prove it in the said prologue.[95]

In quarto. Originals. *3* Another two manuscripts in the *Nahuatl* language, which are cited in the separate items of the history of the Mexican empire. They

93. The author was Bernardo de Riofrío, a canon of Michoacan. On this work see bibliography.

94. José Avilés was a native of New Spain, "maestro de pages" for Archbishop Payo Enríquez de Ribera of Mexico, and author of *Viridarium poeticum* (1669) (Beristáin de Souza, *Biblioteca*, 1:224–25).

95. This may possibly be the annals attributed to the native official Juan Bautista, which give the date for the appearance as 1555. See Poole, *Our Lady of Guadalupe*, 51.

mention in a few lines the apparition in the appropriate year; for the life of me I cannot remember which separate items they are. I will prove their antiquity in the aforesaid prologue.

Original in quarto.

4 Another manuscript cited in section 33, number II. It deals with the history of the miraculous image of Our Lady of Remedios and gives an account of the fifth apparition of Guadalupe to the cacique don Juan Bernardino de Tovar *ce Quauhtzin Tequitlato*[96] of the said town of Los Remedios, which in pagan times was called *Totoltepec.*[97] No author, Indian or Spanish, mentions the fifth apparition except Father Florencia, and I will give the reasons for it in the said prologue.

Copy in folio.

5 Through certain historic fragments that I copied from the originals of the celebrated don Carlos de Sigüenza y Góngora, it is clear to me that don Antonio Valeriano, a native of Azcatpotzalco,[98] a native cacique and former teacher of rhetoric in the Imperial College of *Tlatelolco*, wrote the history of the apparitions of Guadalupe in the *Nahuatl* language, and Sigüenza himself, under oath, admits that he had it in his possession in the hand[writing] of don Antonio, which perhaps is the one that the bachelor Laso de la Vega published, and the Divine Mother can with time strengthen me so that I can establish her history better; and it should be noted that I have in my archive the signatures of the said don Antonio in order to compare them exactly with his original history, provided that it appears.

6 From the said fragments I also discovered another manuscript of the same history of Guadalupe in the Castilian language, its author don Fernando de Alva *Ixtlilxochitl*, whose handwriting I know, which I am searching for with the greatest diligence.

7 The most learned Father Florencia[99] relates in his history of the Most Holy Lady how don Francisco Plácido, lord of *Azcapotzalco*,

96. Literally, "one eagle tribute collector." This apparition did not become part of the Guadalupe tradition.

97. On this see Poole, *Our Lady of Guadalupe*, 193.

98. In margin: "NOTE. *Father Juan Bautista brings forth a Latin letter of the said Indian cacique in the prologue to his Mexican Sermonary, and from it the polished talent of the author is clear.*"

99. In margin: "NOTE. *There is no lack of many other histories and songs of the Most Holy Virgin which with ungrateful distrust the Indians conceal, especially the commoners.*"

at the time that the most holy image appeared and was placed in the first chapel of Guadalupe, composed a song in the Nahuatl language, which was the ancient method of narrating history, and it was found among the interesting papers of don Domingo de San Antón Muñón *Chimalpahin*, and it pained me very much that the said Father had not placed it accurately at the end of his history, because it runs the risk of being lost.[100]

Originals in folios. *8* The account in both the Castilian and Mexican languages of the apparitions of the Divine Lady also belongs here; the comedy in Mexican verse on the same topic; the separate verses in the same language and praise of the Sovereign Queen, all of which were composed by don Joseph Antonio Pérez and are cited in section 24, number 5.[101]

Original in folios. *9* A manuscript of the said apparitions and of the new, celebrated sanctuary that was most recently constructed in Guadalupe to her Divine Majesty; its author, I suppose, must be don something or other Avilés, a priest, although the pastor cacique of Santa Fe, hungry for glory, erased the author's namer and put his own, correcting some of the context and adding some leaves at the end in his own hand.[102]

Originals in folios. *10* Various notebooks of historic notices proven in juridical form with texts in both laws.[103] A work that the pious pen of don something or other Franquis, former oidor of the royal audiencia of Mexico, in pleasant and idle hours dedicated to the Great Lady.[104]

---

100. The original is now in the manuscript division of the Biblioteca Nacional de México, Ms. 1628 bis. The text is reproduced in *Testimonios históricos guadalupanos*, 23; Garibay, "Temas guadalupanas, 3," 295; Bierhorst, *Cantares mexicanos*, 221. For a discussion of this, see Poole, *Our Lady of Guadalupe*, 44–47.

101. This was José Antonio Pérez de la Fuente, author of the play *El portento mexicano.* See Poole, *Our Lady of Guadalupe*, 172–73, 190. Copies of the text are in the New York Public Library, the Bibliothèque Nationale de France, Paris, and Biblioteca Nacional de Antropología e Historia, Mexico City. A translation of the play can be found in *Nahuatl Theater*, 2:108–85.

102. It is not clear what this work is. *Bibliografía*, ed. Grijales and Burrus, no. 62, simply repeats Boturini's information.

103. That is, canon and civil law.

104. It is not clear what this work is. *Bibliografía*, ed. Grijales and Burrus, no. 68, simply repeats Boturini's information.

Copy in quarto.

11 A manuscript that establishes with medical evidence the continuous miracle of the preservation of the *ayatl* or cloth on which the image of Guadalupe is drawn by angelic hands.[105]

12 I also wrote an essay of the history of my Mother and Lady of Guadalupe and of New Spain in general which I was thinking of publishing and communicating to the public to trace the knowledge and materials of both histories.

Public Instruments and other Records

§. XXXVI

1 I said historic fragments of Sigüenza confirm the place where don fray Juan de Zumárraga, the first archbishop of Mexico, was living when the fortunate Indian Juan Diego unfolded the cloak to give him the flowers that he brought on behalf of Most Holy Mary, and the most beautiful image of Guadalupe appeared imprinted on it. The same author proves it with ancient books and a royal cédula[106] given at Monzón, although other Spanish authors were unable to locate it, some of them thinking with feeble conjectures that the said location was in the hospital of Amor de Dios,[107] and others, in the home of the marqués of Soria, formerly oidor of the royal audiencia of *Mexico*, and, following Sigüenza, I labored in the archive of the holy Metropolitan Cathedral and found for this purpose different legal instruments which I copied from the originals, from which it is clear that the archbishop had purchased and lived in the said dwellings at the same time as the apparitions of her Divine Majesty.

2 Likewise I have the copy of the testament of the cacique don Francisco Verdugo *Quetzalmamalitzin*, cited in section 34, number 3, *ad probandum antiquum Deiparæ cultum.*[108]

---

105. This may refer to the inspection of the image on March 28, 1666, by the *protomedicato* of New Spain, the supervisory body for medical and scientific endeavors. See Poole, *Our Lady of Guadalupe*, 142. It is reproduced in Sada Lambretón, Informaciones jurídicas, 375–404.

106. Command or decree.

107. Hospital in Mexico City founded by Cortés.

108. "For proving the antiquity of the devotion to the Mother of God." This will is in the Bibliothèque Nationale de France, Paris, Mexicains, 243. The full text

(*continued*)

Authentic copy. 3 In addition I have an authentic copy of the testament of don Esteban Tomelín, father of the venerable religious María de Jesús, a nun, now deceased, in the convent of the Immaculate Conception of Puebla, whose canonization is being pursued at the present time. In it the said don Esteban left a bequest of some pesos to the blessed image of Guadalupe around the year 1575. It is helpful in proving the fame of the apparitions and the resulting devotion that was given to the Most Holy Lady.[109]

Original. 4 Likewise the original testament of a relative of the fortunate Indian Juan Diego on Indian paper and in the *Nahuatl* language, in which mention is made that the Virgin of Guadalupe appeared on a Saturday, and she [the relative] leaves to the blessed image as a bequest some lands located in the district of *Cuauhtitlan*, and an account is given of María Lucía, wife of the said Juan Diego, and of the conjugal purity in which these two fortunate spouses lived. It is an item of the greatest importance.[110]

Copy. 5 A notice, which I copied from the records of the chapter of the holy Metropolitan Cathedral, of when the Sovereign Image was brought to *Mexico* to stop the great flood that occurred in the said city in the years 1629 and 1630, and the permission that the venerable dean and chapter gave to the devout provincial and religious of Our Lady of Mercy, Redemption of Captives,[111] to be able to celebrate a sung mass at the main altar of the said holy church, where the sacred image was located, and to pay homage to her with a sermon and vespers. It proves the devotion and benefits that the city has received from Her Majesty's most loving hands, and it is the content of the said permission, accompanied by specific clauses.[112]

Copy. 6 Another notice about the blessed image's time and stay in the holy Metropolitan Church on the occasion of the aforesaid flood,

---

is reprinted in Vera, *Tesoro guadalupano*, appendix, 1:5–11 and partially reprinted in *Testimonios históricos guadalupanos*, 96. See Poole, *Our Lady of Guadalupe*, 87.

109. The text of the will can be found in Vera, *Tesoro guadalupano*, appendix, 1:18–22. The name is also spelled Lomelín.

110. The original of this will has not survived. On the question of the wills, see Poole, *Our Lady of Guadalupe*, 195–97.

111. Commonly known as Mercedarians.

112. On this see Poole, *Our Lady of Guadalupe*, 97–98.

and how, once the danger had been removed, it was returned to its sanctuary with great feasts and celebrations, taken from a manuscript book that is found in the library of the Colegio Máximo of San Pedro y San Pablo of the Sacred Company.

Copy. *7* Another notice about the events that happened during the said flood and the devotion that was given to the Most Holy Queen of Guadalupe that I copied from a Dominican author, which I found handwritten in the Grand Convent[113] of his Patriarch of *Mexico*, and it is the second part of his works and has not yet been published.[114]

Copy. *8* A copy of a lead plaque that was placed in the cornerstone when the second church at Guadalupe was constructed.

Originals. *9* A large, bound volume of ancient titles and instruments of a pious work for the humble poor, which was attached to the first chapel of ease and sanctuary of Guadalupe. There are in this volume instruments that prove the devotion from the times contemporaneous with the apparitions and much later.

10 The pictorial manuscript that I cited in section 31, number 2, by which it is proven that the Indian authors left behind a memory of the Most Holy Lady, and that they wrote the history of her apparitions with pictures, according to the style of this nation; and that the Sovereign[115] Virgin, perhaps imitating the usage and customs of the empire, with regard to the manner of writing history, wished to be painted on the *ayatl* of Juan Diego; the Indians were so satisfied with that painted testimony that they always took great pains to serve her. Once I have occasion to interpret this pictorial document, I will show its antiquity and how the natives attributed to her high patronage the spread of the faith in the universal conquest of New Spain.

Cloth no. 4. *11* The original portrait that I have of the fortunate Juan Diego also helps with the proof of her Divine Majesty's history; he is seen painted kneeling, looking at the small hill of *Tepeyacac* where our Mother and Patroness first appeared to him, and next to him he has the miraculous

113. At that time, "convent" could mean a religious house of men or women. It is not clear what document is referred to.

114. John Glass, in an unpublished, unpaginated study indicates that this was taken from a work by the Dominican Alonso Franco, from the second part of his *Chronicle*, book 3, chapter 11.

115. Sobera, conjectured to be an error for soberana.

spring that issued forth with very healthful mineral waters, when above it the Mother of God appeared to him again. I found the said portrait in *Tlaxcala*, where an Indian priest, who was the vicar of the sanctuary of Guadalupe, had transported it.

12 Likewise I have a pictorial document of the present church of Guadalupe and its perspective, with the causeway that extends to Mexico [City], although it is not completely finished. Captain don Luis Navarro, Your Majesty's engineer general, made it that it might serve for the history of the coronation.

13 Also, another by the same engineer for the placement of the houses of the prebendaries,[116] which must have been built on the occasion that the collegiate chapter was established in the sanctuary, something greatly desired; and of the locales that can be put in order for the beauty of the place of Guadalupe, and the change of the source of the river which noticeably narrows it.

14 In addition there are on the shelf of my archive two manuscript notebooks about the history of Guadalupe, that is, of my defensive prologue and its first foundation. *Ab elegantia, & fide historiæ Indicæ*,[117] where I explain the Indians' four modes of writing history, both from pagan times and after them, that is, in songs the historians and rhetoricians composed: *in figures, ciphers, characters, symbols, and hieroglyphs* of a thousand refinements and full of arcane learning; *in manuscripts* in the European alphabet as soon as they were taught by our Spaniards; so that later they would prove, as I shall prove, the apparitions of the Most Holy Virgin, by means of contemporary songs, pictorial documents, and manuscripts; because *in knots*, which were the fourth way of writing history, I have not yet been able to obtain even one of them in the extensive history that I have of New Spain.

116. Canons, here of a collegiate church.

117. "for the distinction and trustworthiness of the history of the Indies."

Observations

§. Final

1 The records in the *Nahuatl* language that are cited in this catalog are understood to be in the Mexican language, although what they speak at present and that the Mexicans spoke in pagan times is not their own, but learned from the other preceding nations, rather, it should be called Toltec because this nation brought it from their wanderings, having perfected it in the third age. Certainly the said language is of exquisite refinement and surpasses Latin in the aptness of its words, having some lofty concepts and very frequent figures of speech, which enhance it; and its poetry is found in the songs that are difficult to explain, because they wrap everything historic in endless metaphors.

2 Indian paper is made from the leaves of the *Maguey*, which in the native language is called *Metl* and in Castilian *pita.*[118] They put it out to rot and after washing its fiber, once softened they spread it out to produce a coarse or thin paper, which they then burnished in order to paint on it. They also made paper from palm leaves, and I have some of them, thin and as soft as silk.

3 Finally, I observe that on my shelf there are many more documents than those specified here; but memory being thin and the stack of papers thick, I cannot remember them all, because when I wrote this catalog I was separated from my archive.

118. Indian paper was ordinarily made from the inner bark of the fig tree and was known as amatl paper.

LAUS DEO
ET VIRGINI
GUADALUPENSI
PER INFINITA
SÆCULORUM
SÆCULA
AMEN[119]

119. "Praise to God and the Virgin of Guadalupe forever and ever."

Bibliography

Alva Ixtlilxochitl, Fernando de. *Obras históricas de don Fernando de Alva Ixtlilxochitl.* Edited by Alfredo Chavero. 2 vols. Mexico City: Editorial Nacional, 1965.

Alvarado Tezozómoc, Fernando de. *Crónica mexicayotl.* Edited and translated by Adrián León. Publicaciones del Instituto de Historia, ser. 1, no. 10. Mexico: Instituto de Historia, 1949.

Antei, Giorgio. *El caballero andante: Vida, obra y desventuras de Lorenzo Boturini Benaduci, 1698–1755.* Mexico City: Museo de la Basílica de Guadalupe, 2007.

Ballesteros Gaibrois, Manuel. *Los papeles de don Lorenzo Boturini Benaduci.* Documentos Inéditos para la Historia de España 5, Papeles de Indias 1. Madrid: Imprenta y Editorial Maestre, 1947.

Bayle, Constantino. "El Caballero Boturini y la fracasada coronación de la Virgen de Guadalupe, México." *Estudios Eclesiásticos. Revista Trimestral Escrita por Padres de la Compañía de Jesús* [Madrid] 2, no. 66 (1923): 183–203.

Beristáin de Souza, José Mariano. *Biblioteca hispanoamericana septentrional.* 5 vols. Mexico City: Ediciones Fuente Cultural, 1883.

Bibliografía guadalupana (1531–1984); Guadalupan Bibliography (1531–1984). Edited by Gloria Grijales and Ernest Burrus. Washington, D.C.: Georgetown University Press, 1986.

Bierhorst, John. *A Nahuatl-English Dictionary and Concordance to the Cantares Mexicanos, with an Analytical Transcription and Grammatical Notes.* Stanford, Calif.: Stanford University Press, 1985.

———. *Cantares mexicanos: Songs of the Aztecs.* Stanford, Calif.: Stanford University Press, 1985.

Boturini Benaduci, Lorenzo. *Catálogo del Museo histórico indiano del cavallero Lorenzo Boturini Benaduci, señor de la Torre y de Hono: quien llegò a la Nueva España por febrero del año 1736.* Sabin Americana: Print Editions 1500–1926.

———. *Historia de la América Septentrional por el caballero Lorenzo Boturini Benaduci, señor de la Torre y de Hono, cronista real en las Indias.* Edited by Manuel Ballesteros Gabrois. Madrid: n.p., 1948.

———. *Idea de una Nueva Historia General de la América Septentrional.* Introduction by Miguel León-Portilla. Mexico City: Editorial Porrúa, 1974.

———. *Idea de una nueva historia general de América Septentrional* [1746]. Mexico City: Instituto de Antropología e Historia, Consejo Nacional para la Cultura y las Artes, 1999.

Burrus, Ernest J. "Clavigero and the Lost Sigüenza y Góngora Manuscripts." *Estudios de Cultura Nahuatl* [Mexico] 1 (1959): 59–90.

Cañizares-Esguerra, Jorge. *How to Write the History of the New World: Histories, Epistemologies, and Identities in the Eighteenth-Century Atlantic World.* Stanford, Calif.: Stanford University Press, 2001.

Clavigero, Francisco Javier. *Historia antigua de México.* Edited by Mariano Cuevas. Mexico City: Editorial Porrúa, 1964.

Codex Chimalpahin. Society and Politics in Mexico Tenochtitlan, Tlatelolco, Texcoco, Culhuacan, and Other Nahua Altepetl in Central Mexico: The Nahuatl and Spanish Annals and Accounts Collected and Recorded by don Domingo de San Antón Muñón Quauhtlehuanitzin. Edited and translated by Arthur J. O. Anderson and Susan Schroeder. 2 vols. Norman: University of Oklahoma Press, 1997.

Covarrubias Orozco, Sebastián de. *Tesoro de la lengua castellana o española.* Edited by C. R. Maldonado. Ed. rev. by Manuel Camarero. 2nd ed. Madrid: Editorial Castalia, 1995.

Cruz, Mateo de la. *Relación de la milagrosa aparición de Nuestra Señora de Guadalupe de México.* Puebla: Viuda de Borja, 1660.

Davies, Nigel. *The Toltec Heritage: From the Fall of Tula to the Rise of Tenochtitlán.* Norman: University of Oklahoma Press, 1980.

Durán, Fray Diego. *The History of the Indies of New Spain.* Edited and translated by Doris Heyden. Norman: University of Oklahoma Press, 1994.

Feingold, Mordechai, ed. *Jesuit Science and the Republic of Letters.* Cambridge: Massachusetts Institute of Technology Press, 2012.

Florencia, Francisco de. *La estrella del norte de Mexico aparecida al rayar el dia de la luz Evangelica en este Nuevo Mundo en la cumbre del cerro de Tepeyacac, orilla del mar Tezcucano, à un Natural recien convertido; pintada tres dias despues milagrosamente en su tilma ò capa de lienzo delante del Obispo y de su familia, en su casa Obispal, para luz en la fé à los Indios; para rumbo cierto à los Españoles en la virtud, para serenidad de las tempestuosas inundancias de la Laguna. En la historia de la Milagrosa imagen de nuestra Señora de Guadalupe de Mexico que se apareció en la manta de Juan Diego. Compusola el Padre Francisco de Florenci de la Compañia de Jesus.* Mexico City: Viuda de Juan de Ribera, 1688.

———. *La milagrosa invencion de un thesoro escondido en un campo, que hallò un venturoso cazique, y escondiò en su casa, para gozarlo à sus solas: patente ya en el Santuario de los Remedios en admirable imagen de ntra. Señora; señalada en Milagros, invocada por patrona de las lluvias, y temporales; defensora de los españoles, avogada de los indios, conquistadora de Mexico, erario universal de las *misericordias de Dios, ciudad refugio para todos los que à ella se acogen.* Seville: Imprenta de las Siete Revueltas, 1745.

García Icazbalceta, Joaquín. *Carta acerca del origen de la imagen de Nuestra Señora de Guadalupe de México, escrita por D. Joaquín García Icazbalceta al Ilmo. Sr. Arzobispo D. Pelagio Antonio de Labastida y Dávalos seguida de la Carta Pastoral que el Señor Arzobispo de Tamaulipas don Eduardo Sánchez Camacho dirigió al mismo eminente prelado.* Mexico, n.p.: 1890.

———. "D. Lorenzo Boturini Benaduci." In *Diccionario geográfico, histórico y biográfico de los Estados Unidos Mexicanos,* edited by Antonio García Cubas. 5 vols. Mexico City: Antigua Imprenta de Murguía, 1888.

Garibay, Angel María. "Temas guadalupanos, 3. El problema de los cantares." *Abside* 9, no. 3 (1945): 243–59.

Genin, Auguste. "Notes on the Dances, Music, and Songs of the Ancient and Modern Mexicans." In *Annual Report of the Board of Regents of the Smithsonian Institution, Showing the Operations, Expenditures, and Conditions for the year ending June 30, 1920,* 657–77. Washington, D.C.: Government Printing Office, 1922.

Gerhard, Peter. *A Guide to the Historical Geography of New Spain.* Cambridge: Cambridge University Press, 1972.

Gibson, Charles. "A Survey of Middle American Prose Manuscripts in the Native Historical Tradition." In *Handbook of Middle American Indians,* vol. 15, *Guide to Ethnohistorical Sources,* edited by Howard F. Cline, 311–21. Austin: University of Texas Press, 1975.

Gibson, Charles, and John B. Glass. "A Census of Middle American Prose Manuscripts in the Native Historical Tradition." In *Handbook of Middle American Indians,* vol. 15, *Guide to Ethnohistorical Sources,* edited by Howard F. Cline, 322–400. Austin: University of Texas Press, 1975.

Glass, John B. "The Boturini Collection." In *Handbook of Middle American Indians,* vol. 15, *Guide to Ethnohistorical Sources,* edited by Howard F. Cline, 473–86. Austin: University of Texas Press, 1975.

———. *Boturini in Spain.* Lincoln, Mass.: John B. Glass, 2005.

———. *Catálogo de la Colección de Códices.* Mexico City: Museo Nacional de Antropología e Historia, 1964.

———. "A Checklist of Institutional Holdings of Middle American Manuscripts in the Native Historical Tradition." In *Handbook of Middle American Indians,* vol. 15, *Guide to Ethnohistorical Sources,* edited by Howard F. Cline, 401–72. Austin: University of Texas Press, 1975.

González de Cossío, Francisco. "Nuevos datos sobre el catálogo histórico de Boturini." *Boletín del Archivo General de la Nación,* 1a. época, vol. 23, no. 1 (January–May 1952): 15–58.

Hassig, Ross. *Aztec Warfare: Imperial Expansion and Political Control.* Norman: University of Oklahoma Press, 1988.

"Inventario de los documentos recogidos a don Lorenzo Boturini por orden del gobierno virreinal." *Anales del Museo Nacional de Arqueología, Historia, Etnografía [*Mexico], 4a. época, vol. 3 (1925): 1–55.

Karttunen, Frances. *An Analytical Dictionary of Nahuatl.* Austin: University of Texas Press, 1983.

Keen, Benjamin. *The Aztec Image in Western Thought.* New Brunswick, N.J.: Rutgers University Press, 1971.

Laso de la Vega, Luis. *Huey tlamahuiçoltica omonexiti in ilhuicac tlatocacihuapilli Santa Maria totlaçonantzin Guadalupe in nican huey altepenahuac Mexico itocayocan Tepeyacac.* Mexico City: Imprenta de Juan Ruiz, 1649.

[Laso de la Vega, Luis]. *The Story of Guadalupe: Luis Laso de la Vega's* Huei tlamahuiçoltica *of 1649.* Edited and translated by Lisa Sousa, Stafford Poole, and James Lockhart. Stanford, Calif.: Stanford University Press, 1998.

León-Portilla, Miguel. Introduction to *Idea de una Nueva Historia General de la América Septentrional*, by Lorenzo Boturini Benaduci. Mexico City: Editorial Porrúa, 1974.

Lockhart, James. *The Nahuas after the Conquest: A Social and Cultural History of the Indians of Central Mexico, Sixteenth through Eighteenth Centuries.* Stanford, Calif.: Stanford University Press, 1992.

———, ed. and trans. *We People Here: Nahuatl Accounts of the Conquest of Mexico.* UCLA Center for Medieval and Renaissance Studies, Repertorium Columbianum 1. Berkeley and Los Angeles: University of California Press, 1993.

López Austin, Alfredo. "Los temacpalitotique: Brujos, profanadores, ladrones y violadores." *Estudios de Cultura Nahuatl* [Mexico] 6 (1966): 97–117.

Mena, Ramón. "La colección arqueológica de Boturini. Ejemplares desconocidos existentes en la Biblioteca Nacional." *Anales del Museo Nacional de Arqueología, Historia, Etnografía.* 4a. época, vol. 2 (1924): 35–70.

Mendieta, Fray Gerónimo de. *Historia ecclesiástica indiana: Obra escrita a fines del siglo XVI.* 3rd. facsimile ed. Mexico City: Editorial Porrúa, 1980.

Molina, Fray Alonso de. *Vocabulario en lengua castellana y mexicana y mexicana y castellana.* Introduction by Miguel León-Portilla. 5th ed. Mexico: Editorial Porrúa, 2004.

Nahuatl Theater. Edited by Barry D. Sell and Louise M. Burkhart. 4 vols. Norman: University of Oklahoma Press, 2006.

Nicoselli, Anastasio. *Relatione Istorica della Mirabile Apparitione della Vergine Santissima Madre di Dio sotto Titolo di Nostra Signora di Guadalupe accaduta nel Messico l'Anno 1531.* Rome, n.p.: 1681.

Our Lady of Guadalupe. Volume 2 of *Nahuatl Theater*, edited by Barry D. Sell, Louise M. Burkhart, and Stafford Poole, 23–24. Norman: University of Oklahoma Press, 2006.

Peperstraete, Sylvie, and Gabriel Kenrick Kruell. "Determining the Authorship of the Crónica Mexicayotl." *The Americas* 71, no. 12 (October 2014): 316, 319.

Poole, Stafford. *The Guadalupan Controversies in Mexico.* Stanford, Calif.: Stanford University Press, 2006.

———. *Our Lady of Guadalupe: The Origins and Sources of a Mexican National Symbol, 1531–1797.* Tucson: University of Arizona Press, 1995.

[Riofrío, Bernardo de]. *Centonicum virgilianum monumentum mirabilis apparitionis Purissimae Virginis Mariae de Guadalupe extramuros civitatis Mexicanae: authore Licto D. Bernardo de Riofrio Michoacanensis Ecclesiae Canonico Doctorali: ad Ilustrissimum, Reverendissimum Principem, M. D. Fr. Payum de Ribera Enriquez, Archiepiscopatus Mexicani Antistitem, Novique Indiarum Orbis proregem nunc Conchensis Ecclesiae Praesulum designatum.* Mexico City: Apud viduam Bernardi Calderon, 1680.

Sada Lambretón, Ana María. *Las informaciones jurídicas de 1666 y el beato indio Juan Diego.* Mexico: Hijas de María Inmaculada de Guadalupe, 1991.

Sánchez, Miguel. *Imagen de la Virgen María, Madre de Dios de Guadalupe. Milagrosamente aparecida en la ciudad de México. Celebrada en su historia, con la profecía del capítulo doce de Apocalipsis.* Mexico City: Imprenta de la Viuda de Bernardo Calderón, 1648.

Silva Galeana, Librado. "Apuntes de los sucesos de la nación mexicana desde el año 1243 hasta el de 1562. Un texto inédito de don Gabriel de Ayala." *Estudios de Cultura Nahuatl* [Mexico] 27 (1997).

Siméon, Remi. *Dictionnaire de la langue Nahuatl ou Mexicaine.* Graz, Austria: Akademische Druck- u. Verlagsanstalt, 1965.

Sullivan, Thelma D. *Compendium of Nahuatl Grammar.* Translated from the Spanish by Thelma D. Sullivan and Neville Stiles. Edited by Wick R. Miller and Karen Dakin. Salt Lake City: University of Utah Press, 1988.

Taylor, William B. *Magistrates of the Sacred: Priests and Parishioners in Eighteenth-Century Mexico.* Stanford, Calif.: Stanford University Press, 1996.

———. *Shrines and Miraculous Images: Religious Life in Mexico before the Reforma.* Albuquerque: University of New Mexico Press, 2010.

Testimonios históricos guadalupanos. Edited by Ernesto de la Torre Villar and Ramiro Navarro de Anda. Mexico City: Fondo de Cultura Económico, 1982.

Thomas, Hugh. *Conquest: Montezuma, Cortés, and the Fall of Old Mexico.* New York: Simon and Schuster, 1993.

Torre Revello, José. "Documentos relativos a D. Lorenzo Boturini Benaduci." *Boletín del Archivo General de la Nación* [Mexico], 1a. época, vol. 7, nos. 1–4 (January–December 1936): 5–45, 229–72, 362–401, 565–95.

Vaillant, George C. *Aztecs of Mexico: Origin, Rise, and Fall of the Aztec Nation.* Revised by Suzannah B. Vaillant. Baltimore, Md.: Pelican Books, 1975.

Vera, Fortino Hipólito. *Tesoro guadalupano: Noticia de los libros, documentos, inscripciones, &c. que tratan, mencionan, ó aluden á la Aparición y devoción de Nuestra Señora de Guadalupe.* 2 vols. Amecameca, Mexico: Imprenta del "Colegio Católico," 1887–89.

Vetancurt, Agustín. *Teatro mexicano: Descripción breve de los sucesos ejemplares, históricos, y religiosos del nuevo mundo de las Indias.* 1st facsimile ed. Mexico City: Editorial Porrúa, 1971.

Villaseñor Black, Charlene. "St. Anne Imagery and Maternal Archetypes in Spain and Mexico." In *Colonial Saints: Discovering the Holy in the Americas, 1500–1800.* Edited by Allan Greer and Jodi Bilinkoff. New York: Routledge, 2003.

"The Wonder of Mexico." In *Nahuatl Theater,* vol. 2, edited by Barry D. Sell, Louise M. Burkhart, and Stafford Poole. Norman: University of Oklahoma Press, 2006.

Zorita, Alonso de. *Breve y sumaria relación de los señores . . . de la Nueva España.* In *Nueva colección de documentos para la historia de México*, edited by Joaquín García Icazbalceta. Mexico: Editorial Chávez Hayhoe, 1941.

Index

Abraham (Abram; biblical patriarch), 77
Acapulco, 41
Acatl: day of the year, 100, 112, 160; east, 109; reed, 63, 90, 163, 165; spring, 109; symbol of water, 110; west, 109; winter, 110; year, 244, 253, 256
acatlxihuitl (year), 90
Achilles, 73
Acosta, José de, 7, 28, 136
age: first, 68–90, 251; second, 91–92; third, 178–79, 189
Agenor, 80
Aguilar, Gerónimo de, 157, 235
Alicante, Dean of. *See* Martí, Manuel, dean of Alicante
Alfonso (king of Aragon and Sicily), 203
Alva Ixtlilxochitl, Fernando de, 142, 154, 155, 159, 188, 207, 209, 211, 252, 259, 267
Alvarado Tezozómoc, Hernando de, 218, 260
Antei, Giorgio, 15
Apollo, 72
Aram (Haran), 77
Archeloos, 81
Atemoztli (altar of the gods; Indian month), 105, 106. *See also* Gemelli Careri, Giovanni Francesco; León, Martín de
Atl (water; day of the year), 100
Atlante, 69
Atlas, 126
Atlcahualo (stopping of the waters), 104, 107. *See also* Gemelli Careri, Giovanni Francesco; León, Martín de
Augustine of Hippo, 35, 174
Axayaca (king of Mexico), 127

Babel, Tower of, 65, 78, 155, 156, 157, 158, 161, 162, 163, 165, 173
Bacchus, 74
Barrientos Lomelin y Cervantes, Manuel, *Epigramma*, 54–55
Bautista, Juan, 248
Becerra Tanco, Luis de, 265
Bellerophon, 74
Betancurt, Agustin de, 221
Boturini Benaduci, Lorenzo: arrested, 6; arrival in New Spain, 201; biography, 3–9; and Black Legend, 12; *Catalog*, 10, 13, 14, 201–74; dedication to the king, 22–23; devotion to Our Lady of Guadalupe, 4, 5, 14, 22; education, 11; *Epigramma*, 54–55;

Boturini Benaduci, Lorenzo, (*continued*) European muses respond, 46; exaltation of Indians, 11; excellence of history of New Spain, 62–65; *Idea*, 7–8, 9, 10, 11, 13, 14, 58; portrait, *59*; prologue for the reader, 60–61; *Sonetto al signor cavalier Boturini*, 50–51; *Sonetto al'medesimo*, 52–53; symbols compared with Gemelli Careri, 109–110; titles, 3; usefulness of his work, 194–200

Burrull, José, 7, 8; declaration, 27–32

Cacontzin (ruler of Michoacan), 225–26

Cadmus, 80

calendars: astronomical year, 252–53; civil year, 251–52; Indian, 64; natural year, 249–50; ritual year, 255–57

Calepino, Ambrogio, 76

California, 167, 168, 221

Calli: autumn, 109; day of the year, 100, 112, 160; east, 109; house, 63, 90, 163, 165, 249; spring, 110; summer, 109; symbol of fire and earth, 110; west, 109; winter, 109

callixihuitl, 90

Camino del cielo. See León, Martín de

Campoy Morata, Antonius Emmanuel (in *Epigramma*), 55

Careri, Giovanni. *See* Gemelli Careri, Giovanni Francesco

Catalog of Historic Indian Museum, 201–74; index, 205–206

Cebrian y Agustin, Pedro, 6

Ce Ehecatl (One Wind), 83, 254. See also *Ehecatl* (wind; day of the year)

Centeotl inopiltzin (orphan god), 94

Ce xochitl. See *Xochitl*

Chalchiuhcueitl (native deity), 83, 250, 254, 255

Chalchihuitlicueyohua (lord of the water; nocturnal symbol), 112

Chaldeans, 63, 77

Charles II (king of Spain), 28

Charles VI (emperor), 4

Chichimeca Indians, 123, 124, 129, 143, 155, 180–81, 182, 183, 191, 198, 207, 208; history, 205, 209–12, 213, 224

Chimalpahin, Domingo de San Antón Muñón, 188, 217, 218, 252, 260, 268

Cicero, Marcus Tullius, 46, 150

Cihuatlicue (woman's skirt; native deity), 107–108

Cinteotl (god of maize), 108. *See also* Gemelli Careri, Giovanni Francesco

Cinteucyohua (lord of the maize; nocturnal symbol), 112

Cipactli (day of the year), 100, 101, 256

Coatlatona. *See* Cihuatlicue (woman's skirt; native deity)

Cohuatl (serpent; day of the year), 100

Columbus, 50

Concepción, Juan de la (Discalced Carmelite), 8; American Muses, 40–44; approbation, 34–37

conquest, by Spaniards, 188–89, 205, 214, 215, 219, 230; history, 258–60

Cortés, Fernando, 34, 35, 46, 65, 142, 156, 157, 188, 218, 231, 234, 235, 258, 259

Cruz, sor Juana Inés de la, 165

Cuberos, Manuel, bishop, 158, 159

Cueztpallin (lizard; day of the year), 100

culturanismo (literary style). *See* Góngora y Argote, Luis de

Cyparissus, 72, 119

Daedalus, 75

Danae, 81

Daphne, 72, 119
David, psalmist, 68
Diego, Juan, 139, 143, 192–93, 269, 270, 271. *See also* Guadalupe, Our Lady of
Dionysius of Halicarnassis, 150

Ecatonatiuh (course of the sun), 64
ecclesiastical history, 261–62
Egyptians, 63, 67
Ehecatl (wind; day of the year), 100
Erysichthon (king of Thessaly), 86
Europa, 80

Favonius, 47
Ferdinand II (king of Aragon), 37
Fernández de Echeverría y Veytia, Mariano, 6–7
Fernández Munilla, Miguel, 38, 39
Festus, 76
Florencia, Francisco de, 262, 244, 265, 267
Fresneda, Pedro (Jesuit), 8; evaluation by, 24–25
Fuenclara, count of, 6

Ganymede, 74, 94
Gaona, Juan, 247
García, Gregorio (bishop-elect), 146
Garcilaso de la Vega (El Inca), 7, 28, 29n8
Gemelli Careri, Giovanni Francesco, 30, 71, 102, 107, 121, 127, 131, 134, 160, 161, 250, 253; compared with Boturini, 109–10; symbols of the Indian months according to, 106, 109
Genebrardo (Gilbert Genebrard), 137
giants, 170–74
Glass, John, 5, 14
Gómez de Escobar, Miguel (licentiate), 26
Góngora y Argote, Luis de, 10
gongorismo (literary style). *See* Góngora y Argote, Luis de
Guadalupe, Our Lady of, 5, 139, 143, 188, 189, 192–93, 240, 243, 258, 259; history, 206, 242, 263–72

Hahuiatlteotl (native deity), 86
Hakluyt, Richard, 12, 184
Ham, 77, 172, 173
Heraclitus, 151
Hercules, 81n142, 82, 148
Herrera y Tordesillas, Antonio de, 7, 28, 29n8, 31
Homer, 138; *Iliad*, 134
Huehuetlapullan (city), 63, 176, 253
Huejotzinco, history of, 205, 224, 229
Hueipachtli (fully grown moss; Indian month), 106. *See also* Gemelli Careri, Giovanni Francesco
Hueymicaylhuitl (greater commemoration of the dead; Indian month), 88. *See also* Gemelli Careri, Giovanni Francesco; León, Martín de
Hueytecuilhuitl (feast of the great lord; Indian month), 105. *See also* Gemelli Careri, Giovanni Francesco; León, Martín de
Hueytotzotzontli (great fast; Indian month), 104. *See also* León, Martín de
Hueytozoztli (great letting of blood; Indian month), 106, 108. *See also* Gemelli Careri, Giovanni Francesco
Huitzilopochtli (native deity), 84, 85, 86n161, 114, 139, 190, 236, 250, 255. *See also* Teoyaotlatohua-Huitzilopochtli (native deity)
Huitziton (ancestral captain), 113–14

Itzaqual, 98
Itzcalli (when it sprouts, rebirth; Indian month), 105, 107, 139. *See also* Gemelli Careri, Giovanni Francesco; León, Martín de

Itzteucyohua (lord of the fire; nocturnal symbol), 111
Ixtlilxochitl, Fernando de Alba. *See* Alva Ixtlilxochitl, Fernando de
Izcocauhqui, 79
Izcuintli (dog; day of the year), 100

Jerome (Eusebius Sophronius Hieronymus), 77, 78n132, 137
Josephus, Flavius (historian), 157, 162, 165, 166
Joshua (biblical patriarch), 96
Jupiter, 44, 72, 80, 81, 94, 95, 96n190. *See also* Ganymede; Zeus
Justinian (emperor), 195

Keen, Benjamin, 7
Kino, Eusebio Francisco, 168, 221
Kircher, Athanasius, 163, 186
knots, and songs, historical and poetic, 135. See also *quipu*

Lactantius, 35
las Casas, Bartolome de, 11
Laso de la Vega, Luis, 14, 263, 264, 266, 267. *See also* Guadalupe, Our Lady of
Lázaro, Diego, 13, 261–62
Livy, Titus, 150, 175
lunisolar year, 63
León, Martín de: as Dominican author, *Camino del cielo*, 103, 248; symbols of the Indian months according to, 104–105
León-Portilla, Miguel, 4, 14, 70n99
Lyra. *See* Nicholas of Lyra

macana (native sword), 85, 127
Macuilxochiquetzalli (native deity), 72, 147, 253, 255
Malinalli (twisted cords; day of the year), 100
Mange, Juan Mateo, 221
Martí, Manuel (dean of Alicante), 30
Matlaltzinco, history of, 205, 224, 228
Mazatl (deer; day of the year), 100
Medea, 46
Medusa, 81, 82, 125
Mestra, 86, 87n165
metl (native paper), 66, 156, 273
Mexican Indians, 183–86; history, 205, 211, 213, 214–21, 224, 230–33, 252
Mexico (city), 97, 203, 225, 31
Meztitlan (town), 150
Meztli: moon, 96; symbol of month, 102
Meztli itzaqual (house of the moon), 98
Micaylhuitl (lesser commemoration of the dead), 88. *See also* Gemelli Careri, Giovanni Francesco
Michoacan, history of, 205, 224, 225–27
Mictlanteuctli (native deity; ruler of the underworld), 87, 147, 159, 254
Mictlanteucyohua (lord of the underworld; nocturnal symbol), 112
Minotaur, 75
Miquiztli (death; day of the year), 100
Molina, Alonso de, 247
momacpalitohticque (sorcerers), 83
mometzcopinqui (witches), 83
Moteuczoma Xocoyotzin (Xocoyotl), Mexican emperor, 4, 49, 65, 160, 184, 185, 214, 215, 259
Motolinía, Toribio de, 11
Muñoz Camargo, Domingo, 232, 259

Nahuatl (Aztec language), 12, 89, 143, 146, 179, 181, 184, 196, 206, 209, 210, 212, 216, 217, 218, 220, 223, 231, 232, 233, 241, 242, 244, 245, 259, 264, 270, 273; manuscripts in, 266, 267; printed books in, 247–48

Nanahuatzin, the Venereal One, 93, 94, 97
Nemontemi, 64; symbol of the months, 102
Nenontemi. See *Nemontemi*
neomenias lunares, 64, 64n76, 70, 109. *See also* Gemelli Careri, Giovanni Francesco
nepohualtzitzin, 62, 135, 136. See also *quipu*
Nereides, 48
Netzahualcoyotl (king of Texcoco), 127, 129–30, 131, 139, 142, 160, 181, 182, 209, 210, 211, 212, 244
New Spain, 47, 114, 125, 131, 135, 136, 155, 156, 161, 173, 174, 175, 176, 180, 183, 184, 191, 194, 198, 201, 211, 212, 219, 224, 230, 232, 244, 253, 258, 272; origin of the Indians of, 146–66
Nezahualpiltzintli (ruler), 134, 181, 210, 212
Nicholas of Lyra, 77, 78n132, 165
Nicoseli, Anastasio, 265
Nimrod, 77
Nopaltzin (son of Xolotl), 124, 180
Núñez de la Vega, Francisco (bishop), 157, 158
Nyades, 81

Oca Silva y Moctezuma, Manuela de. *See* Santibáñez, countess of
Ocelotl, Septenario, 101
Ochpaniztli (sweeping; Indian month), 105, 106, 140. *See also* Gemelli Careri, Giovanni Francesco; León, Martín de
Ollin Tonatiuh: movement of the sun, 99, 254; Septenario, 101
Olmec Indians, 175–76, 191
Orpheus, 69, 88, 138, 211
Osiris, 45
Our Lady of Guadalupe. *See* Guadalupe, Our Lady of
Our Lady of Remedios. *See* Remedios, Our Lady of
Ovid (Publius Ovidius Naso), 10, 13, 75, 80, 81n144, 83, 83n149, 84, 85, 86, 87n166, 90, 92, 96; *Fasti*, 200; *Metamorphoses*, 94, 95, 114, 115, 116, 118, 119, 120, 121, 124–25, 126, 138, 151, 153, 172; *Tristia*, 145
Oxipe (god of flaying), 107. *See also* Gemelli Careri, Giovanni Francesco
Ozomatli (monkey; day of the year), 100

Pachtli: moss, 141; Indian month, 106, 140. *See also* Gemelli Careri, Giovanni Francesco
Pallas, 80
Pan, 75
Panormitanus, 203
Panquetzaliztli (gold banner; Indian month), 86, 139. *See also* León, Martín de
Papahua Tlemacazque, 97
passage of Indians to America, 167–69
Peleus, 73
Pérez de la Fuente, Joseph, 13, 242
Peru, 47, 135, 136, 149, 169
Phaethon, 95, 95n187, 96, 96n190
Philip V (king of Spain), 4, 47
Philo (Jewish scholar of Alexandria), 77, 165
Piltzinteuctli (native deity), 74, 147, 254
Piltzinteucyohua (lord of the children; nocturnal symbol), 111
Placido, Francisco, 139, 267
Pliny, 76
Puerto Rico, 41
Purchas, Samuel, 12, 184, 185, 186
Pyrrha, 73

Quauhtli (eagle; Septenario), 101
Quecholli (turkey; Indian month), 105, 106. *See also* Gemelli Careri, Giovanni Francesco; León, Martín de
Quetzalcohuatl (native deity), 82, 192, 244, 250, 254, 255
Quiahuitl (rainwater; Septenario), 101
Quiauhteucyohua (lord of the rain; nocturnal symbol), 112
quipu, 62, 135

Remedios, Our Lady of, 267

Saenz de Aguirre, Joseph, 28, 28n7
Sahagim, Bernardino de, 11, 246
Sanchez, Miguel, 14, 263. *See also* Guadalupe, Our Lady of
San Juan de Ulúa, 48
San Juan Teotihuacan, 97
Santibáñez, countess of, 4
Seneca (Lucius Annaeus Seneca), 61, 62, 70, 76, 176
Septenario, 101
Septuagint, 66, 164, 165, 179
Sigüenza y Góngora, Carlos de (Mexican scholar), 30, 102, 109, 165, 211, 243, 267, 269
Sincero (Jacopo Sannazaro), 144–45
solar cycle, Indian, 63
Solís y Ribadeneyra, Antonio de, 7, 29, 31
Sonetto al'medesimo, 52–53
Sonetto al signor cavalier Boturini, 50–51
symbols: divine heroic nocturnal symbols of the year, 111–12; divine heroic symbols of the days of the year, 99–101; divine heroic symbols of the months, 102–103; divine heroic symbols of the planets, 93–98; heroic military symbols, 23–27; heroic political symbols, 128–34; symbols of the Indian months according to fray Martín de León, 104–105

Tacitus (Roman historian), 148, 171–72
Tapia, Andres de, 235
Tecpatl: autumn, 109; flint, 63, 90, 112, 160, 163, 164, 165, 173, 186, 249, 253; midday, 109; north, 109; Septenario, 101; spring, 109; summer, 109; symbol of air and fire, 110; winter, 110
Tecpatlxihuitl, 90
Tecuilhuitltzintli (lesser feast of the lord; Indian month), 105. *See also* Gemelli Careri, Giovanni Francesco; León, Martín de
Temetlatl (grinding stone), 101
Tenochtitlan, Mexico (native capital), 114, 121, 129, 216, 262
Teochichimeca Indians, 187, 191
Teotecpatl (Divine Flint), 85
Teotlacanexquimilli (native deity), 74
Teotlamacazqui: god of the underworld, 70, 159; god of the priests, 253
Teotleco (arrival of the gods; Indian month), 105. *See also* León, Martín de
Teoyaominqui (native deity), 85, 254
Teoyaotlatohua-Huitzilopochtli (native deity), 84, 254
Tepanec Indians, 181–83, 191; history, 205, 213, 224
Tepeyoloyohua (lord of the innermost mountains; nocturnal symbol), 112
Tepilhuitl (feast of the mountains; Indian month). *See also* León, Martín de
teponaztli (native drum), 65, 142
Tetzauhteotl (frightful god; native deity), 113, 114, 254
Teuhtli. *See* Teuhtile (governor of Cuetlachtlan)
Teuhtile (governor of Cuetlachtlan), 65
Tezcatlipoca (native deity), 70, 71, 114, 146, 147, 190, 253